A Visitor's Companion to Tudor England

A Visitor's Companion to Tudor England

SUZANNAH LIPSCOMB

EBURY
PRESS

1 3 5 7 9 10 8 6 4 2

Published in 2012 by Ebury Press, an imprint of Ebury Publishing
A Random House Group company

Copyright © Suzannah Lipscomb 2012

Suzannah Lipscomb has asserted her right to be identified as the author of
this Work in accordance with the Copyright, Designs and Patents Act 1988

The Random House Group Limited Reg. No. 954009

Addresses for companies within the Random House Group can be found at
www.randomhouse.co.uk

A CIP catalogue record for this book is available from the British Library

The Random House Group Limited supports the Forest Stewardship
Council® (FSC®), the leading international forest certification organisation.
All our titles that are printed on Greenpeace approved FSC® certified paper
carry the FSC® logo. Our paper procurement policy can be found at
www.randomhouse.co.uk/environment.

Designed and set by seagulls.net

Illustrations by Angela Beale angiebealdesigns.com

Printed and bound by CPI Group (UK) Ltd, Croydon, CR0 4YY

ISBN 9780091944841

To buy books by your favourite authors and register for offers visit
www.randomhouse.co.uk

To my husband, Drake,
for his long-suffering of my sojourns in the
sixteenth century, and for having unwittingly
become a Tudor traveller himself.

Contents

South East

South West

Introduction

*'I have so travelled in your dominions both
by the seacoasts and the middle parts... that there
is almost neither... cities, burgs, castles, principal
manor places, monasteries, and colleges, but I have
seen them, and noted in so doing a whole
world of things very memorable.'*
John Leland's *Itinerary*, written 1539–45 and dedicated to Henry VIII

I grew up very near the site of Nonsuch Palace. Its very name, 'None-such', conjured up a mythical, fabled palace without parallel. The streets nearby had names like 'Anne Boleyn's Walk', 'Aragon Avenue' and 'Tudor Close'. Hampton Court, with its profusion of twisted chimneys, was not all that far away. I remember as a child going to fairs, riding and even ice-skating in its shadow. Somewhere along the line, these childhood moments sowed the seeds of a lifelong fascination with the Tudors. I don't think I'm the only one.

As a nation, we have a continuing obsession with our notorious 'Bluebeard' Henry VIII, and our famed 'Gloriana' Elizabeth I. Their lives – one much married, the other unmarried – are part of our common currency of ideas. Their age attracts us because it has all the best stories: the break from Rome and Catholicism, wives beheaded or cast aside, boy-kings, dissolved monasteries, Protestant martyrs, the Spanish Armada, New Worlds, and some of the best characters: Shakespeare, Holbein, Anne Boleyn, Francis Drake and Walter Ralegh.

Somewhere in this mix, the Tudors define what it means to be English. Through the translation of the Bible into English, the establishment of the Church of England, the founding of the navy, the beginnings of empire and the defence against the threat of foreign invasion, the Tudors represent the foundations of much of our corporate culture and historic identity. When the Channel Tunnel opened in 1994, the two figures chosen to represent England and France in great mock-ups were the sixteenth-century rival kings Henry VIII and Francis I. Who else but Henry VIII could capture Englishness so completely?

The sixteenth century is also one of the first periods from which we have an overwhelming amount of surviving material. Our documentary sources are vast: chronicles, letters, ambassadorial accounts, poems, plays, treatises and state papers fill our National Archives. We have portraits of the Tudor monarchs painted from life, unlike those that came before, and sixteenth-century houses are still the ideal cottages in the countryside to

TUDOR TIMELINE

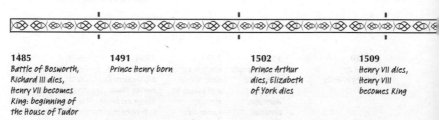

1485
Battle of Bosworth,
Richard III dies,
Henry VII becomes
King: beginning of
the House of Tudor

1491
Prince Henry born

1502
Prince Arthur
dies, Elizabeth
of York dies

1509
Henry VII dies,
Henry VIII
becomes King

which middle England aspires. Above all, we have extraordinary grand houses, palaces, churches and castles that evoke a time past and a heritage shared. This book is a way into exploring that history.

❋

This book is intended to be both a practical handbook to fifty of the best and most interesting Tudor houses, palaces and castles, and a colourful introduction to the key characters, stories and events of the Tudor age. It is designed to be a companion both to the visitor to these fifty sites, and to the historical visitor to the Tudor period.

Any attempt to draw up a list of fifty Tudor places would find its critics, but there has been reason at work in the choosing, and I thought it might be helpful to explain the criteria by which places have made it into this book.

The first principle was that there must exist something worth seeing.

Not every important Tudor site has been preserved. So many Tudor houses, palaces and buildings did not survive: William Cecil, Lord Burghley's great house at Theobalds (pronounced 'Tibbles'); Thomas Howard, Duke of Norfolk's mansion at Kenninghall;

1516
Princess
Mary born

1537
Prince Edward born,
Jane Seymour dies

1520
Field of
Cloth of Gold

1529
Henry appeals
to Pope to
annul his
marriage,
Cardinal
Thomas
Wolsey dies

1533
Henry marries
Anne Boleyn
and annuls his
marriage to
Katherine,
Princess
Elizabeth born

1536
Dissolution of
the monasteries
begins, Anne
Boleyn executed,
Katherine of
Aragon dies,
Henry marries
Jane Seymour

1540
Henry VIII marries
and divorces
Anne of Cleves,
Thomas Cromwell
executed

Nonsuch Palace; Greenwich Palace; the Old St Paul's Cathedral; Bedlam Hospital for the mad. In London, only sacred sites like churches and the stone-built Guildhall survived the Great Fire of 1666. The London houses of Sir Thomas More and Thomas Cromwell, Earl of Essex, among many others, have been lost to us. When something does survive of these lost places from the sixteenth century, such as the Gatehouse at Richmond Palace, the panels from Nonsuch Palace at Loseley Park or the arches at Holdenby, I have included them.

This means that some of the sites I have chosen are ruins: Tutbury Castle, Hailes Abbey and Kenilworth, Pontefract and Ludlow castles, but they are evocative, and the places important.

Many are, however, glorious buildings of great architectural importance: Montacute House, Hardwick Hall, Hampton Court, Burghley House and Kirby Hall are all spectacular, and I've included some gems like Little Moreton Hall and Gawsworth Hall – beautiful examples of black and white wattle-and-daub gentry housing – or the simple yet elegant Sandford Orcas Manor House, a sixteenth-century stone house in Somerset.

But not all are houses. There are fortresses and castles such as the Tower of London, Pendennis Castle and Rochester Castle. There are also abbeys and monasteries such as Fountains Abbey,

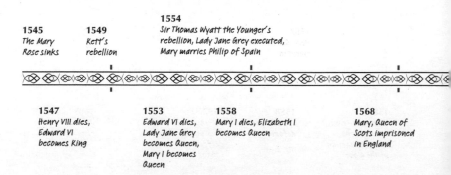

1545
The Mary
Rose sinks

1549
Kett's
rebellion

1554
Sir Thomas Wyatt the Younger's
rebellion, Lady Jane Grey executed,
Mary marries Philip of Spain

1547
Henry VIII dies,
Edward VI
becomes King

1553
Edward VI dies,
Lady Jane Grey
becomes Queen,
Mary I becomes
Queen

1558
Mary I dies, Elizabeth I
becomes Queen

1568
Mary, Queen of
Scots imprisoned
in England

Walsingham, Glastonbury and Charterhouse, which have important stories to tell about the religious changes afoot in sixteenth-century England.

Some too are tombs: we travel to the tomb of Mary Tudor, Henry VIII's sister, in Bury St Edmunds; to the many graves at Westminster Abbey; to the unadorned tomb of Katherine of Aragon at Peterborough; and the simple black slab that marks the resting place of Henry VIII and his third wife, Jane Seymour, in St George's Chapel at Windsor Castle.

I am also a firm believer in the value of *things*. There are occasional entries where little remains from the period except tantalising shreds of evidence that evoke a particularly strong or striking story: whether they are portraits at the National Portrait Gallery, Arundel Castle or the Walker Art Gallery, or objects at Bosworth Battlefield. In one case, our story centres on a 500-year-old tree in Wymondham; in another, it is a simple memorial in the road in Broad Street, Oxford and sixteenth-century doors licked by the flames of the martyrs' pyres that tell our tale.

The book attempts to draw attention to the most fascinating parts of the architecture, or to the best parts of the collections but, above all, I hope you'll feel a sense of walking in the footsteps of the great iconic figures of the Tudor age.

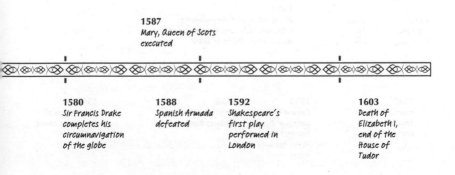

1587
Mary, Queen of Scots executed

1580
Sir Francis Drake completes his circumnavigation of the globe

1588
Spanish Armada defeated

1592
Shakespeare's first play performed in London

1603
Death of Elizabeth I, end of the House of Tudor

The second principle was that each place should tell a fascinating tale about an important character, event or story from the turbulent Tudor period.

This does mean that some beautiful places were not included, including some of my favourites, such as Haddon Hall, Longleat, Broughton Castle and Oxburgh Hall, but this was never intended to be merely a guidebook to architecture. The stories, as well as the places, are important.

The stories and places intersect in different ways. For Thornbury Castle, Kirby Hall, Buckland Abbey, Sherborne Castle and Hardwick Hall, the buildings are very closely tied up with the fates of their owners. It is as if the destiny of the owner has been played out in stone and glass.

Others are places that shaped people, not places shaped by people. Trinity and St John's Colleges in Cambridge and Lincoln's Inn in London were the training grounds of the astrologer Dr John Dee and the martyr Sir Thomas More. Hever Castle, Eltham Palace, Shakespeare's birthplace, Gawsworth Hall and Hatfield Old Palace were all childhood homes, though in every case our protagonists returned as adults too.

Sometimes there was just a moment that changed everything. Anne of Cleves's meeting with Henry VIII at Rochester determined her fate. Winchester Cathedral was the scene of Mary I's happiest day. Henry VIII and his entourage stopped for just one night at Leeds Castle on their way to the Field of Cloth of Gold. Prince Arthur's death at Ludlow Castle altered the entire course of Tudor history.

Some stories will be well known, others will be less familiar; all are, I hope, compellingly and divertingly retold. I have drawn on primary sources and on the latest research to direct you to interesting treasures and overlooked titbits. Being confined by the evidence means I have not included tales unless I can verify them (so the apocryphal tale of Sir Francis Drake playing bowls at Plymouth when the Armada arrived didn't make the cut!): I want you to be able to trust what you read, even if the text, designed for the general reader, is written without the scholarly apparatus of references.

The third principle was that the list must cover the geographical diversity of England, as far as possible.

In some ways, my hands were tied: the Tudor monarchs rarely ventured north and had a preference for London and the South East, so the northern regions are the least well covered, but this is an inevitable consequence of the material.

I chose to cover England, rather than Britain, because it would be anachronistic to do otherwise. Scotland was very certainly not Tudor in this period, and the Irish were fighting the colonialist powers of the English: I didn't think that either nation would appreciate coming under the erroneous blanket heading of 'Tudor Britain'. Wales, it is true, after the Acts of Union of 1536 and 1543 was joined to England, but Wales and England were still uncomfortable bedfellows – despite having Welsh Tudors on the throne – so I have confined myself to England alone. But, within these confines, I've tried to give coverage of as many regions and counties as possible.

Finally, the fourth principle was that taken together, these stories would represent virtually every significant person and event of the Tudor age, to ensure that there were not, for example, fifteen entries on Henry VIII and nothing on Shakespeare.

This was harder. Many great characters left no fixed abode, or didn't build houses. Sir Francis Walsingham invested his fortune not in palaces, but in people: in Elizabeth I's spy network, rather than a lasting edifice to his name. Many places that were built do not survive. There are two men that I feel particular chagrin about not covering in any depth – Thomas Cromwell, Earl of Essex and Edward Seymour, Duke of Somerset – but there had to be something to *see*.

Christopher Marlowe, another fascinating character, was murdered by Ingram Frizer in a lodging in Deptford: but where is that now?

This is fundamentally a book about *where* history happened.

For several years, I was a curator at Hampton Court Palace and one of the things I grasped while working for Historic Royal Palaces was the value of telling 'history where it happened'. There is something undeniably powerful about walking along the Processional Gallery at Hampton Court in the very steps that Henry VIII would have taken as he emerged from his privy chambers and went to the Chapel Royal, or standing where Sir Christopher Hatton stood at Kirby Hall as he yearned to return to his 'holy saint' and great love, Elizabeth I. When I was discussing this book with Natalie Grueninger of www.onthetudortrail.com, she put it perfectly: when in those places, only time, not space, separates us from the people whose lives we seek to understand. The great historian G. M. Trevelyan once wrote:

> the poetry of history lies in the quasi-miraculous fact that once, on this earth, on this familiar spot of ground, walked other men and women, as actual as we are today, thinking their own thoughts, swayed by their own passions, but now all gone, one generation vanishing after another, gone as utterly as we ourselves shall shortly be gone, like ghosts at cock-crow.

In the places featured in this book, the veil between the past and the present seems very thin. It feels possible to see the past re-enacted before one's eyes – as if one could almost reach out and touch it.

Finally, I've observed several things in my search for Tudor places. In some ways, they rarely exist. There are precious few buildings that are exclusively Tudor, and have not been changed in any way since Elizabeth I sat on the throne. In fact, the standard story for England's great houses is something along the lines of: what you see now is a 1930s renovation of a Victorian restoration of a sixteenth-century building that was slighted (partially destroyed) during the Civil War, and originally stood on a Norman site!

There are so many different scenarios a building can go through. At the end of all of these, what appears to us today is an accident of happenstance and history that has depended on the whims of a building's individual owners, the mishaps of time (fires play a large part) and the fashions and politics of the day. Many originally Tudor buildings have been substantially altered in the intervening centuries: the interiors of Burghley House, for example, were overhauled in the late seventeenth century by John Cecil, the fifth Earl of Exeter, while at Hampton Court the private apartments of the Tudor palace were demolished to make way for William and Mary's new baroque palace.

Our attitudes towards conservation today are very different from those of our forebears. I was fortunate enough to be married at Hampton Court Palace, but the opportunity came with an understandable list of things we could not do, among them eat red-coloured jam on our scones in the Little Banqueting House or stand up with a glass of red wine in the Great Hall. Compare this with the fate of Nonsuch: what was allegedly one of the greatest palaces in all of Europe was given by a disinterested king to a negligent mistress (Charles II to Barbara Villiers), who set about dismantling it to pay off her gambling debts.

This leads to a question that many a historic house owner has had to answer: do you leave buildings in their historic state, even when they need interventions to preserve them, or do you restore them and risk destroying what remains? Over the years, even some well-meaning 'restoration' has damaged original Tudor fabric, as at the Old Hall at Lincoln's Inn. William Morris founded the Society for the Protection of Ancient Buildings in 1877 precisely to stop what he considered the 'feeble and lifeless forgery' of restoring buildings to some imagined past. Given the necessity of restoration in most cases, to what period do you restore a building? All buildings with a Tudor history have a story since, and it's rather hit-and-miss which ones retain their Tudor features or are represented in their Tudor state. Therefore, for the places in this book, although I've tried to contextualise each building within their longer histories, I've focused on picking out the Tudor parts and explaining why the buildings – and the places, people and events associated with them – are significant from a Tudor point of view.

The book doesn't attempt to be a substitute for a comprehensive guidebook to each site through its ages but, in what follows, I attempt to explain how to experience these buildings as a visitor to Tudor England. What I hope this book accomplishes is that it shows you how to peel back the layers and experience the history of each place from a Tudor perspective, looking at it through Tudor eyes and with Tudor stories in mind. I will be your guide and companion.

London
and
Greater
London

The Tower of London

*'These bloody days have broken my heart...
The bell tower showed me such a sight'*

The Tower of London is one of the most famous buildings in the world. With William the Conqueror's eleventh-century White Tower at its centre and its many other towers largely completed in the reign of Edward I (1272–1307), it has been a fortress and a royal palace, and even, in the thirteenth century, housed a menagerie of exotic animals, including an elephant and a polar bear that fished in the Thames. It is famous for its ravens, the Crown Jewels, the Yeoman Warders (known universally as 'Beefeaters') and the fabled murder of the young 'Princes in the Tower', whose bones were found two centuries after their deaths. Henry VIII was the last monarch to invest in repairing and refurbishing the Tower, and all the Tudor monarchs processed from the Tower to Westminster for their coronations.

The Tower's chief distinction in the Tudor period was, however, as a place of imprisonment and execution. Many Tudor prisoners would have arrived by boat and entered through the water gate in St Thomas's Tower, now commonly known as Traitors' Gate, which was reached from a tunnel under the wharf from the Thames. Compared to many Tudor prisons, the Tower was relatively comfortable. That it may also have been terribly boring is attested to by the extraordinary graffiti left by Tudor prisoners. Most of it, like tagging in modern graffiti, shows a fixation with leaving a record of one's name. In the Tower, however, prisoners had a much more compelling motive than today's graffiti artists: they feared, many quite rightly, that they would only leave their imprisonment to die.

Beauchamp (pronounced 'Beecham') Tower has some beautifully inventive graffiti: Thomas Abel, chaplain to Katherine of Aragon, was imprisoned for refusing to accept the annulment of her marriage to Henry VIII, and depicted his surname with the letter 'A' on a bell; the Dudley brothers, imprisoned after their failed attempt to crown Lady Jane Grey queen, carved an elaborate rebus to the right of the fireplace with their coat of arms in a floral border, where each flower represents one of the Dudleys. Another supporter of Jane's carved the simple word 'IANE', while Sir Philip Howard, Earl of Arundel [see ARUNDEL CASTLE] – one of the many Catholics imprisoned in the Tower in Elizabeth's reign – spent his ten years of confinement carving the Latin phrase, 'The more suffering for Christ in this world, The more glory for Christ in the next.' In the Salt Tower, you can see the most incredible carving of an astrological sphere or clock and inscription by Hugh Draper, imprisoned on an accusation of sorcery in 1561. Here, too, are indications of Catholic faith: 'Maria' carved into the walls, and a bleeding foot to indicate the five wounds of Christ. Henry Walpole, a Jesuit priest, was imprisoned here in 1593 and inscribed the walls with the Latin names of St Paul and St Peter, and the four fathers of the Church. Walpole's story also reminds us of why the Tower was so feared in the sixteenth century: it could be a place of torture.

Perhaps surprisingly, torture was relatively rare, as only the Privy Council could authorise it. Nevertheless, there were forty-eight sanctioned cases of torture between 1540 and 1640. The Lower Wakefield Tower has a display of the weapons of torture: usually the rack; contorting irons for the legs, wrists and neck; or the manacles, from which a prisoner was suspended from the hands or wrists. Walpole was hung from the manacles fourteen times, and had the middle finger of his right hand torn off, but still refused to inform on other English Catholics [for more on English Catholics, see HARVINGTON HALL]. Ralph Ithell, a Catholic priest whose engraving from 1586 can be seen in Broad Arrow Tower, was racked for plotting to overthrow Elizabeth I. Earlier in the century (and contrary to a woman's normal exemption from torture), the Protestant Anne Askew, who was imprisoned in the Cradle Tower, had also been racked. After her trial of June 1546, and in the hope that she would denounce a number of noble-women for sharing in the heresy of which she was accused, two royal councillors, Thomas Wriothesley and the devious Sir Richard Rich, even turned the rack themselves.

More famous prisoners include Sir Walter Ralegh, gaoled three times in the Bloody Tower (as the Garden Tower was renamed after the murder of the Princes); Sir Thomas More [see LINCOLN'S INN], Bishop John Fisher and the poet Sir Thomas Wyatt the Elder who was interned in the Bell Tower (sadly, not open to the public). Wyatt wrote of seeing those accused of adultery with Anne Boleyn executed on Tower Hill:

> These bloody days have broken my heart…
> The bell tower showed me such a sight
> That in my head sticks day and night.
> There did I learn out of a grate,
> For all favour, glory, or might,
> That yet *circa regna tonat* [thunder rolls around the throne
>   of kings].

The Tower was also a place of death. In 1536, Anne Boleyn was imprisoned in the Queen's lodgings, which ran from the Lanthorn Tower up towards the White Tower: precisely where she had stayed before her coronation three years earlier. She was tried in the medieval Great Hall: you can see where this would have been as you emerge from the Wakefield Tower. Anne was one of only seven people in the Tower's history to be executed on Tower Green and she was then buried under the altar in the chapel of St Peter ad Vincula (the parish church of the Tower). She was also the only one to be executed with a sword, rather than an axe.

Tower Green, within the Tower itself, was chosen over Tower Hill for private, secure executions of high-ranking individuals. Two other queens of England died in this way: Henry VIII's fifth wife, Katherine Howard, and Lady Jane Grey. The other victims were Margaret Pole, Countess of Salisbury, formerly governess to Princess Mary, who was chased across the scaffold by her executioner – 'a wretched and blundering youth... who literally hacked her head and shoulders to pieces in the most pitiful manner'; Jane Boleyn, Lady Rochford, who had abetted Katherine Howard in her adultery; and Robert Devereux, Earl of Essex for his uprising against Elizabeth I. The Devereux Tower still bears his name.

The others buried at St Peter ad Vincula were executed in public on Tower Hill, on what is now Trinity Square Gardens. They included Edward Stafford, Duke of Buckingham, in 1521 (see THORNBURY CASTLE); George Boleyn, Lord Rochford, Anne Boleyn's brother, in 1536; Thomas Cromwell, Earl of Essex and Henry VIII's first minister, in 1540; Edward Seymour, Duke of Somerset and Lord Protector in 1552; and Thomas Howard, Duke of Norfolk in 1572. All died on charges of treason.

Strangely, the place instantly recalled when thinking of the Tower – the iconic White Tower itself – is that least associated with captivity and execution. Today it houses the collections of the

Royal Armouries, including Henry VIII's armour. Look out for the exquisite horse armour made for Henry in 1515: beautifully engraved all over with foliage, Tudor roses and pomegranates, its skirt bears the intertwining initials H and K, for Henry and Katherine of Aragon. As it was made to measure, it also shows that in 1515 Henry had a chest of just thirty-six inches, in contrast to the enormous size of his field and tournament armour of 1540, which you can also see here. In 1540, when Henry VIII turned fifty years old, his chest had expanded to an obese fifty-seven inches.

The Tower, as a place of incarceration, death and final rest for many, is a must-see for the Tudor visitor. The passing of time alone accounts for the fact that a place characterised by suffering, cruelty and death is now experienced as beautiful and impressive by those of us who, unlike many of its residents, can choose to leave.

National Portrait Gallery
London

*'Holbein's manner of limning (watercolour painting)
I have ever imitated and hold it for the best.'*

Miniaturist Nicholas Hilliard, in his *Treatise on the Art of Limning*, 1600

The remarkable collection of Tudor portraits at the National Portrait Gallery is second-to-none. The gallery is like a *dramatis personae* of the period, giving us the chance to come face-to-face with well-known characters of the period in vivid colour and extraordinary detail.

The portraits begin, appropriately, with a portrait of Henry VII [see RICHMOND PALACE] from 1505, holding a red rose. Although his closed mouth hides his black and rotting teeth, it is probably otherwise a good likeness as it was painted by Margaret of Austria's court painter as part of Henry's (rejected) marriage proposal to her after the death of his wife, Elizabeth of York: Margaret's court painter would have had no reason to flatter. Elizabeth of York, meanwhile, is depicted in a late sixteenth-century copy of the original holding the white rose of the House of York, and looking every inch like a queen on a playing card.

There are two contrasting portraits here of Henry VIII. His portrait of 1520 makes him appear (much like his father's portrait) weak and wan, but the hugely impressive cartoon by Hans Holbein the Younger from 1536/7 dwarfs it. The cartoon – a full-size, masculine image of Henry – is a detailed preparatory drawing for the Whitehall Mural, which measured nine feet by twelve feet [see THE WALKER ART GALLERY]. The detailing on the classical interior in the background and the clothing is unusually fine. Holbein would have transferred the image to the wall by pricking tiny holes along the ink lines, and brushing charcoal through the holes to leave dots on the wall behind.

Three of Henry VIII's wives are represented here, too. Katherine of Aragon was painted in miniature [see PETERBOROUGH CATHEDRAL] in 1525, probably by Lucas Horenbout, and is also depicted in an unflattering eighteenth-century copy of another picture that, judging by her clothing, was painted in the same year. A portrait of Anne Boleyn dates from the late sixteenth century (no agreed portraits survive from her lifetime): she wears her famous 'B' pendant. Given her reputation as a dowdy old widow, the image of Kateryn Parr [see SUDELEY CASTLE] is perhaps the most surprising. This full-length image from 1545, attributed to Master John, shows an elegant woman with a tiny waist and immensely fashionable clothing: the wide neckline, the lynx-fur sleeves, the red embroidery on her shift, the decorative faces on her girdle, the abundance of pearls. If you look carefully, you can see that even her overskirt is lined with fur.

Nearby, there are important pictures of Henry VIII's court, including Richard Fox, Bishop of Winchester; Thomas Cranmer, Archbishop of Canterbury [see BROAD STREET], who has been painted by Gerlach Flicke suitably holding St Paul's *Epistles*; and Thomas Cromwell, Earl of Essex, in a portrait after Holbein, and in a miniature attributed to Holbein from 1532–3.

The two portraits of Edward VI are worth noticing. The portrayal by William Scrots in 1546, in its original frame, is shown in a distorted, stretched perspective (called an anamorphosis – the skull at the bottom of Holbein's *Ambassadors* from 1533, next door in the National Gallery, is a famous example of this technique). If you stand at a certain angle and look down the viewfinder, you can see Edward in proper perspective. Perhaps the painting was designed to amuse the soon-to-be boy-king, as well as show off Scrots's skills. Edward's portrait of a year later is a much more regal affair: he looks just like a little version of Henry VIII in Holbein's cartoon. To exaggerate his manliness, his clothes have evidently been stuffed.

Mary I is well represented across her lifetime, first in a miniature by Lucas Horenbout from around 1525, when she was only seven, and then in her twenties, by Master John. Her cabinet portrait (a painting of a sitter's head and shoulders) by Hans Eworth from 1554 dates from her queenship, soon after her marriage to Philip II of Spain [see WINCHESTER CATHEDRAL]. Finally, the couple are depicted alongside each other. There is also a much later image of England's Spanish King in ceremonial armour with gilt etchings, dating from 1580. This is the man who ordered the Armada to sail against Elizabeth's England.

Elizabeth I's portraits show Tudor portraiture at its zenith. The image of her coronation (15 January 1559) actually dates from 1600. She is shown with crown, orb and sceptre, and exquisite robes woven with gold and silver thread, lined with ermine and decorated with the Tudor rose and fleur-de-lis of France (the robes had been used at Mary I's coronation in 1553, when England still owned Calais). Elizabeth's hair is loose, her hairline plucked high and her alabaster face made pale with white powder. The appearance of blue veins at her temples was the Tudor way of emphasising the flattering translucent quality of her skin.

Elizabeth is portrayed more simply in Nicholas Hilliard's miniature of 1572, and in the important Darnley portrait of 1575, when
she was painted from life, providing a type that would be copied
for years and keep Elizabeth's portraits looking young while she
aged. Although her snow-white face is striking in its ghost-like,
anaemic quality, recent research suggests that her face would not
have been quite as uniformly pale as it appears to us now: the red
pigments in the paint used to depict her cheeks have faded and she
has lost some of her healthy glow. The portrait by Marcus Gheeraerts the Younger, from 1592, is much more symbolic. It was
produced for Sir Henry Lee, her Master of Ordnance, and was
designed to flatter, with Elizabeth standing astride the globe as a
symbol of the sun.

Elizabeth's court is also represented here in great numbers.
There is John Astley, her tutor, from 1555; and William Cecil,
Lord Burghley, her Secretary of State and, later, Lord Treasurer
[see BURGHLEY HOUSE] wearing the rich, black velvet that signified
wealth. There are also notable portraits of her favourites. Two of
the many portraits of Elizabeth's favourite, Robert Dudley, Earl of
Leicester, are here: one from 1575, the year he last wooed her [see
KENILWORTH CASTLE], and a Hilliard miniature from 1576. In the
portrait, Leicester wears the somewhat effete clothing of the Elizabethan male: a figure-hugging doublet in red and gold thread,
and short, wide breeches, with his legs unabashedly on show in silk
stockings. Another of Elizabeth I's favourites, Sir Christopher
Hatton [see KIRBY HOUSE], is depicted in a Hilliard miniature from
1581, as is the upstart Robert Devereux, Earl of Essex, who has
also been painted life-size by Gheeraerts.

Here, too, are the great and good of her court: Sir Francis
Drake, in miniature and in life-size with his hand resting on a globe
to mark his circumnavigation, which he'd completed just before
these portraits were painted [see BUCKLAND ABBEY]; and Sir Walter

Ralegh, dashing in his miniature of 1585, but greyed in his image of 1602, where he's pictured with his son (also named Walter), who would later die in the search for El Dorado [see SHERBORNE ABBEY]. Sir Philip Sidney, the soldier-courtier-poet whom the Elizabethans adored [see PENSHURST PLACE], is flatteringly depicted (with no sign of his acute childhood smallpox scars) in neck armour. Surprisingly, given that facial hair fashions at the time worked on the basis that beards equalled masculinity, Sidney is barefaced, maybe as a symbol of his youth.

Also, be sure to spot Thomas Howard, fourth Duke of Norfolk, executed for treason in 1572 [see ARUNDEL CASTLE]; the miniature of Francis Bacon, Viscount St Alban, the English philosopher, from 1578; and an unbecoming portrait of his father, Sir Nicholas Bacon, Lord Keeper of the Great Seal, painted a year later. Sir Henry Lee is also shown in a fascinating picture painted by the great artist Antonis Mor, with his sleeves decorated with armillary spheres and lovers' knots symbolising Elizabeth, and three mysterious rings.

Finally, there are two portraits that tell wider stories. The portrait of Anne, Lady Pope, pregnant and with her three children, was probably painted before she entered the dangerous period of childbirth (which one in four women did not survive). Notice that two of her children, although in skirts, are actually boys: boys would only be 'breeched' – taken out of girls' clothes and put in breeches – at the age of six or seven. The last is a very unusual narrative portrait of the minor courtier, soldier and diplomat Sir Henry Unton, from 1596. Commissioned by his widow, Dorothy Wroughtson, and read right to left, it shows his whole life and death, including his travels, banqueting, music-making and an Elizabethan masque. It is a wonderful summary, in oil, of the amusing and arduous world of the Tudor gentry.

TUDOR PORTRAITURE

It was only in the sixteenth century that portraits of monarchs and courtiers became popular: the earliest painting in the National Portrait Gallery's collection is of Henry VII, and dates from 1505. Many Tudor portraits are life-sized, but some are smaller 'cabinet' paintings of the sitter's head and shoulders, or tiny miniatures, designed to be worn on clothing in glittering jewelled cases. Full-length portraits began as the preserve of the monarchy, chiefly Henry VIII, but by the 1590s, when canvas was increasingly used for painting instead of expensive oak panels, these larger pictures became more common for those outside the royal family.

Portraits had many purposes in Tudor times. They could be a faithful likeness of the sitter at a moment in time, and were nicknamed 'counterfeit' by the Tudors for the way they provided a duplicate likeness of an absent person. Others were painted in order to demonstrate status, power and wealth: people were painted in their best clothes, wearing their most expensive jewellery, and bearing symbols of their position or achievements. Many paintings bore a coat of arms or a personal motto. Portraits of monarchs were often commissioned as a way of showing loyalty to the Crown: it was the ultimate flattery. As monarchs didn't sit for portraits often, this means that many of the portraits of Elizabeth I, for example, are copies of one original. Others were produced to send to foreign monarchs as a way of cementing diplomatic ties, in the hope of arranging political marriages, or to advertise one's dynasty.

Although tapestry weavers and goldsmiths were regarded as superior in the pecking order to painters, several portraitists came to be known and respected. Many of the best were from northern Europe: Hans Holbein the Younger and Gerlach Flicke were German; William Scrots, Marcus Gheeraerts the Younger and Antonis Mor were Dutch; Hans Eworth and the court miniaturists Lucas and Susanna Horenbout were Flemish; while Nicholas Hilliard, George Gower and an artist known only as 'Master John' were native English painters. They had distinct styles that attracted followers, whose paintings we describe for example, as being, 'after Holbein'.

Portraits can tell us many things, yet there is one thing that we expect from portraits that they generally can't tell us: the character or personality of the sitter. We must not mistake them for photographs!

Westminster Abbey
London

'Partners both in throne and grave, here we sleep, Elizabeth and Mary, sisters, in hope of the resurrection.'

Westminster Abbey is home to 1,000 years of royal history. Edward the Confessor first founded an Anglo-Saxon abbey here in 960, and the present abbey dates from 1245 when it was built by Henry III to house Edward the Confessor's shrine. The pointed arches, flying buttresses and rose windows are typical of the French-inspired Gothic style that was fashionable in thirteenth-century architecture, and nearly every addition to the Abbey since – including the eighteenth-century West Towers by Nicholas Hawksmoor – have copied the thirteenth-century original. The one exception is the beautiful sixteenth-century fan-vaulted Lady Chapel in the east end of the Abbey behind the High Altar, which was built by Henry VII after the death of his beloved wife, Elizabeth of York, in 1502. He, too, was subsequently buried here.

Henry VII chose Westminster Abbey as his wife's resting place because the couple had solemnised their momentous union here on 18 January 1486. (This was the last royal wedding at Westminster Abbey until 1919, when the Abbey was readopted by the modern royals with Princess Pat's – one of Queen Victoria's granddaughters – nuptials.) The marriage between the nineteen-year-old Elizabeth and the recently crowned King Henry VII was cause for celebration indeed. It marked the coming together of the warring houses of York and Lancaster: an end to the bloody Wars of the Roses that had torn England apart on and off for over thirty years. A strikingly attractive and intelligent woman, with long golden hair, Elizabeth wore her finest robes for the wedding – described as glowing 'with gold and purple dye' – and a necklace 'framed in fretted gold'. She carried symbolic white and red roses.

As with HRH Prince William and Catherine Middleton's – the Duke and Duchess of Cambridge – wedding in April 2011, Henry and Elizabeth's nuptials were marked by festivities and street parties. Accounts say that the wedding was 'celebrated with all religious and glorious magnificence at court and by their people with bonfires'.

Westminster Abbey is not only famous as a place for royal weddings. It is, of course, the country's coronation church: thirty-eight English and British monarchs have been crowned here since 1066, including all the Tudor monarchs, except Lady Jane Grey. The only other exceptions are the boy-king, Edward V, one of the 'Princes in the Tower' who was murdered before he could be crowned, and Edward VIII, who abdicated in 1936 to marry the American divorcée Wallis Simpson. The coronation chair, dating from 1298, on which every subsequent crowned monarch sat, can be seen at the Abbey, while the first monarch to introduce English into the coronation ceremony, Elizabeth I, also gave the Abbey its special status as a 'Royal Peculiar', answerable directly to the monarch.

The Abbey is also significant in Tudor history for being the burial place for many of the period's famous and most important figures.

If the Tudor dynasty has a founder, it is probably Margaret Beaufort, Countess of Richmond and Derby, and Henry VII's mother, through whom he derived his claim to the throne (she was Edward III's great-great-granddaughter through John of Gaunt's son, John Beaufort). On her tomb, in the south chapel aisle of the Lady Chapel, her effigy is a delicate gilt bronze sculpture by the Italian Pietro Torrigiano, with an impressively lifelike face and wrinkled old hands, dating from 1511.

Nearby, Edward VI, Henry VII's grandson, was buried under the altar in the Lady Chapel by his half-sister, Mary I, thereby deliberately avoiding an elaborate tomb, which could have become the locus of Protestant pilgrimage.

In turn, Mary and Elizabeth are buried at the Abbey, too. In the north chapel aisle of the Lady Chapel, one can see their large white marble tomb, on which Elizabeth lies in effigy. It is decorated with gilt Tudor roses, fleurs-de-lis, portcullises (the symbol of a 'strong fort', representing the Beaufort line of Henry VIII's grandmother) and even, interestingly, the falcon: Anne Boleyn's badge. In a final twist of fate these two rivalrous half-sisters are buried not only together, but with Elizabeth on top of Mary. Part of the Latin inscription reads in translation: 'Partners both in throne and grave, here we sleep, Elizabeth and Mary, sisters, in hope of the resurrection.'

The obvious missing Tudor is Henry VIII himself, who can be found at St George's Chapel in Windsor. Somewhat ironically, the most prestigiously placed Tudor tomb is that of Henry VIII's most overlooked wife, Anne of Cleves [see ROCHESTER CASTLE]. Anne's tomb, erected in her memory by Mary I (probably because Anne was one of the only people who showed the adult Mary affection), is to the right of the thirteenth-century mosaic pavement in front of the High Altar, and befits her wisely adopted status as the 'King's sister'.

Another splendid tomb is that of James VI of Scotland and I of England's mother, Mary, Queen of Scots. James had also paid for Elizabeth I's tomb – a generous gesture given that she had executed his mother at Fotheringhay in 1587 – but he retaliated a little by making his mother's tomb more magnificent than Elizabeth's.

James I also erected the monument and effigy to Margaret Douglas, Countess of Lennox. Margaret is a rather under-recognised figure at the Tudor court, but her lineage and succession were of vital importance to the future of England. She was the daughter of Henry VIII's elder sister, Margaret Tudor, and of Archibald Douglas, the sixth Earl of Angus. After her fiancé (or possibly even husband), Lord Thomas Howard, died in the Tower – where both he and Margaret had been imprisoned in 1536 for contracting marriage without Henry VIII's permission – Margaret married Matthew Stewart, Earl of Lennox. Their son, Henry, Lord Darnley, would go on to marry Mary, Queen of Scots and father the future James VI and I. Margaret herself, however, died in 1578 in poverty, as none of her eight children who kneels by her side on her monument survived her. Her fine and colourful alabaster effigy is a fitting tribute to a king's niece and grandmother, who experienced little of such favour in life.

Finally, there is another important Tudor woman buried at the Abbey. Frances Brandon was the daughter of Charles Brandon, Duke of Suffolk, and his third wife, Mary: Henry VIII's younger sister and widow to the French King, Louis XII. Married first to Henry Grey, Marquess of Dorset, later Duke of Suffolk, Frances was the mother to three girls, among them Lady Jane Grey. It is through her that Lady Jane Grey had a claim to the English throne. Frances's second husband, her lowly Master of Horse, Adrian

Stock (or Stokes), had the alabaster monument that you can see in St Edmund's Chapel built for her, in 1563.

There is one last discovery for the Tudor visitor to make, but you have to go next door to St Margaret's to see it. At the east end of the church is a dazzling Flemish stained-glass window, commissioned as a gift by King Ferdinand and Queen Isabella of Spain to mark the engagement of their daughter, Katherine of Aragon, to Henry VII's eldest son, Prince Arthur. By the time the window arrived, in 1509, Arthur was long dead, and Katherine had married his brother, Henry. Like many of the tombs in the Abbey, this window represents a cold and lasting memorial of the often frustrated hopes and loves of the Tudors.

Charterhouse
London

*'They were dragged [to the place of execution] in their habits,
to the great grief of the people. They were hanged,
cut down before they were dead, opened, and their bowels and
hearts burned. Their heads were then cut off,
and their bodies quartered.'*

Charterhouse (simply meaning 'Carthusian monastery') is one of London's great secrets. Its historic buildings, some dating back to the late fourteenth century, are well preserved, despite surviving a direct hit from a bomb during the Second World War. Yet not everyone knows about this incredible site in the middle of the City, and even fewer know about the sad and terrible fate that met some of its Tudor inhabitants.

Work began on the Carthusian priory of Charterhouse in 1371, next to the site of a burial ground of victims of the Black Death that had ravished London in 1349. The remains of this phase of building can be seen in the Norfolk Cloister: the rubble-stone wall was part of the original monastic cloister and you can still see the doorway to the first monastic cell to be built in 1371, Cell B, complete with serving hatch for the monk's food. The current chapel was the original priory's Chapter House and dates from the early fifteenth century.

By the time of the Tudors, the austere priory was thriving. The young Thomas More spent time at Charterhouse between 1499 and 1503, and the famous Tudor medical writer Andrew Boorde also passed thirteen years here. By the early 1530s, there was a healthy community of sixty-three souls under the prior, John Haughton. You can spot Haughton's influence on the architecture: Wash-House Court has both medieval stonework and brick buildings that were added in 1531–2, with characteristic diaperwork (the diamond or lozenge-shaped crisscross pattern made in brickwork using black or glazed bricks) among the red bricks, and the initials 'IH', for John Haughton, also picked out in black.

Haughton's name is noted here for a far more sobering reason, however, and it is one to remember as you approach Charterhouse gateway. In 1535, Haughton died a terrible death, and one of his limbs was hung outside this very gate – as a foreign reporter noted at the time – to 'terrify the other monks' into submission.

Haughton's crime was that he refused to accept in conscience Henry VIII's position as Supreme Head of the Church of England. In order to have his marriage to Katherine of Aragon annulled, and to marry Anne Boleyn, Henry VIII and his government had passed a series of Acts of Parliament in the early 1530s that effected the 'break from Rome', and established Henry VIII as the Supreme Head of the new Church of England. In April 1534, every man in the country had been required to swear the Oath of Succession, in which they promised 'to be true to Queen Anne [Boleyn], and to believe and take her for the lawful wife of the King and rightful Queen of England, and utterly to think the Lady Mary daughter to the King by Queen Katherine, but as a bastard, and thus to do without any scrupulosity of conscience'.

This incredible attempt by Henry VIII to make the whole king-dom complicit in his decision – even in their very thoughts – meant that everyone was forced to agree to the King's divorce from Katherine of Aragon and, according to the oath's preamble, to his position as Supreme Head of the Church (in place of the Pope).

After some early resistance, Haughton and most of his monks agreed to swear to the oath, but with some undisclosed conditions, which obviously came to Henry VIII's attention for, in April 1535, he required them to swear further oaths recognising his position as Supreme Head of the Church (and therefore, his displacement of the Pope). Haughton and a number of other Carthusians refused.

Punishment was swift. On 20 April, ten Charterhouse monks were sent to Newgate Prison, including Robert Lawrence, prior of the Charterhouse of Beauvale in Nottinghamshire, and Augustine Webster, prior of the Charterhouse of Axholme, Lincolnshire. Less than three weeks later, and the day after Bishop John Fisher declared that he also could not, in conscience, consent to the King's supremacy over the Church, Haughton, Lawrence and Webster were tried, convicted of treason and executed.

The foreign report on the gruesome event was graphic: 'they were dragged [to the place of execution] in their habits, to the great grief of the people. They were hanged, cut down before they were dead, opened, and their bowels and hearts burned. Their heads were then cut off, and their bodies quartered.' Another shocking report added the horrific detail that the executioner 'caused them to be ripped up in each other's presence, their arms torn off, their hearts cut out and rubbed upon their mouths and face'. The barbarity of the act was blamed directly on the King of England himself.

In June, three more monks: Sebastian Newdigate, William Exmew and Humphrey Middlemore suffered the same horren-dous fate.

By May 1537, some two years later, with the memory of the martyrs still fresh and with ongoing deprivations – their food restricted, their books removed – twenty of the monks at Charterhouse agreed to sign an acknowledgement of the King's supremacy. Incredibly, there still remained ten brave monks willing to deny it: a testament to their extraordinary faith given the certainty of their punishment. They were taken to Newgate Prison and put in chains. By mid-June, three were dead, and four perilously sick. By September, all but one had died. The survivor was executed at Tyburn in August 1540. It seems highly likely that the others had starved to death.

It is fitting, therefore, that on the east wall of Chapel Court there is a memorial to the Carthusian martyrs who suffered for their conscience.

In 1537, Charterhouse was surrendered to the Crown, and went the way of all monasteries in November 1538. But it was to have a new lease of life in the second half of the sixteenth century as a private home.

In 1545, Sir Edward North, Chancellor of the Court of Augmentations – a kind of select committee responsible for disposing of monastic lands – took Charterhouse for himself, and converted it into a sumptuous aristocratic mansion. He demolished the church and cloisters, and built Master's Court in 1546. The Long Gallery that he put on the first floor of the south range was destroyed as a result of a 1941 firebomb, as was the hammer-beam ceiling of the Great Hall, but the rest of the Hall – its high windows, oriel window and interior décor complete with Tudor roses – is from North's original scheme. Elizabeth I came to stay with North in 1558, soon after her accession, and again in 1561.

North's son sold Charterhouse in 1565 to Thomas Howard, fourth Duke of Norfolk [see ARUNDEL CASTLE], and, as Norfolk's primary London establishment, it became known as Howard

House. Norfolk added the beautifully carved wooden screen to the Great Hall. Look out for his initials and the date of the installation: 1571. Norfolk also enlarged the Great Chamber left by North, adding in the fireplace, elaborate chimneypiece and the decorated plaster ceiling (unfortunately, only the part within the bay is original; the rest did not survive the 1941 fire, but is a faithful reproduction). Norfolk also added the brick wall and vault to the Norfolk Cloister, to create a striking entrance to his tennis court, and it still bears his name. Unfortunately, like the fortunes of so many Tudor courtiers, Norfolk's luck took a turn for the worse, and Howard House became Norfolk's prison: in 1571 he was put under house arrest and was executed for treason at the Tower in 1572.

The house passed to his son Philip Howard, Earl of Arundel, spent a brief period as the Portuguese embassy (of all things) in the 1570s and returned to the Howard family in 1601. Elizabeth stayed once more soon before her death. In James I's reign, the then owner, Lord Thomas Howard, sold it to Thomas Sutton. Sutton set up a school, which was the forerunner of the famous Charterhouse public school in Godalming, and an almshouse for eighty elderly men, 'the Brothers', still known as Sutton's Hospital in Charterhouse.

Lincoln's Inn
London

*'Pluck up thy spirits, man, and be not afraid
to do thine office. My neck is very short.'*

At the centre of bustling London, Lincoln's Inn is a leafy,
peaceful eleven-acre enclave that has housed law students,
barristers and Benchers (the highest rank of membership of the
Inn) for nearly 600 years. It is by far the oldest of the four Inns of
Court. Its oldest records, the 'Black Books', date from 1422, and
there is evidence of an even earlier history in the form of an arch-
way surviving from a previous building: the London palace of the
Bishop of Chichester. Many of the Inn's buildings look outwardly
Tudor, including both the Lincoln's Inn Fields Gatehouse and the
Great Hall with its chimneys, onion domes and diaperwork, but
they are actually Victorian, constructed in a Tudor style.

Nevertheless, there are two pieces of architecture here that
provide a tangible connection to one of the most revered men of
the Tudor age: Sir (or Saint, depending on your theological inclin-
ation) Thomas More.

Born in 1478, More was sent as a child to the household of
Cardinal John Morton – who, legend has it, prophesied that More

would 'prove a marvellous man' – before being educated at Canterbury College, Oxford and New Inn. He was then admitted to Lincoln's Inn, where his father was already a Bencher, on 12 February 1496, having just turned eighteen years of age. He was called to the Bar five or six years later.

The Lincoln's Inn that More knew centred on the Old Hall, built between 1489 and 1492, only a few years after Henry VII came to the throne and before Christopher Columbus headed for the New World. This beautiful building would have been where the young More ate and drank, debated with his friends, or watched the Christmas revels when a 'Lord of Misrule' (often some lowly person, dressed in motley) presided over the Feast of Fools, a bacchanalian time of drinking and partying. The hall was enlarged with two bay windows in 1582, and has been remodelled over the years (in the eighteenth century, a disproportionately heavy plaster ceiling was added which was removed when the hall was rebuilt stone by stone in 1924–8), but it would still be familiar to More, whose arms are now shown in two of the windows. In later years, More would also have regularly walked into the Inn through the old gatehouse on Chancery Lane, which was built in 1521 (the gates themselves date from 1564).

It was Thomas More's early adult life at Lincoln's Inn that fundamentally shaped both his identity and destiny. Here, More made some influential friends: scholars like John Colet, the future Dean of St Paul's, and Thomas Linacre, the noted physician. They were humanists, which in the sixteenth century did not imply atheism but an intellectual focus on the rediscovery of classical learning, including an interest in reforming the Church by turning to the original Greek scriptures. Through another scholar, Lord Mountjoy, More met the greatest humanist of the age, Desiderius Erasmus, who became his lifelong friend, and in whose company, in 1499, More walked from Lincoln's Inn to Eltham Palace to meet the young Prince Henry, who would ultimately determine his fate.

More was attracted to the austere monastic life and spent time at nearby Charterhouse. Later, his son-in-law recorded that More wore a hair shirt and practised self-flagellation. More, however, decided against the monastic life and chose instead to marry – in 1505 to Jane Colt and, after her death in 1511, to Alice Middleton – and accounts of his character suggest a cheerful, charismatic and intelligent man. Erasmus called him 'a man for all seasons' – the moniker Robert Bolt used as the title to his famous play and film about More's life – because of his jovial disposition, while in 1521, Richard Whittington described him as 'a man of angel's wit and singular learning'. This wit found its apogee in his book *Utopia* ('utopia' is an ambiguous word that suggests both the Greek for 'no place' and 'happy place'). This is a satirical account of a traveller in a fabled land in which pride and greed do not exist, war is thought only fit for beasts, all property is communal and potential spouses can inspect each other's naked bodies before deciding to marry. The book remains one of the founding texts of political science and philosophy, and is still on undergraduate reading lists around the world.

More eventually entered the public sphere. He sat in Parliament, acted as a diplomat and became a member of Henry VIII's council. Henry was very fond of More: there are accounts of the two going up onto a palace's lead roofs to study the stars and planets together, and of Henry visiting More at his house in Chelsea and walking with him in the garden 'by the space of an hour, holding his arm about his neck'.

Henry was particularly pleased with More's help in composing the riposte to Martin Luther that won the King the title of 'Defender of the Faith'. It was the first of More's many anti-heretical actions: in 1525, More was involved in raids on Lutheran books, and four years later produced a sharp and brilliant volume called *Dialogues Concerning Heresies* which challenged and refuted the teachings of William Tyndale, among others. After Cardinal Thomas Wolsey fell from grace [see CHRIST CHURCH] and More took his role as Lord Chancellor, he used his new powers to further his campaign against heretics, including approving several executions.

Despite the honour of his elevated position, More knew better than to trust the man who had deposed the 'wise and honourable' Wolsey. His remarks – that he couldn't rely on Henry's favour for 'If my head could win him a castle in France... it should not fail to go', and that 'Politics be King's games... and for the more part, played upon scaffolds' – show a shrewd understanding of the corrupting nature of power and, in particular, Henry's tendency to punish failure in those on whom he most relied.

Yet More also had a conscience: one that proved to be his downfall. He felt unable to accept Henry's repudiation of his marriage to Katherine of Aragon, both resigning from his post as Lord Chancellor in May 1532 and refusing to attend Anne Boleyn's coronation in June 1533. Like John Haughton and the monks of Charterhouse he then refused to consent to the King's displacement of the Pope in the role of Supreme Head of the Church by swearing the Oath of Succession. As a result of this disloyalty, he was imprisoned in the Tower, and tried over a year later under an act passed in the interim that made it treason to deny the King's supremacy. Silent in the face of his accusers, he was eventually convicted by the perjury of the villainously named Sir Richard Rich [also see THE TOWER OF LONDON].

On 6 July 1535, More was beheaded. His wit did not desert him at the last. He joked with an officer on the scaffold, 'I pray you, master lieutenant, see me safe up, and for my coming down, let me shift for myself', and comforted the executioner, 'Pluck up thy spirits, man, and be not afraid to do thine office. My neck is very short.' Four hundred years later, Pope Pius XI canonised More as a Catholic saint and martyr.

Lincoln's Inn remembers its famous son. A copy of Hans Holbein's portrait of More as Lord Chancellor, with his rich gown and chain of office, hangs in the Great Hall, but the greatest treasure is hidden in a nearby committee room. Here, a prized Holbein miniature of More ensures that in this place, where many great men and women have studied and worked, More's profound determination to act according to his conscience will never be forgotten.

Guildhall
City of London

'On 18 July, in the first year of our reign.'
Letter signed 'Jane the Queen', from July 1553

Guildhall, which is situated at the centre of the City's square mile on the site of an old Roman amphitheatre, is one of London's great survivors. It was the only secular building to escape the Great Fire of London in 1666 and it survived the Blitz in 1940, though in both instances it lost its roof and windows. In the fifteenth century, it was the second largest edifice in London, after the Old St Paul's Cathedral, and the formidable Great Hall and undercroft date from that period. It is now on its fifth roof, designed by Sir Giles Gilbert Scott to recreate what the medieval roof may have looked like, but everything beneath window-height is to the design of the original master mason, John Croxton, who built the Great Hall between 1411 and 1430. It is Gothic perpendicular in style, and an impressive 151 feet long, 48 feet wide and 89 feet high. The five-foot-thick walls may partly explain its durability.

In the Tudor century, it was the setting for important trials: notably the momentous trial of Thomas Cranmer, Archbishop of

Canterbury [see BROAD STREET, OXFORD]; Guildford Dudley and his wife, Lady Jane Grey.

The traditional version of Jane's story is littered with misapprehensions, not least of which is that she is known as the 'Nine Days' Queen'. In fact, her reign extended for thirteen days, from the death of Edward VI on 6 July 1553 to the declaration of Mary as Queen on 19 July. She is also known to history as Lady Jane Grey, but after her marriage on 25 May 1553, she always signed herself with her husband's surname, Jane Dudley. Most tellingly of all, she is thought of as a rebellious pretender to the throne, thrust into the limelight by her ambitious father-in-law, John Dudley, Duke of Northumberland.

The truth is that, according to the provisions of Edward VI's 'device for the succession', Jane was Edward's rightful chosen heir and Mary the illegitimate rebel, and it was not only Northumberland, but the whole political establishment who originally backed Jane. When Edward died, it looked likely that Queen Jane would have a long and prosperous rule.

Instead, Jane became one of history's victims. Just sixteen years old, pretty, petite and slender, with brown eyes, auburn hair and fair, lightly freckled skin, she seems to have been a serious but charming bluestocking. Her extraordinary gift for study and languages is best illustrated by the fact that when Roger Ascham, Elizabeth I's tutor, arrived at the Greys' house at Bradgate in August 1550, he found everyone out hunting except for the fourteen-year-old Jane, who sat alone, reading Plato in the original Greek.

But Jane's eventual downfall had nothing to do with her character: it was a matter of birth. Her parents were Henry Grey, Marquess of Dorset (later Duke of Suffolk), and Lady Frances Brandon, daughter of Henry VIII's younger sister, Mary [see THE CHURCH OF ST MARY, BURY ST EDMUNDS]. When the sick and childless Edward VI was looking to provide himself with a legitimate heir, his gaze landed on Jane, and her fate was sealed.

Under Henry VIII's last will, and a statute from 1544, if Edward died without children, the English throne was to pass to Mary, and then to Elizabeth. But Edward's half-sisters were only in the line of succession because in 1536 Henry VIII had established that it was the king's right to determine his successor beyond the usual principle of male primogeniture. This meant Henry could later add Mary and Elizabeth to the line of succession while retaining his profound belief in their illegitimacy – for they had been declared bastards when his marriages to their mothers failed. Their claim to the throne was not by right: it was a gift from the King, and what one monarch had given another could take away.

As King, Edward also had the right to determine the succession, and since his half-sisters were officially bastards, he never seems to have considered their claim. Edward was also desperate not to hand the crown to his Catholic sister Mary, for he had been busy entrenching the Protestant reformation in England. When he fell ill in early 1553, and his mind turned to his mortality, his first plan for the succession intended that only male heirs would succeed. Later, when he realised his illness was terminal, he – or someone with his consent – made a crucial change to his 'device for the succession', amending it in favour of 'Lady Jane and her heirs male'. On 21 June 1553, Edward signed and sealed this legal document, and 102 witnesses added their support.

Yet, when Edward died a fortnight later on 6 July, the government was unprepared. For several days Edward's death remained a badly kept secret. Jane was not informed that she was queen until Sunday 9 July. The council also underestimated Mary, failing to anticipate her bold and rebellious actions after sources told her that Edward was dying. When Robert Dudley was sent to collect her the day after Edward's death, he found that Mary had already escaped to her strongholds in East Anglia and, a day later, had had herself declared queen [see FRAMLINGHAM].

Meanwhile, in London, Jane was proclaimed queen on 10 July, and escorted, with her husband, Guildford Dudley, to the Tower in great pomp and ceremony to await her (and possibly his) coronation.

Having let Mary escape, the government now needed to muster an army to tackle her rebellion, but they failed to do so with sufficient speed. Northumberland was given charge of the troops but, taking the long way towards Mary's base at Framlingham, via Cambridge, in the hope of picking up reinforcements, he didn't reach Suffolk until 18 July. In the interim, Mary had amassed a force of close to 10,000 and had probably even acquired artillery.

To both the council in London and Northumberland on the march, it became evident that might was on Mary's side. In the afternoon of 19 July, sensing their hand had been forced, the council performed a volte-face and proclaimed Mary queen. On 20 July, Northumberland followed suit. Ten days after being told she was queen, Jane was told she was not.

Keen to evade punishment, the council looked for a scapegoat and pointed the finger at the absent Northumberland. After Mary had taken full power, he was tried for treason on 18 August, even though most of the jury had been just as committed to Queen Jane as he.

Jane remained in the Tower, now a prisoner, until her trial on 13 November 1553. Staging the trial at Guildhall, rather than in the privacy of Westminster or the Tower, was in itself an act of humiliation. Dressed in black and carrying a Bible, Jane maintained her composure, even when the sentence to be 'burned alive on Tower Hill or beheaded as the Queen should please' was pronounced in Guildhall's cavernous Great Hall.

Few, however, believed it would end that way. It was still

expected that Jane, whom even Mary accepted had done little wrong herself, would, in time, be released.

This all changed after Sir Thomas Wyatt the Younger's rebellion in early February 1554 [see WINCHESTER CATHEDRAL]: an uprising about which Jane had no knowledge and with which she could not have been involved, imprisoned as she was in the Tower. Seeing her as a target for rebellion, and perhaps in revenge at Jane's father's involvement, Mary decided to execute Jane and Guildford. The sentence was carried out almost immediately: both were beheaded on 12 February 1554. Jane had not yet reached her seventeenth birthday.

In the years after her death, Jane's story was rewritten by the victors: their guilt obscuring her legal claim to the throne. At Guildhall, remember the young, bright Jane Dudley, whose fate was decided by forces greater than herself.

Eltham Palace
London

'The Prince of Wales was kept under such strict
supervision that he might have been a young girl.'

Eltham Palace was the childhood home of Henry VIII. Perched on a hill with magnificent views over London, it was built as a moated mansion for Anthony Bek, the Bishop of Durham in 1295, and became a royal home ten years later. Among its many royal residents and builders were Edward III, Richard II, Henry IV – who spent most of his Christmases as King here – and Edward IV. At its zenith, it was a vast palace, far bigger than Hampton Court, with an outer court (you can see the Lord Chancellor's lodgings, which made up part of this court, to the left over the moat bridge), substantial chapel, apartments for the King and Queen, a Great Hall, an array of kitchens and lodgings for courtiers. Edward IV and his wife, Elizabeth, entertained 2,000 people here during Christmas 1482. Now, it is a masterpiece of a different sort, having been turned into an art deco wonderland by the Courtauld family in the 1930s. Nevertheless, there is an important Tudor history to the palace to discover.

Henry VIII was born on 28 June 1491 at Greenwich Palace (which sadly no longer stands). He was the third child and second son of Henry VII and Elizabeth of York. Like his elder brother,

Arthur [see LUDLOW CASTLE], he had symbolic titles bestowed on him as an infant, becoming the nominal Constable of Dover Castle, Lord Warden of the Cinque Ports, Earl Marshal and Lieutenant of England, Duke of York, Warden of the Scottish Marches and Knight of the Garter. The most memorable of these investitures for him must have been when as a child of nearly three and a half (doting parents take note), he rode a great warhorse through London and was bathed in a wooden tub in order to be dubbed a Knight of the Bath the following day.

Throughout his childhood at Eltham, Henry was often separated from his father, who had his hands full dealing with the threat posed by pretenders to his throne. He also lived almost entirely apart from his elder brother, who had been given a separate establishment at Farnham and was then shipped off to Ludlow at the age of six. Henry was left with his mother, Elizabeth, his two surviving sisters, Margaret and Mary, and the overbearing figure of his grandmother, Lady Margaret Beaufort.

Into this female world came the poet John Skelton, who was Henry's tutor from the mid-1490s to 1502. Under his influence, Henry became an accomplished musician and linguist. He learnt to play the lute, virginals and organ, to sing well, and to speak and write a number of languages, including Latin. When the renowned humanist Desiderius Erasmus visited the young Duke of York with Thomas More in 1499 [see LINCOLN'S INN], he was so impressed that he later noted 'when the King was no more than a child... he had a vivid and active mind, above measure to execute whatever tasks he undertook'. 'You would say,' he added, 'that he was a universal genius.' Skelton also entrusted Henry with a dedicated book of advice, *Speculum Principis*, or *The Mirror of Princes*, in which he exhorted him to 'pick a wife for yourself and love but her alone' – advice that Henry imperfectly followed on a total of six occasions.

In these seminal years of education and female affection, Henry would have walked under the spectacular oak hammer-beam ceiling of Eltham's Great Hall, erected by Edward IV and still there today. In Henry VIII's youth, it would have been partly gilded and we know it had an impact on the young Henry, because he recreated it at his pleasure palace of Hampton Court thirty years later. He would also have known the medieval stone bay windows in the Great Hall, but little else would have been exactly as it is now. The timber screen at the dais end with the carved beasts is a good guess – it is based on a fifteenth-century rood screen – but it was added by the architects John Seely and Paul Paget in the 1930s, while the stained glass in the windows dates from 1936.

Henry's world changed when he was ten years old. In the first of several losses, his brother Arthur died before Henry turned eleven. Less than a year later, his mother died on 11 February 1503, on her thirty-seventh birthday and, four months after that, his elder sister, Margaret, moved to Edinburgh to marry James IV. Henry never saw her again. In the place of relatives came further titles – Duke of Cornwall, Prince of Wales, Earl of Chester.

The spate of deaths in the family – including five infant mortalities – in so short a time also rocked Henry's father. He responded by sheltering his remaining son from danger. Unlike Arthur, who had been sent to the Welsh Marches (the part of England bordering Wales) as a training for kingship, Henry was to receive no such apprenticeship. In early 1508, a Spanish envoy called Gutierre Gomez de Fuensalida visited England and reported that 'the Prince of Wales was kept under such strict supervision that he might have been a young girl' and was 'so subjected that he does not speak a word except in response to what the King asks him'. It is not wild to speculate about a link between his sheltered and repressed childhood and his extravagant adulthood, or the excessive masculinity he displayed as a grown man compared with his upbringing 'like a young girl'.

Henry continued to prize Eltham as a young man, extending and remodelling the palace during 1519–22. It was at Eltham that Cardinal Thomas Wolsey formulated a famous set of rules to regulate the royal household and court in 1526: the Eltham Ordinances. But Henry VIII was the last monarch to spend any considerable time at the palace, drawn back, no doubt, to his place of childhood abandon.

It is particularly regrettable then, that after the early sixteenth century, the palace was allowed to fall into decay. By the seventeenth century, parts of the palace had collapsed. During the eighteenth century, the ruined palace became a farm, and the Great Hall was used as a barn. Today, only the ragstone Great Hall, three fifteenth-century gables and the foundations of the royal apartments remain from the grand palace of Henry's boyhood. Eltham may be famous now as a quintessentially art deco house but, with a little imagination, we can picture the place as the formative boyhood home of England's most notorious monarch.

Richmond Palace
Surrey

*'Upon each side of this goodly court… there are galleries
with many windows full lightsome and commodious.'*

All that remains of Henry VII's great palace at Richmond is the red-brick palace gatehouse on Richmond Green (now in a road called The Wardrobe, testament to the buildings that once stood there) and the outer courtyard, now known as Old Palace Yard. As you look around you'll see several signs marking the area where the palace once stood. Much of it was torn down during Oliver Cromwell's Commonwealth and, in the eighteenth century, new buildings such as Trumpeter's House were constructed out of the surviving Tudor materials. Yet, it is possible to get a sense of what this grand palace must have been like and see a glimpse of the character of the King whose coat of arms – the red dragon of Wales and the greyhound of Richmond – is still above the gate.

Henry VII became King at the Battle of Bosworth [see BOSWORTH] in 1485 at the age of just twenty-eight. He is chiefly remembered, when he is remembered at all, for his miserly avarice, secretive nature and sombre court, but these are qualities that should be more fairly associated with him only in the last few years

48

of his life when, suffering from a recurrent illness, he grieved the loss of his wife, his firstborn son and many of his infant children, and feared greatly for the succession. Founding a dynasty is not without its anxieties.

Consider his position in 1485: having grown up in Wales, he had only once briefly been to England; he had no experience of governing, or training as a prince; he had spent fourteen years as a captive in exile in Brittany; and he had neither wealth nor land. Yet, this usurper rallied people around him and, once King, made prudent and effective decisions to consolidate his rule. He must have been a natural leader: confident, capable and charismatic enough to inspire support, and clever enough to maintain it. Sixteenth-century historian Polydore Vergil tells us that his 'mind was brave and resolute', that he was gracious and kind, and generous in hospitality, but severe with those who failed him. His appearance helped, as he was above average height (a Tudor trait), slender but strong and was 'remarkably attractive' with a cheerful face and small, blue eyes, though his teeth were 'few, poor and blackish'.

One of his wise decisions was to marry Elizabeth of York, Edward IV's eldest daughter, four months after Bosworth: in one stroke he finally managed to unite the warring houses of York and Lancaster. Eight months after their wedding, Elizabeth gave birth to the first of their eight children: Prince Arthur, born 19 September 1486.

But a king needs an heir *and* a spare, and Henry still faced threats to his throne. He established a 200-strong armed bodyguard for himself (the forerunners to the Yeomen of the Guard), as he was acutely aware that his claim to the throne was weaker than that of the Yorkist pretenders who would emerge during his reign.

The first was Lambert Simnel, who claimed to be Edward, Earl of Warwick, the son of Edward IV's brother George, Duke of

Clarence. Simnel was supported by John de la Pole, Earl of Lincoln, and was crowned King of England in Dublin in May 1487, before landing on the Cumbrian coast with 2,000 Dutch mercenaries in June. But, when it came to battle at Stoke, Simnel's army was squarely defeated. What was more, Henry could demonstrate that he had the real Warwick in the Tower of London!

Another pretender to the throne, on the other hand, was not so easily dispatched. The curious case of Perkin Warbeck is shrouded in mystery to this day, and we will probably never know for sure whether he was in fact Richard, Duke of York – or Richard IV – the younger brother of Edward V, one of the 'Princes in the Tower' who had miraculously escaped, or simply a rank imposter. Certainly, it is true that Warbeck managed to convince Charles VIII, King of France; Margaret of York, who welcomed him as her nephew; Isabella of Spain; and Maximilian, the new Holy Roman Emperor, that he was the rightful king of England.

This foreign support created great instability for the new Tudor King, and it was a threat that rumbled on and on. Henry decided to act ruthlessly. In early 1495, he arrested and beheaded those he suspected of plotting Warbeck's usurpation, including Sir William Stanley, his step-uncle who had courageously defected from Yorkist ranks in order to help him at Bosworth.

The destruction of local support meant that when Warbeck finally landed at Deal, Kent, in July 1495, his troops were quickly obliterated. And when – despite having the support of the Irish Earl of Desmond and James IV of Scotland – Warbeck's second attempt to invade at Land's End in 1497 with 8,000 men was met by the full force of Henry's army, James IV saw the error of his ways. Warbeck's troops were crushed, and he was finally executed in November 1499.

These had been troubling times and coupled with a Cornish insurrection (defeated in battle on Blackheath) and one final pretender, Ralph Wilford, the majority of Henry VII's reign was marked by uncertainty and constant danger.

Henry cleverly used the marriages of his children to strengthen the new dynasty: Prince Arthur was betrothed to Katherine of Aragon in 1497 and they were married with great pomp in 1501. Subsequently, Princess Margaret married James IV of Scotland in August 1503. Nevertheless, despite the elimination of claimants to his throne, after 1500 the succession became more precarious: Henry's third son died as an infant in June, and two years later his eldest son, Arthur, followed, leaving only Prince Henry as a male heir. Henry and Elizabeth comforted themselves with the prospect of more children: a daughter was born ten months after Arthur's death, but both the baby and her mother died just days after the birth. Henry was plunged into years of grief and anxiety, during which he searched unsuccessfully for a new wife (even considering Katherine of Aragon's sister, the unpromising-sounding Joanna the Mad), while his health steadily declined.

Richmond Palace, however, was a product of the rare period of his reign when Henry was most secure and contented. There had been a royal manor at Sheen since the twelfth century: Edward III had built a palace there, and died in it in 1377; Henry V had rebuilt it in 1413–1422, but the palace had burned down during Christmas 1497. This is when Henry VII decided to rebuild it, naming it after the title he held before he became King: Earl of Richmond.

Henry retained the shell of Henry V's stone moated keep and added red-brick lodgings that went to three storeys high, with an enchanting series of four-storey turrets topped with gilded domes and pinnacles. Inside, the rooms were richly decorated with tapestries, painted ceilings and walls decked with gold roses and portcullises. Henry added, naturally, a Great Hall, chapel, fountains and a large outer courtyard. A visitor in 1501 noted that 'upon each side of this goodly court... there are galleries with many windows full lightsome and commodious'. Such extravagant use of glass was rare – and expensive. Set in a deer park and surrounded by 'most fair and pleasant' gardens, Richmond cost Henry £20,000 (around £6 million today). Some of the oaks in the present-day Richmond Park are old enough to have been seen by Henry VII, and he might even have hunted some of the ancestors of the deer that still roam here.

The palace was a way of signalling Henry's magnificence and invulnerability. Like his constant warfare against pretenders, it depended on his creative brilliance in finding new ways to extract revenue from his subjects: such brilliance that, by the end of his reign, many felt him to be, in fact, greedy and rapacious. It was not for nothing that Lord Mountjoy wrote on Henry VIII's accession, 'Avarice is expelled from the country.' How wrong Mountjoy's proclamation would prove to be by the time Henry VIII was finished with the throne!

Henry VII died late at night on Saturday 21 April 1509 at Richmond Palace. It was also at Richmond that his granddaughter, Elizabeth I, died in 1603. But while Elizabeth is remembered, Henry VII, like Richmond Palace itself, was quickly forgotten. This incomplete monument reminds us of the Tudor we have neglected: Henry VII, the first monarch of the dynasty.

Hampton Court Palace
Surrey

'Hampton Court is a Royal Palace,
magnificently built with brick…consisting
of noble edifices in very beautiful work.'
Paul Hentzner, visiting German tourist, 1598

Hampton Court Palace is arguably the finest remaining Tudor palace; it was certainly one of Henry VIII's favourites. In the sixteenth century, this Tudor palace was even more magnificent, but William III and Mary II demolished some of the Tudor buildings in the late seventeenth century, replacing them with their baroque palace, meaning that today Hampton Court is a palace of two halves.

The first sight of the Tudor palace is of the Great Gatehouse, built by Cardinal Thomas Wolsey – Lord Chancellor of England, papal legate and Henry VIII's right-hand man – in 1522, and lowered in 1772 from its original five storeys. The Gatehouse bears two terracotta roundels featuring busts of Roman emperors (there are another nine in the palace) that were commissioned by Wolsey from Florentine sculptor Giovanni da Maiano to symbolise Henry's good rule. Unfortunately, Wolsey unwittingly chose two of Rome's worst tyrants, Nero and Tiberius, as his exemplars!

Externally, early Tudor houses often give the impression of being fortified and defensible. You will usually see crenulations, battlements, turrets and gatehouse towers. For the most part, however, these were decorative features, rather than offering any real hope of defence.

Hampton Court is a good example: crenulated like a castle, it is nevertheless utterly indefensible, and was from the very beginning intended to be a palace of pleasure, where Wolsey and Henry VIII could entertain foreign ambassadors, feast, hunt and joust. The first courtyard, Base Court, built by Wolsey, testifies to this role: it is surrounded by forty apartments, which, with their two rooms, private garderobe (or lavatory) and fireplace, would have been the height of luxury for visiting guests. The wine fountain you can see in this courtyard is a recent installation on the site of an original fountain or conduit, and is modelled on the fountain in the Field of Cloth of Gold painting in the permanent 'Young Henry VIII' exhibition [see also LEEDS CASTLE]. Wolsey also built Clock Court, now named after the wonderful astronomical clock made for Henry VIII in 1540 by Nicholas Oursian, Deviser of the King's Horologies (or 'clockmaker'), that you can see on Anne Boleyn's gatehouse. As well as showing the time and date, it displays the phases of the moon and the times of the tides, and features the sun orbiting the earth. (Just three years after it was made, Copernicus would discover that it was, conversely, the earth that orbited the sun.)

Although Wolsey had always referred to Hampton Court as Henry's palace, and had built suites for both the King and Queen, Henry properly acquired the palace when Wolsey fell from grace in 1529. He spent £60,000 extending it over ten years: roughly equivalent to £19 million today. Among his additions were tennis courts, bowling alleys, a tiltyard (for jousting), the extraordinary Great Kitchens and his magnificent Great Hall with its spectacular hammer-beam ceiling. Of these, only the Great Kitchens and Great Hall survive today (although you can see some remaining towers from the tiltyard in the grounds, one of them emerging from the eponymously named Tiltyard Café).

The Great Hall was used for feasts, masques and revels, and twice-daily meals when the court was in residence. On the most lavish occasions, it would have been hung with the priceless tapestries that adorn it today. These Abraham Tapestries that Henry had woven in the Brussels workshop of Willem de Kempaneer at vast expense in the early 1540s, signify that, like Abraham, Henry saw himself a patriarch, making a new covenant with God and being granted, in return, a son and heir late in life. If you look closely at the tapestries on the walls of Hampton Court's Great Hall, now tarnished by age, you can still see they are woven with threads of real gold and silver and would have glittered dazzlingly in candlelight.

Although the Great Hall was built for Henry VIII and Anne Boleyn, Anne was not alive to see it when it was finished in 1536. Indeed, the workmen had to quickly knock out the carvings of her heraldic beast, the falcon, and replace them with the panther of Henry's new Queen, Jane Seymour; but they missed a couple, which can still be seen high in the rafters today.

There are, in fact, visual cues and lingering memories of all Henry's wives in the palace. Look out for the pomegranate of Katherine of Aragon above the buttery door and the leather mâché badges on the ceiling of the Great Watching Chamber (completed in 1537), some of which feature Jane Seymour's badge of a crowned phoenix rising from a castle between two rose bushes. Further down the Processional Gallery, Henry VIII's Council Chamber (possibly one of two) was where a treaty of marriage between Henry VIII and Anne of Cleves was signed in 1539, and it was in the Royal Pew, or Holyday Closet, of the Chapel Royal that Henry reportedly found a letter left for him by Archbishop Thomas Cranmer, detailing the infidelities of his fifth wife,

Katherine Howard – the day after the kingdom had given thanks in prayer for his happy marriage [see PONTEFRACT CASTLE]. Since her subsequent beheading, visitors have reported seeing Katherine's ghost running screaming up and down the 'Haunted Gallery', attempting to plead with Henry for her life. There are also happier memories here: Henry married his last wife, Kateryn Parr on 12 July 1543 in the Queen's Privy Closet at Hampton Court, before a select audience of only nineteen people.

The central story of Hampton Court, as the commissioning of the Abraham Tapestries reveals, is that this was the birthplace of Henry's only legitimate son and heir, Edward, later King Edward VI. After an excruciating labour of two days and three nights, Jane gave birth to Edward on 12 October 1537. These glad tidings were long awaited, and one letter to Henry VIII expressed the mood of the kingdom when it congratulated him on 'the most joyful news that has come to England these many years of the birth of a prince'. Prince Edward's christening in the Chapel at Hampton Court on 15 October was an ostentatious and impressive affair. Under its gorgeous blue and gold-starred ceiling, with its baby-faced gilt cherubs, the great and good of Tudor England assembled for a ceremony that lasted for hours.

The apartments that were built for the new young prince are still standing, and you can see them on the left of Chapel Court. The Royal Collection paintings at Hampton Court also evoke this heritage. In the Processional Gallery, you can see a seventeenth-century copy of the Whitehall Mural by Remigius van Leemput [see THE WALKER ART GALLERY] that recreates, in miniature, a painting that was almost certainly finished when Jane was pregnant with Edward. A full-length portrait of the boy-king, nearby, mimics his father's famous stance in the mural. Finally, *The Family of Henry VIII* painting of 1545 outside the Chapel Royal depicts Henry VIII at the proud centre of his family, between the young

Edward, his favourite wife, Jane Seymour, and Princesses Mary and Elizabeth. (The other two figures are almost certainly Henry's court fool, Will Somer, and a female fool called Jane.)

The only trouble is that this last picture is fictional. Jane Seymour did not live until 1545; in fact, she never left the childbed where she had so victoriously given Henry his much desired son. Just two weeks after Edward's birth, she died of puerperal sepsis, or childbed fever. Her heart and innards are buried in the chapel, while the procession to her funeral at St George's Chapel in Windsor Castle started from Hampton Court. The joys and griefs of Henry VIII echo off the walls of this, his most incredible surviving palace.

AN HEIR AND A SPARE

Henry VIII's life was dogged and determined by his hope of having sons. He, and most people of his time, believed that one of his most important tasks as King was to provide at least one adult male heir to succeed him peacefully when he died.

This was not misogyny on Henry's part; rather, there was no precedent of female rule: England had never had a crowned queen regnant (a ruling queen, as opposed to a queen consort). In the twelfth century, Matilda, the daughter of Henry I, had succeeded to the throne and was immediately challenged by her cousin, Stephen of Blois. Their struggle for the throne led to civil war in England, and Matilda was never crowned. Henry VIII feared that if one of his daughters succeeded him, it would prompt civil war or, worse, she would marry a foreign prince and bring England under the rule of a foreign power (as indeed did occur when Mary I married Philip II of Spain). For this reason, in sixteenth-century France, under the 'Salic law', women were not able to succeed to the throne.

So Henry needed a son. He also needed that son to be at least fifteen years old by the time of his death. Children could not rule alone and, instead, would be governed by a regent or group of councillors. This was never ideal – as the example of Richard III and the 'Princes in the Tower' had shown, regents were not always to be trusted, and if there were many councillors, their tussle for power over a young king might also endanger the peace and security of the country.

Henry VIII had grown up aware of his history: he knew that in the thirty years before his father became king, England had been in an on-off state of bloody civil war, fought between the Lancastrians and the Yorkists (the Wars of the Roses). The marriage of his father and mother, he a Lancastrian, she a Yorkist, had brought peace, and the last thing that Henry VIII wanted was to return England to bloodshed. He needed a line of adult princes to prevent it from happening again.

This meant making haste: Henry himself had been only seventeen when his father died at the age of fifty-two. He was worried that if he didn't have a son by his early thirties, he might die in his fifties without an adult male heir. Sadly, that was exactly what came to pass. His son Edward was only nine when Henry died. Nor was one son enough. Children died easily. Henry's own brother, Arthur, had died at the age of fifteen. Henry's own sons – the illegitimate Henry Fitzroy [see

FRAMLINGHAM], and his legitimate heir, later King Edward VI –
died aged seventeen and fifteen respectively.

So, having sons remained a priority for Henry VIII until the
end; the peace and prosperity of England rested on the fruit of
his wives' wombs. Ironically, he could never know that all three
of his legitimate children would reign; that his youngest daughter would prove to be one of England's greatest monarchs; and
that his dynasty would, nevertheless, end after his children's
generation.

South East

St George's Chapel, Windsor Castle
Berkshire

'Divine Providence has mingled my joy with the bitterness of the death of her who brought me this happiness.'

St George's Chapel at Windsor Castle has played a unique role in British history as the burial place for many kings and queens, among them Edward VII and Queen Alexandra, George V and Queen Mary, and George VI and Elizabeth, the Queen Mother. The stunning perpendicular chapel was the brainchild of Edward IV, and work started in 1475, but Henry VII added the intricate vaulted ceiling and Henry VIII completed the chapel. It is Henry VIII's magnificent coat of arms that features above the organ loft between the nave and the quire. Above all, it is a place of pilgrimage because it is the burial place of King Henry VIII and his third and favourite wife, Jane Seymour.

There is an extraordinary amount of beautiful detail to spot in the chapel, and you could while away many hours taking it all in. Like Henry VII's chapel at Westminster Abbey, which features the

Knights of the Bath, the quire at St George's displays the carved and painted crests of the Knights of the Garter (the more recent female Knights have coronets and no swords, with the exception of Her Majesty the Queen). Henry VIII's 'stall plate' (bronze plaque) marking his own infant elevation to the Garter is here (you can spot it as the highest and one of the largest in the stall, two to the left of the Sovereign's). The beautiful, wooden oriel window in the quire was built for Katherine of Aragon, and is carved with intertwining roses and pomegranates.

The south quire aisle is a veritable treasure trove. Look out for the panel painting of four kings, including Henry VII, and the recovered stall plate of Thomas Howard, fourth Duke of Norfolk, created a Knight of the Garter (KG) in 1559, but convicted of treason in 1572, when his plaque was removed. A stained-glass window nearby features Henry VIII, Edward VI, Jane Seymour and Elizabeth I (notably, no Mary I), each with their motto. Elizabeth's motto '*Video taceo*' means 'I see and remain silent' – perhaps advice for tourists browsing the chapel? Of particular note, also, is the Lincoln Chapel with its sixteenth-century alabaster tomb of Edward Fiennes de Clinton, Earl of Lincoln KG, Lord High Admiral and Governor of the Tower of London under Elizabeth I. His third wife, Elizabeth FitzGerald, is buried with him. At her feet there is an unusual burial mascot: a monkey, which alludes to the role one played in rousing her family during a thirteenth-century fire.

The central attraction is, however, plainer than all these fine effigies and decorations. Beneath the gorgeous fan-vaulted ceiling, a simple black marble slab on the floor at the centre of the quire is inscribed in gold letters:

In a vault beneath this marble slab are deposited the remains of Jane Seymour, Queen of King Henry VIII 1537. King

Henry VIII 1547. King Charles I 1648. And an infant child
of Queen Anne. Memorial placed by William IV 1837.

Henry VIII chose to be buried with his third wife, Jane Seymour.
Her significance in his life was chiefly dynastic: she gave him his
long-awaited legitimate male heir, but our knowledge of Henry's
favourite wife and a queen of England is otherwise rather limited.

We know that Jane came from respectable, but not grand,
parentage. Born in 1509, the year Henry became King, to Sir John
Seymour and Margery Wentworth at their house, Wolf Hall, she
was one of ten children. Two of her brothers would earn their own
degree of fame and power; both would also die as traitors: the
charming Thomas, Baron Seymour of Sudeley, fourth husband of
Kateryn Parr [see SUDELEY CASTLE], was executed 1549 and the
elder Edward, later Duke of Somerset and Lord Protector of
England, was executed in 1552.

Jane, on the other hand, seems to have been unremarkable. The
Imperial ambassador to England, Eustace Chapuys, described her as
'of middle stature and no great beauty, so fair that one would call
her rather plain than otherwise', and 'not a woman of great wit'.
Her pre-eminent quality was her docile, modest and amenable
nature. Her motto, 'Bound to obey and serve', epitomises her nicely.

It is possible that Henry met Jane in September 1535, when
he visited Wolf Hall, but she is not mentioned in any accounts by
name until 10 February 1536, when Chapuys reported that after
Anne Boleyn's miscarriage in January 1536 Henry had sent 'great
presents' to Jane. In March, he records that she had refused a purse
of coins and letter sent by the King. This last action, perhaps
cunning in its coyness, has been taken by some historians to indicate that Jane was no mere submissive fool, and was manipulating
Henry into marrying her, as Anne before her had done. But there
is little other evidence of anything beyond a cheerful, bovine
tractability to Jane. No doubt after the fierce, opinionated and

passionate Anne, this demeanour was part of Jane's appeal – she could hardly have been more different.

Henry could literally not wait to marry her. Archbishop Thomas Cranmer issued a dispensation for marriage (Henry and Jane were fifth cousins) on 19 May 1536, the very day of Anne's execution. The couple were betrothed the following day and married privately at Whitehall Palace on 30 May. She was the first wife to whom Henry could convince himself he was legitimately and unquestionably married (both his previous marriages, to Katherine and Anne, having been annulled). Henry may therefore have intended for her to be crowned, but an outbreak of plague in London and her subsequent pregnancy removed any opportunity.

Of her short reign, we know that she went on progress with Henry to Kent in the summer of 1536, and spent an enjoyable Christmas at Whitehall. She encouraged Henry to be reconciled with Princess Mary, and rumour has it that she once begged Henry to save the abbeys during the huge rebellion of October 1536, known as the Pilgrimage of Grace [see PONTEFRACT CASTLE], but was warned by him not to meddle in politics as her predecessor had done.

By February 1537, it was known that she was pregnant. The quickening – the first movement of the baby in the womb, thought by the Tudors to mark the beginning of life – was celebrated on 27 May, Trinity Sunday. On 16 September, she retired into her rooms on the second floor at Hampton Court, for her 'lying-in' (women in Tudor times retired to a closed, dark and warm environment to await the birth), and after a terrible labour of two days and three nights, she gave birth to a healthy son at 2 a.m. on 12 October. He was baptised Edward three days later. For Henry, it was the greatest gift Jane could ever have given him, but it cost her everything. She never rose from her childbed and died on 24 October 1537, probably of puerperal fever and septicaemia. She was twenty-eight.

Henry was devastated. He wrote to Francis I of France, 'Divine Providence has mingled my joy with the bitterness of the death of her who brought me this happiness.' He wore black mourning clothes well beyond the expected time, until February 1538.

Her body was eviscerated and embalmed (her heart and innards were buried in the chapel at Hampton Court), and Jane lay in state until 12 November, when her funeral procession took her body to Windsor for burial. Through her untimely death, she earned a perpetual sanctity in the eyes of the King. It is no wonder, then, that Henry chose to be buried next to her. He joined her a decade later. Having died on 28 January, he was buried on 16 February 1547.

There is a rather gruesome story about Henry VIII's corpse. Two nineteenth-century writers, apparently quoting lost original documents, recorded that two weeks after Henry's death, while his coffin lay in state at St George's, his body exploded and the lead casing burst, leaking putrefied matter onto the floor, and stray dogs wandered in to lick up the fluids. It may be true – after two weeks, his decomposed body would have been swollen and could theoretically have exploded – but this rumour also circulated after the deaths of William the Conqueror, Pope Alexander VI and Elizabeth I.

Other Tudor treasures to see at Windsor Castle: the quire aisle chantries have notable fifteenth-century panel paintings. In the State Apartments of the castle, look out for paintings by sixteenth-century artists including Pieter Brueghel and Lucas Cranach, and portraits of Henry VIII (by Joos van Cleve), Mary I (by Antonis Mor), Edward VI and Elizabeth I as a girl (by William Scrots). In the Lantern Lobby, you can see Henry VIII's stout 1540 field and tilt armour, made at Greenwich. Look carefully to see the fine engraving and note the space for a codpiece. (German tourists standing behind me when I visited remarked, '*Das ist nicht von Weight Watchers.*')

The Mary Rose
Hampshire

*'The Great Harry sailed as well as any ship that
was in the fleet, and rather better, and weathered them
all save the Mary Rose. And if she go by the wind,
I assure your grace, there will be a hard choice
between the Mary Rose and her.'*

Letter from royal servant William Fitzwilliam to Henry VIII,
comparing the flagship *Great Harry* to the *Mary Rose*

In 1982, the world watched as the hulk of the *Mary Rose* was
lifted, in the world's largest underwater excavation, from the
seabed 437 years after she sank in the Solent during an encounter
with an invading French fleet on 19 July 1545. Buried in the silt,
the *Mary Rose* proved to be an invaluable time capsule of over
1,000 preserved artefacts that now give insight into the lives of
the ordinary soldiers and sailors on board. Her surviving starboard
side, which will be housed from autumn 2012 in a brand new
museum in Portsmouth's Historic Dockyard, also reminds us that
she was an English flagship, a symbol and example of Henry VIII's
innovative standing navy. It is for this reason that Henry VIII is

considered the founding father of the Royal Navy, whose later rule of the waves was a key factor in establishing Britain's global empire. The *Mary Rose* is also testament to Henry's great desire for martial glory.

The *Mary Rose* was built between 1509 and 1511, and was one of two ships that Henry ordered at the very start of his reign, signalling the new King's intentions with regards to naval warfare and to defeating the French, England's traditional enemy. Although Henry VIII had only inherited a small number of ships (between five and seven) from his father, when he died he left a navy of 57 ships of the 106 that had served during his reign.

There are two myths about the *Mary Rose*: the first is that she sunk on her maiden voyage, and the second is that she was named after Henry VIII's younger sister [see ST MARY'S, BURY ST EDMUNDS]. The first is an injustice, simple to disprove: Henry's *Mary Rose* put in thirty-four years of active service after she was launched in 1511, while the clue to the real origins of her name can be found in the fact that the *Mary Rose* was built at the same time as the ship *Peter Pomegranate*. The rose and the pomegranate were the emblems of Henry and his new wife, Katherine of Aragon; the names Peter and Mary are likely to have been allusions to the saints, especially as Henry's visit to the Shrine of Our Lady of Walsingham in January 1511 shows his allegiance to the Virgin Mary at this time.

The *Mary Rose*, built from elm and oak, was a carrack: a four-masted ship with a high forecastle and aftercastle and a low waist, which meant she was excellent for hand-to-hand fighting alongside an enemy vessel. Besides her surviving hulk, we have a good idea of what she looked like in her prime because she is included in a set of depictions known as the Cowdray Engravings, which was the roll of Henry's fleet made by Anthony Cowdray, a Clerk of the Ordnance in 1546. She is also portrayed in the *Embarkation at*

Dover painting (at both LEEDS CASTLE and HAMPTON COURT PALACE) where Henry stands on his great warship, *Henry Grace à Dieu*. The *Mary Rose* is on the far right.

The Cowdray Engravings show that she was indeed a flagship: she would have been decked with flags, banners and pennants, including the three gold lions of England, the three gold fleurs-de-lis of France (Henry's paltry holdings in Calais meant he claimed to be the King of France too), the red cross of St George and impressive billowing pennants in the Tudor livery colours of green and white, up to fifty yards in length. Camouflage was not the overriding concern here.

The *Mary Rose* first saw service in 1512, in the first of Henry VIII's rather futile wars against France. The decision, unusual at the time, to keep her after the cessation of hostilities meant that she could be regularly recaulked and pumped out, ready to sail whenever Henry needed her, including to the Field of Cloth of Gold in 1520. Or, as when Henry entertained the Holy Roman Emperor, Charles V, on board in May 1522.

She was, however, a warship above all. According to an inventory of 1541, she was loaded with ninety-six guns in total, over three decks. These were the single-bored muzzle-loading guns preferred by the early Tudors; the largest recovered from the *Mary Rose* is a 4,783lb bronze cannon. Others are smaller and more ornate, decorated with the Tudor rose and inscriptions praising Henry VIII. Tudor warfare did not rely wholly on artillery: 172 longbows were also found in the ship, reminding us that by law, all English men were required to practise archery.

Looking at some of these items of war, you can see the individuality of the men who wielded them. For example, the linstocks – carved poles along which a slow fuse was wrapped in order to ignite gunpowder from a safe distance – have been whittled into garish animal mouths by the gunners who owned them. There are personal items found on board, too, and now on view at the museum: more than eighty combs for brushing hair and removing lice, manicure sets, ear scoops for wax, wooden bowls, ballock knives (the suggestive shape of the hilt was intentional), tankards and sewing kits. Musical instruments, such as the shawm (an early type of oboe), dice for illegal gambling, Bibles and rosary beads attest to how the sailors on the ship spent their spare time. Although most of them slept uncomfortably on deck, their lot was better than that of most ordinary people in Tudor England, who faced the rising prices and rents, poor harvests and enclosure of common land that contributed to Kett's Rebellion of 1549 [see KETT'S OAK].

Having been 'new made' in 1536, the *Mary Rose* was brought out again in 1545 to face the French peril. The renewed threat from Catholic Europe after Henry VIII's break with Rome and the subsequent publication of a papal decree authorising the invasion of England in 1538 was one reason why Henry VIII invaded France in 1544 and seized Boulogne. The other was his ongoing desire to achieve the legendary military glory won by former kings of England: Edward III and Henry V at Agincourt. The French responded by sailing into the Solent (the strait that separates the Isle of Wight from mainland England) in 1545 with a fleet of 324 vessels: more ships than the Spanish Armada. It was the single greatest foreign threat of Henry VIII's reign, and it was during this battle that the *Mary Rose* sank.

It has never been fully clear why. The French claimed it was a result of their cannon, but the recovered hulk shows this could not have been the case. One probable factor was the refitting of 1536 itself as she was made heavier, to nearly double her original tonnage, and over-laden with a large number of crew the morning of 19 July. The extra weight, high up in the ship, decreased her stability and manoeuvrability. She seems likely to have been either turning stern-on to face her eight large guns towards the French galleys, or trying to steer out of the way of their shot, but in the violent act of manoeuvring the ship, this great weight may have overbalanced her, causing water to rush in through her open gun-ports and capsize her.

Only thirty men were rescued. The vast majority of her crew, including the commander Sir George Carew, the captain Roger Grenville [see BUCKLAND ABBEY] and 500 other men unable to escape because of anti-boarding nets and heavy chain-mail jerkins, went down with her. From Southsea Common, Henry VIII, with Lady Carew besides him, watched helplessly as the tragedy unfolded. For years afterwards, the tops of her masts remained visible at low tide.

Their loss is our great gain. The remains of the *Mary Rose* give us hints of just how impressive Henry's ships were in their heyday, but what an irony that only by being destroyed can a warship be preserved.

Winchester Cathedral
Hampshire

'She would be, while her father lived...
the most unhappy Lady in Christendom.'

The soaring, majestic and vast cathedral at Winchester was the setting of one of the most impressive weddings of the Tudor age: Mary I to Philip of Naples (later Philip II of Spain) on 25 July 1554. Built by a kinsman of William the Conqueror, William Walkelin, and transformed into a fine example of Gothic perpendicular architecture in the thirteenth century, this beautiful medieval cathedral would be a place of great hope for Mary, after a lifetime of painful trials.

Mary's decision to marry a foreign prince was not popular. Parliament and a number of her councillors had expressed their concerns, and a more violent reaction came in the form of an armed rebellion led Sir Thomas Wyatt the Younger, which reached the walls of the Palace of Westminster in the early hours of 7 February 1554. Mary was, however, determined to marry the man of her choosing, and with excellent reason: not only because she wanted to join England to Catholic Europe once again, but because she had been moved around like a marital pawn from early childhood.

Born on 18 February 1516, Mary was the only child of Katherine of Aragon and Henry VIII to survive infancy. Aged just two and a half years old, she was betrothed to the French dauphin, Francis. The ceremony was by proxy (the dauphin was just twenty-eight weeks old, after all), and Mary was given a tiny diamond engagement ring for the occasion. When she was five, the engagement was broken off: it was decided that she would become not a French queen, but instead be betrothed to Charles V, the Holy Roman Emperor. In a miniature by Lucas Horenbout, Mary is shown wearing a brooch over her heart that says simply 'the Emperor'. However, Mary would not be of marriageable age for another eight years, and after three years of waiting – during which Mary had become quite attached to the idea of her grown-up husband-to-be – Charles decided that he wanted to marry a different cousin, Isabella of Portugal, instead.

It was a shame, as Mary was developing into a good catch. Highly educated, she spoke Spanish, French and Latin, and read Greek. Her accomplishments as a dancer and musician were demonstrated to the French envoys arriving to discuss a second French engagement in 1527. They praised her 'silver tresses' and 'great and uncommon mental endowments' but, again, a match could not be engineered.

If Mary felt rejected after these fruitless betrothals, it was nothing compared to what happened next. In 1531, after her father had determined to marry Anne Boleyn, Mary was separated from her mother, Katherine, in a callous effort to persuade both mother and daughter to accept the new situation. Mary was only fifteen, and although she couldn't know it, she would never see her mother again. She then suffered the indignity of being downgraded from 'Princess' to 'the Lady Mary, the King's daughter' within a week of her half-sister Elizabeth's birth in 1533. To make matters even worse, she was sent to Hatfield to serve in Elizabeth's court, under the stewardship of Anne Boleyn's aunt and uncle.

After Katherine died in early 1536, Mary reluctantly agreed to swear both to Henry's position as Supreme Head of the Church of England, and that her parents' marriage had been incestuous and unlawful, making her a bastard. As a result, in July 1536, she saw her father for the first time in five years. It is not wildly speculative to imagine that the awful treatment she suffered at her father's hands shaped her psyche and informed her later rejection of her father's institutions when she came to the throne.

It was not long before Henry was pushing her around the marriage board again. In 1539, at the age of twenty-six, she was told to consider another match, this time to the Lutheran duke, Philip of Bavaria, whose religion she could not countenance. She told one of her ladies that, 'she would be, while her father lived... the most unhappy Lady in Christendom'.

Nor did life get much easier for Mary during her brother Edward's reign. She retreated to East Anglia, where her continued celebration of the Latin Mass in her chapel at Kenninghall put her in direct opposition to the new Protestant establishment. At one point, she considered fleeing the country, but her decision to stay meant that when Edward died at the age of fifteen, she was available to contest his 'device for the succession' that named Lady Jane Grey as his heir [see GUILDHALL and FRAMLINGHAM]. On 19 July 1553, she was declared England's first Queen regnant and, three months later, the Spanish ambassador knelt and offered her Philip's hand in marriage. (The irony of marrying the son of her first fiancé cannot have been lost on her.) At thirty-seven, Mary was eleven years older than he.

Philip eventually arrived in England, with a personal entourage of around 4,000, in July 1554. When he reached Winchester, he was housed in the Dean's lodging in the cathedral precinct, where Henry VII's eldest son, Prince Arthur, had been born. The couple met two days before their wedding. Mary, who by this point must have thought she would never marry, was delighted with him, and if Philip found Mary badly dressed or pale and sagging, as his attendants reported, he didn't comment on it.

On the day of their wedding, both were sartorially resplendent. Philip wore a white doublet and breeches, with a mantle of cloth of gold (a fabric woven with threads wrapped in fine spirals of gold) adorned with pearls and precious stones, given to him by Queen Mary. Mary's wedding dress was 'rich tissue with a border and wide sleeves, embroidered upon purple satin, set with pearls... lined with purple taffeta', with a high collar, partlet (sleeveless jacket) and a kirtle of white satin.

At half past ten in the morning, Mary entered through the west door and walked the length of the cathedral, past the rich hangings of arras and cloth of gold, to the quire which had been built by Richard Fox, Bishop of Winchester, thirty years or so earlier. The couple stood before the fifteenth-century Great Screen on a specially constructed dais. The carved figures in the screen had been removed and destroyed during the Reformation (the current figures date from the nineteenth century), but above Mary's head remained colourful wooden bosses on the ceiling that proclaimed, through the ubiquitous Tudor rose, portcullis and fleur-de-lis, her right to rule. As sovereign, she stood on Philip's right side, and the Bishop of Winchester, Stephen Gardiner, married them. In the Triforium Gallery you can see an X-frame armchair that is thought to have been the chair that Mary sat on during the wedding ceremony.

Now, at last, England was safely tied to Catholic Spain and, before long, they could hope for a Catholic heir. But it was not to be. Soon after the wedding, Mary believed she was pregnant and withdrew for her lying-in but, humiliatingly, no baby came. Mary was heartbroken when Philip left to govern the Netherlands. He only returned after seventeen months, and then only for four. During this time, once again, Mary believed she had become pregnant and, once again, it turned out to be a phantom pregnancy, the product of hope and anxiety.

When, a year later, in 1558, Mary succumbed to a fever that would prove to be fatal, she may legitimately have felt that life had been cruel to her. She was unloved and mistreated as a daughter, horse-traded by her father for political gain, separated from her beloved mother and abandoned by her only husband. Posterity remembers her as 'Bloody Mary'. Better perhaps to look on the glory of Winchester Cathedral and think of Mary's one day of love, hope and faith.

The Vyne
Hampshire

'[Sandys] so translated and augmented it, and beside built a fair Base Court that at this time [it] is one of the Principal Houses in all Hamptonshire.'
John Leland, 1542

William, Lord Sandys, is not a name that most of us are familiar with. It is a shame: this soldier and courtier was a regular Tudor 'Flashman', constantly popping up for a front-row seat at an improbably large number of key events during Henry VIII's reign. The Vyne was the house he rebuilt to celebrate and chart his success, and it retains some incredible and unique treasures of the Tudor age.

Lord Sandys was one of those few lucky men who managed to pass from one reign to the next without losing royal favour. Born in 1470, he rose under Henry VII and after his marriage to Margary Bray became a Knight of the Body (an honorary bodyguard to the monarch), a ceremonial and coveted post that he continued to hold after Henry VIII's accession. Sandys was evidently seen as a safe pair of hands as Henry VII entrusted him with two crucial roles: receiving Katherine of Aragon when she landed in England, and accompanying his daughter, Margaret, to Scotland to marry James IV.

For Henry VIII, Sandys was an early and long-time favourite, and the King heaped positions of status upon him. Several pieces of evidence point to Sandys's privileged standing: Henry went to stay with Sandys at The Vyne less than a year after his coronation and later charged Sandys with accompanying his sister Mary to France in October 1514 to marry Louis XII. In 1517, Sandys was given the prestigious position of Treasurer of Calais, which he held for nine years and, like anyone who mattered in 1520, he attended the Field of Cloth of Gold [see LEEDS CASTLE]. He was also made Knight of the Garter, created Baron Sandys and returned to court in 1526 as Lord Chamberlain. This role meant, as Wolsey's Eltham Ordinances decreed, that he was required to give 'continual attendance in the causes of [the King's] counsel, unto what place so ever his Highness shall resort': he was one of Henry's right-hand men, always present to advise.

It was during this fortunate and comfortable phase that Sandys started to renovate his brick and stone mansion in Hampshire. The house today has seen much change since: chiefly, it was originally far larger; possibly even as big as Hampton Court. It was much reduced by Chaloner Chute, when he bought The Vyne in the mid-seventeenth century, and further changed over the following 200 years. Nevertheless, three of the prized features that Sandys introduced remain as distinct and wonderful evidence of both his eye for design, and his lofty associations.

The first is the extraordinary floor-to-ceiling oak linenfold panelling (wood carved to mimic the folds of cloth) in the Long Gallery. Look closely and you will see that each panel is carved with the heraldry of one of Sandys's contemporaries or patrons, thereby creating a visual *Who's Who* of Tudor England in the 1520s. Although painted much later (probably in the nineteenth century), it can be dated to between 1515 and 1529 not only through dendrochronology (dating by counting tree rings), but also through the coats of arms and insignia that have been chosen. Taken together, it represents an almost complete corpus of Tudor heraldry. Thus, you can hunt for: fleurs-de-lis; portcullises; Tudor roses and 'HR' standing for Henry VIII (the Latin *Henricus Rex*); the pomegranate (the symbol of Granada) and castle (for Castile) of Katherine of Aragon; the rose and pomegranate growing together on one stem; a cardinal's hat and initials 'TW' for Thomas Wolsey (giving us our start and end dates); the mitres and initials for Richard Fox, Bishop of Winchester, William Warham, Archbishop of Canterbury and Cuthbert Tunstall, Bishop of Durham; three sickles and 'WH' for Sir Walter Hungerford (who in 1540 suffered the ignominy of being the first person executed under a new law outlawing buggery and sodomy); and Lord Sandys's own devices, which include a winged half-goat, a rose merging with the sun and a ragged cross.

The carving of the royal arms over a doorway is thought to mark the entrance to Henry's chambers on the three occasions that he stayed at The Vyne and, like the gallery as a whole, is a proud demonstration of Sandys's close alliance with the King and his court: Sandys included so many badges of honour to Henry in his house that were this practice to be replicated by someone today, we might suspect them of an unhealthy obsession! But such shrines to living people were not uncommon for Tudors: a grown man of the court would think nothing of inscribing and carving his monarch's symbols or initials into his own residence. (Many of Elizabeth's male courtiers had whole manor houses built in the shape of an 'E' [see MONTACUTE HOUSE].)

In the Stone Gallery, you will find a stunning terracotta roundel of a Roman emperor, likely to be Probus, which is a real treasure, as it has survived in remarkably good condition. He was probably chosen for The Vyne because Probus was famous for introducing viticulture – the vine – to England. He has looked down on visitors to The Vyne for nearly 500 years and now, as then, is a visual association with Wolsey and Henry VIII, and a symbol of Sandys's artistic patronage and powerful connections. It was sculpted in the 1520s by the Italian craftsman Giovanni da Maiano: the same man who carved matching roundels at Wolsey's Hampton Court Palace.

Finally, Sandys commissioned one last piece of brilliant art to reflect his relationship with Henry VIII. In 1525, he ordered three wonderful stained-glass portraits of the royal family to be made for the chapel. These vivid, colourful depictions were created just down the road in Basingstoke, and show Katherine of Aragon in the left window, Henry VIII in the centre and his sister, Margaret, Queen of Scotland, on the right. The portrayal of a barefaced king with long, ginger hair is particularly interesting. All are kneeling in prayer, and Henry VIII himself would have knelt to pray in this chapel when he visited in 1531, and again with Anne Boleyn in 1535.

Although Sandys had been something of an Aragon supporter, he was first and foremost loyal to Henry: he both faithfully attended Anne's coronation on 1 June 1533, and served as one of the jurors at Anne's trial three years later. His role as eyewitness to history did not stop there: he was one of only three barons to receive gifts of monastic land from Henry VIII during the period of the dissolution; he was present at the baptism of Henry's long-awaited heir Edward in October 1537 at Hampton Court; and, a month later, attended Jane Seymour's funeral at Windsor Castle; he even tried those involved in the Exeter conspiracy of 1538–9. Only death – his wife's in March 1539, and his own in December 1540 – could end his extraordinary talent for ubiquity.

❁

Other Tudor sights to see at The Vyne: the chimneypiece in the Tapestry Room is almost certainly Tudor; it was moved from the Dining Parlour in the 1840s. Concealed behind the panelling in the Strawberry Parlour, there is a small Tudor doorway. Parts of the original, larger Tudor house were found in the lake, and are displayed in the Stone Gallery. The panelling in the Dining Parlour is Tudor too, and there are some lovely pictures here, all copies, depicting Charles Brandon, Duke of Suffolk; Mary Neville, Lady Dacre; Henry VIII; and my favourite, the six-year-old Chrysogona Baker, Lady Dacre in 1579, looking like a little Elizabeth I. The choir stalls in the Chapel are of early Tudor design; look out for the give-away roses and pomegranates.

ROYAL PROGRESSES

The Tudor monarchs never stayed in one place for long, and especially not during the summer months. Their peregrinations had more one than purpose. To some extent, it was a logistical and hygienic necessity. Moving around was seen as a way to avoid the seasonal bouts of plague or the 'sweating sickness' in London. Moreover, the court could number over 1,000 people – the population of a small town – and ate such vast quantities of food that they easily exhausted an area's resources. Meanwhile, their waste and rubbish mounted up. As a friend wrote to Sir John Harington in the 1590s, Elizabeth's 'palace at Greenwich and other stately houses… are oft annoyed with such savours as where many mouths are fed, can hardly be avoided': the court needed to move to another palace to escape its own excrement.

Progresses were also an important opportunity to be seen. In an age before mass communication, these progresses fulfilled the crucial political function of displaying a monarch's magnificence to his or her subjects, and allowing local gentry and officials a chance to access and display loyalty to their sovereign. The chronicler Edward Hall wrote of Henry VIII in 1515:

> This summer the King took his progress westward & visited his towns, castles there & heard the complaints of his poor commonality & ever as he rode, he hunted & liberally departed with venison; & in the middle of September he came to his manor of Woking & thither came to him the Archbishop of York whom he heartily welcomed and showed him great pleasures.

Hall also reveals another key purpose of the progress: pleasure. Henry VIII travelled in order to hunt; Elizabeth to enjoy the hospitality and extraordinary entertainments of her subjects. The Imperial ambassador, Eustace Chapuys, wrote in June 1531 that he had 'sent one of [his] men to Hampton Court to ask for an audience from the King, but he was already gone to Windsor and other places to amuse himself and pass away the time... For the last fortnight he has done nothing else but go from place to place...'

The crucial difference between the progresses of Henry VIII and Elizabeth I was that Henry stayed, for the most part, in his own houses. By the time of his death, Henry VIII had acquired or built over sixty great houses and palaces in which he stayed as he travelled around his realm. This is one reason why Henry VIII seldom left the south and east of his kingdom, although there were exceptions. Henry's long progress to the West Country in 1535 took him as far as Gloucestershire where, as well as staying in his castle at Thornbury (acquired from the Duke of Buckingham in 1521), he also stayed with Sir Nicholas Poyntz, who built an entire new wing onto his manor house, Acton Court, for the occasion: quite an undertaking given that Henry rarely remained in one place for longer than a few days. Henry VIII's furthest progress north was in 1541 when he travelled to York to meet James V. Not only did the Scottish King not show up, but soon after he returned home, Henry discovered that his wife, Katherine Howard, had betrayed him en route [see PONTEFRACT CASTLE].

Elizabeth I was even more enthusiastic about travel. She went on progress every summer of her forty-five-year reign, but she too confined her expeditions to twenty-five of England's forty counties. Elizabeth, however, preferred to stay in her courtiers' houses. Clergyman William Harrison wrote in 1577 of Elizabeth I, 'when it pleaseth her in the summer season to recreate herself abroad, and view the estate of the country, every nobleman's house is her palace'.

Although technically a sign of favour and an opportunity to seek patronage, having the Queen to stay was something of a dubious honour. It put one to great expense and inconvenience, did not necessarily result in new offices or grants and could easily go disastrously wrong.

The Queen did not travel light. Foreign visitor Jacob Rathgeb commented in 1592 that 'when the Queen breaks up her Court with the intention of visiting another place, there commonly follow more than three hundred carts laden with bag and baggage'. Others estimated the figure to be nearer 400 or even 600 carts. Elizabeth brought with her a minimum of 150 people, who needed to be housed and fed, and this demanding Queen also required lavish entertainment, often at great cost. William Cecil, Lord Burghley knew this well: Elizabeth visited his house at Theobalds thirteen times; her ten-day visit in 1591 cost him £1,000 (equivalent today to more than £125,000). The most extravagant example is Elizabeth's nineteen-day visit to Robert Dudley, Earl of Leicester's, house in 1575 [see KENILWORTH].

Elizabeth's lack of tact could also prompt further outlay. When Elizabeth visited Sir Nicholas Bacon's house at Gorhambury in 1572, she remarked, 'My Lord, what a little house you have gotten.' By the time she returned five years later, he had built a new wing. Sir Thomas Gresham was quicker to act. Elizabeth came to his house at Osterley, Middlesex, in 1578, and opined that the courtyard would look better if divided by a wall. Gresham sent immediately for workmen from London who quickly and quietly built the wall during the night as a surprise for Elizabeth when she awoke. Some men went further. It was Elizabeth's love of progresses that led to the building of the great 'prodigy' houses of the age. Sir Christopher Hatton built the huge and magnificent Holdenby House in the hope that Elizabeth would visit. The building of it bankrupted him [see KIRBY HALL], and the house waited ten years for a queen who never came.

Hever Castle
Kent

'Le temps viendra / Je anne boleyn.'
('The time will come / I Anne Boleyn)

Set in the midst of the beautiful countryside of the Weald of Kent, and with landscaped grounds that include a lake, a walled rose garden and playful animal topiary, Hever Castle makes an excellent day out. It is also a must for Anne Boleyn's acolytes. Despite the fact that one of Henry VIII's other wives, Anne of Cleves, owned this house from after her 'divorce' settlement of 1540 until her death in 1557, it is as the childhood home of Anne Boleyn that Hever is chiefly memorialised. It was substantially remodelled and restored by William Waldorf Astor in the early twentieth century.

Unfortunately for Hever, Anne was very probably not born here but at Blickling in Norfolk. Anne's date of birth is unknown: historians have quarrelled over 1501 or 1507 as the most likely date, deciding recently on the former because of a sophisticated letter sent by Anne from France in 1513: the handwriting is not that of a five or six-year-old, and Anne was abroad as a maid-of-honour (an unmarried lady-in-waiting), a post suitable for a young adolescent. The Boleyn family moved to Hever in 1505. This does mean, nonetheless, that Anne spent a good eight years in the moated manor house at Hever as a child, and she also returned to her parents' home at certain times during the 1520s. There is a bedroom on the first floor with a fifteenth-century half-domed ceiling that is thought to have been Anne's bedroom as a child. It is this close association of Anne and Hever that makes this the ideal place to tell her tale.

In 1513, Anne went to be maid-of-honour to Margaret, Archduchess of Austria, in Brussels, but remained in her service for a mere fifteen months before joining the court of Henry VIII's younger sister, Mary, on her marriage to King Louis XII of France. At Hever, there is a tapestry in the Book of Hours room dating from 1525 which commemorates this marriage; as one of Mary's ladies at the time, Anne may well feature. When the eighteen-year-old Mary was widowed three months later, Anne chose to stay in France at the court of the French Queen Claude. These years were pivotal in Anne's development and character: she not only learnt exquisite French, but all the cosmopolitan glamour of the French court – from dancing and singing, to witty banter and a taste for fine clothes. It was this sophistication that would later make the black-haired, dark-eyed Anne so attractive to Henry VIII.

She returned to England in 1521, and is first recorded as appearing at the English court on 1 March 1522, rather aptly playing the part of 'Perseverance' in a masque called the 'Château Vert'. At this time, it was, however, another Boleyn girl who had caught Henry's eye: Anne's sister, Mary, was the King's mistress from around 1522 to 1525. (In later years, Henry VIII was charged with having had a relationship with Anne's mother and sister. He replied gruffly, 'Never with the mother.') In these years, while negotiations were being made for Anne to marry her Irish cousin, James Butler, a 'secret love' grew between her and Lord Henry Percy, the son of the Earl of Northumberland. Exactly how this love manifested itself is unknown – Percy and Anne would both later deny exchanging promises to marry – but the King's minister, Cardinal Thomas Wolsey, intervened to prevent the match (acting for Percy's parents who wanted him to marry Mary Talbot, daughter of the Earl of Shrewsbury, instead). For two years, Anne returned to Hever to nurse her wounds.

The King's affection for Anne appears to have started around 1526. An ardent letter from Henry VIII to Anne, which can probably be dated to 1527, declares that he has been 'for more than a year now struck by the dart of love'. He beseeches her to 'give yourself body and heart to me' and to become his 'sole mistress'. Anne's refusal of that position meant that by the summer of 1527, the couple had pledged to marry each other.

In fact, many of Henry VIII's love letters to Anne, which survive by quirk of fate in the Vatican Library, were written in the late 1520s when the couple were parted by illness. Anne retired to Hever Castle when afflicted with the 'sweating sickness', a virulent and often fatal disease that the heirless Henry desperately needed to avoid. Originally written in French, one of these passionate letters can be seen in translation on the wall in the Book of Hours room at Hever. (Ignore the one from Anne to Henry, which is of dubious veracity.)

Nearby, two books of hours – beautiful, illuminated personal prayer books – bear Anne's signature. Does her inscription: '*Le temps viendra / Je anne boleyn*' ('The time will come / I Anne Boleyn') refer to this period of longing and waiting while Wolsey and then Thomas Cranmer tried to work out how to free Henry from his marriage to Katherine of Aragon so he might marry Anne? Did Anne pace Hever's Long Gallery in frustration?

As history shows, the Pope was unwilling to listen to Henry's appeals to Leviticus 18:16 and 20:21 – that it was unlawful for him to be married to his brother's wife. Ultimately, after seven years of waiting and many Acts of Parliament enabling the break with Rome, Henry's marriage to Katherine was annulled by Thomas Cranmer on 23 May 1533.

Henry had in fact already married Anne: once secretly in Dover in November 1532, and again privately but officially in January 1533. Their child, Elizabeth, was born in September 1533. Two of the best portraits of the many at Hever are of Anne herself (a late sixteenth-century portrait by an unknown artist) and of her daughter Elizabeth (a portrait from c.1580 by John Bettes the Younger).

Henry and Anne were frequently described as 'merry together', but after Anne miscarried a male child in January 1536, an accusation of adultery dislodged Anne from her place in Henry's affections. Although Anne was almost certainly innocent of any sexual misdemeanours, her witty, flirtatious banter with the men of the court – the very quality that had attracted Henry to her in the first place – sealed her fate. Following the execution of the five men accused with her, including her brother, George Boleyn, Lord Rochford, Anne was beheaded at the Tower of London on charges of adultery, incest and conspiring the King's death on 19 May 1536.

The disgrace of the Boleyns meant that Hever passed into the Crown's possession, to be given away in turn to Anne of Cleves and, after her death, to the Waldegrave family. The Waldegraves were secretly recusant Roman Catholics, and they built a hidden Catholic oratory chapel at Hever in 1584 – that you can still see – and this in the childhood home of the proto-Protestant who caused the break with Rome.

Leeds Castle
Kent

'The most noble and royal lodging…
that passed all other sights before seen.'

In this green little corner of England, 6,000 people and 3,000 horses gathered one day in late May 1520. Imagine the hubbub: the frenetic activity of men rushing to erect tents to house everyone before nightfall, the whinnying and stamping of the horses, the impatient demands from the highest nobility in the land as lords and ladies wait around in their silks, velvets and furs, despite the spring sunshine. What could be further from what you now see at Leeds Castle? Peacefully set amidst its pretty Kentish gardens, romantically isolated on an island surrounded by a moat, it is like a miniature fairytale fortress. The only sounds to break the stillness are the cries of the peacocks and black swans that strut around the grounds, and the parrots and cockatiels chattering away in the aviary.

Much of the castle, it's true, is not Tudor, either inside or out, but the historical pedigree of it is impeccable: six medieval queens, from Eleanor of Castile, wife of Edward I, to Catherine of Valois, Queen of Henry V, made this their home. After Henry V's death, Catherine would go on to marry Owen Tudor, starting the Tudor dynasty, and it is her great-grandson, Henry VIII, and his first wife, Katherine, whose visit to Leeds Castle secures this diminutive fortress an important place in the Tudor story.

In order for this royal couple to stay, certain architectural improvements were required in the original late thirteenth-century *gloriette* (the name given to any elevated garden building). Under Henry VIII's orders, Sir Henry Guildford, the Master of the Revels, oversaw the installation of an upper floor, fireplaces and large windows in the newly created Banqueting Hall. Evidence of this renovation remains in the spandrels of the ragstone mantle-piece in the Queen's Gallery, which are decorated with engravings of the castle of Castile and the pomegranates from Katherine of Aragon's coat of arms and heraldic badge. There are early Tudor tapestries hanging on the walls, and a Latin service book said to have been owned by Katherine in the chapel, while the four marble busts in the Gallery representing the Tudor monarchs (with Henry VII and Queen Jane silently dropped) date from Elizabeth's reign.

The central importance of this castle is, however, represented by a large, stunning painting that you can see in the Banqueting Hall. It probably dates from around 1550 (the fashions depicted suggest the date), which is a sister copy to a painting at Hampton Court. This is *The Embarkation at Dover*, painted by Vincenzo Volpé and his workshop, which depicts Henry VIII and his retinue – including the *Mary Rose* – setting sail from Dover on 31 May 1520, bound for a meeting with the French King just outside Calais. You can spot Henry VIII ornately dressed in gold; his ship has gold sails. All the architectural alterations at Leeds Castle had been made specifically so that several days earlier, on 22 May 1520, on their way to Dover, Henry and Katherine and their entourage of up to 6,000 could stay at the castle overnight. They were en route to the Field of Cloth of Gold.

The Field of Cloth of Gold was a magnificent party without parallel in the Tudor period. Cardinal Thomas Wolsey, Henry VIII's astute Lord Chancellor, had arranged this first personal meeting between Henry VIII and the French King, Francis I, to inaugurate the Anglo-French alliance made in 1518 [see CHRISTCHURCH]. The alliance had been agreed under the international Treaty of Universal Peace, sworn between France, England and the Holy Roman Empire, to enable the European powers to focus their combined resources on resisting the Ottoman Empire.

As England was a puny country by comparison to the great might of France or the Holy Roman Empire, Wolsey had done well to give England such an important role in brokering the peace. Now, England and her King had an opportunity to prove that their peace-making was a choice, not a necessity, through a lavish display of wealth, culture, and sporting and military prowess.

For two and a half weeks, from 7 to 24 June 1520, 12,000 people (equivalent to the population of England's second largest city at the time, Norwich) gathered in a field between Guînes and Ardres. As England had held Calais since 1347, the meeting technically took place on English soil in northern France.

Every aspect of the meeting was designed to demonstrate magnificence. If the improvements to Leeds Castle were noteworthy, the construction of a temporary palace, made of brick, timber, canvas and glass to house Henry VIII at Guînes was jaw-dropping. The chronicler Edward Hall described it as the 'most noble and royal lodging... that passed all other sights before seen'. A full 300 feet square, it was covered with such 'sumptuous work' that it '[il]lumined the eyes of the beholders'. Everyone else, Francis I included, was housed in rich tents made of cloth of gold. Outside the palace, the English even constructed a gilt fountain crested by the figure of the god of wine, Bacchus, for the fountain ran with wine, not water, and one night a 'flying dragon' – probably a firework – was seen in the sky.

The company ate and drank their way through prodigious amounts of food and wine. The expenses for food during the whole trip, from 31 May to 16 July, run to many pages. A mere snippet from this shows that the English consumed: 373 oxen; 2,014 sheep; 51 pigs; 82 pheasants; 3,003 quail; 506 geese; 2 peacocks; 92 cygnets; 633 pigeons; 30,700 eggs; 5,500 oranges and at least 122 'tuns' or 40,320 imperial gallons of wine! Over 210 gallons of beer were provided for the consumption of the English king alone.

The Field of Cloth of Gold was above all, though, a tournament. There was jousting every day (except Sundays), archery, wrestling and other feats of arms including combat on foot and horseback. It was designed so that the two kings would never meet directly in combat and both could be extolled as champions. 'Course after course,' Edward Hall notes, 'the King lost none,' and 'the French king on his part ran valiantly breaking spears'.

Despite this, underneath everything ran a current of rivalry between the two monarchs. They were similar ages – Henry twenty-nine, Francis twenty-six – and had heard much about each other before their meeting. They were keen to know who was the tallest? Who could grow the best beard? And who had the finest calf?

In two important respects, Francis triumphed. Any comparison of the French Queen Claude, aged twenty, with a brood of three children and another on the way, and the thirty-five-year-old English Queen Katherine of Aragon, with her one daughter and lacking a son, must have been wretched for both Katherine and Henry. Also, if an account by one French eyewitness is to be believed, Henry defied the terms of the encounter by drunkenly challenging Francis to a wrestling match: Henry was heavier, but Francis threw him to the floor, using a famous Breton technique.

At the tranquil Leeds Castle, it may be a stretch to imagine the clamour, tumult and stench of the swarming throngs of people and horses amassed here in May 1520 to pitch golden tents across the grounds. The huge logistical exercise of transporting 6,000 people from London to Calais – and all the food and materials needed to maintain and shelter them – is almost inconceivable – but here they were.

After such vast expense, it is chastening to consider that this extravagant celebration of military power and stupendous wealth in the name of peace, between two such great rivals, had few lasting political consequences. Within three years, England and France were once again at war.

FOOD IN TUDOR ENGLAND

Many people have a vision of Tudor food and eating habits drawn straight from Hollywood's depiction of Charles Laughton as Henry VIII throwing a greasy, gnawed chicken leg over his shoulder. Instead, people in Tudor England had a pronounced sense of table etiquette and ate a rich and varied diet, even if they didn't consider it desirable to consume their 'five a day'.

Red meat was the linchpin of the Tudor diet, and beef most important of all. Thomas Cogan's *The Haven of Health* of 1589 states that beef 'of all flesh is most usual among English men', while physician Andrew Boorde considered that, once salted, beef 'doth make an Englishman strong'. All Tudor food was, of course, organic, and farm animals and game raised solely on pasture and other vegetation would have had a rich flavour. The second most popular meat was mutton, while capons – young castrated male chickens – and pigeons were also regularly on the menu. Pig meat, once cheap and commonly available, declined in favour in the sixteenth century, while rabbit eating greatly increased. The wealthy Willoughby family of Wollaton Hall employed their own 'coninger' (named after 'conies' or full-grown rabbits) Thomas Hill. Those at the high end of the social scale, especially the monarch, had access to a wide range of other meats, including venison, pheasant, partridge, quail, swan, goose and stork. Our Christmas bird, the turkey, was an exotic novelty: it was first mentioned in accounts in the 1570s.

Meat was supplemented by the 'white meats'. Tudor diets were rich in butter, cheese and eggs, which were eaten with a large quantity of bread. One of the best breads was 'white manchet', made with fine white wheat flour, though it was sometimes adulterated with chalk.

Meat was not eaten on fast days, which were every Friday and Saturday, and throughout Lent and Advent except Sundays. Instead, the Tudors ate fish, both salted fish such as cod, ling and pollock, and fresh fish such as haddock, turbot and plaice. A visitor to England in 1598 noted the large quantities of oysters on sale in London.

Fruit and vegetables were not thought to agree with man's digestion. *The Book of Keruynge* [*Carving*] of 1508 warned its readers to 'beware of green salads and raw fruits for they will [make] your souerayne [stomach] sick', and Sir Thomas Elyot had the same message in his book from 1541, *The Castle of Health*. 'All fruits generally,' he wrote, 'are noyfull [harmful] to man and do engender ill humours.' Such attitudes naturally encouraged relatively low consumption of fruit and vegetables for those who could afford otherwise but, nevertheless, the kitchen garden featured in every diet to some extent. Tudors had access, if they chose, to apples, pears, damsons, peaches, oranges, lemons and berries; and cabbages, beans, peas, leeks, turnips, onions and parsnips, although garden produce was, of course, seasonal and not all fruits and vegetables were available all year round. Carrots were still relatively new, and potatoes only arrived in England from the New World via Seville around 1570. The poor relied on pottage – a broth or stew of whatever meat was available with leeks, onions, herbs and the local cereal grain – to fill themselves up.

Water was not thought to encourage digestion, so most people drank ale, made of water and malted grain, or the foreign hop-infused ale, beer. Wine was a luxury import. The rich enjoyed French wines from Gascony or Bordeaux, 'sack' or sherry from Xeres and sweet Malmsey wine from Greece.

Those at the top end of society also enjoyed other treats. At Henry VIII's court, popular sweetmeats included marchpane (an early version of 'marzipan') made of ground almonds, rosewater and sugar, and 'subtleties': elaborate model decorations, probably made of sugar plate (or paste), sometimes with the addition of wax. A conceit was to make realistic nuts or cinnamon sticks from sugar plate dusted with cinnamon, or to serve wine in a goblet made of sugar; once the wine had been consumed, the goblet could be eaten. George Cavendish reports that to impress visiting French ambassadors in 1527, Cardinal Wolsey served up 'so many dishes, subtleties, and curious devices, which were above a hundred in number, and of so goodly proportion and costly, that I suppose the Frenchmen never saw the like', including a chessboard made of 'spiced plate', and a model of the then St Paul's Cathedral, complete with towering spire.

If this weren't enough sweetness, at the end of meals, the King and Queen enjoyed sugar-coated spice, and a spiced wine called hippocras. No wonder many rich Tudors ended up with blackened teeth!

Penshurst Place
Kent

'Built of fair and strong stone, not affecting so much
any extraordinary kind of fineness as an honourable
representing of a firm stateliness; handsome without curiosity
and homely without loathsomeness.'

'Built of fair and strong stone,' as Sir Philip Sidney described it, Penshurst Place is a gorgeous medieval and Tudor manor house, set in beautiful gardens. Early in the sixteenth century, it belonged to Edward Stafford, third Duke of Buckingham; he entertained Henry VIII here at exorbitant expense (spending £2,500 or the equivalent of £1.2 million) in 1519. Today, Penshurst Place is chiefly remembered as the home of the Sidney family, whose most famous representative, Sir Philip Sidney, was fêted as the perfect courtier-soldier-poet of his day, owing in part to his early death at the age of thirty-one.

After Buckingham's untimely demise in 1521 [see THORNBURY CASTLE], Penshurst remained in the possession of the Crown until Edward VI bequeathed it to Sir William Sidney in 1552, who died two years later and passed it to his son, Sir Henry Sidney. Sir Henry was connected to the highest echelons of Tudor society: he had been educated with the boy-king, Edward, and married Mary, daughter of John Dudley, Duke of Northumberland. When Northumberland engineered the marriage of his son, Guildford, to Lady Jane Grey and acclaimed her as Queen in 1553 [see GUILD-HALL], the Sidneys were lucky to escape the aftermath unscathed.

With the twists and turns of Tudor history, the Dudley connection became one of honour when Queen Elizabeth I fell in love with Mary's brother, Robert Dudley, later Earl of Leicester. There are portraits of them all here: Sir Henry and Mary Sidney (the former by Hans Eworth); Leicester in older age; Ambrose Dudley, Earl of Warwick; Edward VI; and Elizabeth in the Long Gallery. Meanwhile, Mary had given birth at Penshurst in 1554 to the first of the Sidneys' seven children, Philip, named after his godfather, the Catholic-Spanish King of England. The young Philip would become famed at the Elizabethan court, but only really after his death.

At the heart of the house in which Philip spent his childhood is the Barons' Hall, a marvellous room with a central octagonal hearth and a sixty-foot roof timbered with chestnut beams, constructed by Sir John de Pulteney in 1341. The hall's wooden eavesdroppers (the word comes from the sense that the eaves might drop down to listen in) are life-size satirical peasant figures and would surely have caught the child's eye as he sat at the two long oak refectory tables that have been here since the fifteenth century and are the only surviving examples of their kind. The Minstrels' Gallery was then newly added and the expensive and exquisite tapestries from Tournai and Brussels were still in their first flush of colour.

Before he was six years old, Philip suffered a terrible bout of smallpox, which an early biographer described as having 'laid waste, as with little mines, [to] the excellence and fashion of his beauty'. His mother, Mary, was also terribly scarred by the disease while nursing Elizabeth I through it in 1562.

As Lord President of the Council of the Welsh Marches, effectively the ruler or 'pro-rex' of Wales, Sir Henry Sidney and his family lived for a time at Ludlow Castle, though retained Penshurst as their main home. Philip was schooled at Shrewsbury School, with his future friend and biographer Fulke Greville, before going to Christ Church, Oxford.

Aged just eighteen years, Philip was given an important duty in the realm of international diplomacy. In 1572, Elizabeth I dispatched him to accompany Edward Fiennes de Clinton to Paris to sign the Treaty of Blois, which promised that neither England nor France would aid their mutual enemy, Spain. This meant that Philip was in Paris for the August wedding of King Henri of Navarre (later Henri IV of France) to Marguerite de Valois, and for the terrible massacre of Protestants on St Bartholomew's Day that followed it. Philip then spent three years on an extended proto-Grand Tour of Europe, during which he met the great and good of European society and saw the European Renaissance – painters like Titian and Tintoretto – first hand.

Philip returned to England in May 1575, glittering with cosmopolitan glamour, and possibly a little full of himself, given his widespread international recognition as the son of the ruler of Wales and nephew and heir to the Queen's paramour, Robert Dudley, Earl of Leicester. Quite an adventure for a young man of just twenty-one. The Tudor loggia (gallery of columns) built by Sir Henry at Penshurst, which can be seen from the window of the Tapestry Room, is one of the imports from Philip's travels in Italy. Philip joined the Queen on progress that year and witnessed Leicester's spectacular entertainments to win her hand [see KENIL-WORTH CASTLE].

In the Solar Room and Long Gallery at Penshurst, there are portraits of Philip, showing him at around the time of his return, with his strawberry-blond hair and effete moustache, dressed in a huge (though fashionable) ruff. English antiquary John Aubrey described him as 'extremely beautiful'. In these portraits and the one at the National Portrait Gallery, there is no sign of smallpox devastation. There is also a fascinating picture in the Solar Room from 1581 of Elizabeth dancing *la volta* with Leicester (remember Cate Blanchett and Joseph Fiennes in the film *Elizabeth*?), in which Philip can be seen pointing out to his uncle that the Duc d'Alençon, one of the men courting Elizabeth, has his arm around another lady.

Although Aubrey added to his description that Philip looked 'not masculine enough', in fact, part of the trouble during his years as a courtier was that he was a little too macho and too easily angered. At court, he quarrelled with the earls of Ormond and Oxford, and was rebuked by Elizabeth for acting with contempt to his social superiors. Had his years of entertaining kings and dukes around Europe given him a restless haughtiness when dealing with the earls of England? This may have been a reason why, along with his failure to advance the foreign interests of the Queen, he remained without an official post or knighthood until 1583. Though he was famed abroad, he was a courtier without honour in his own country.

In 1579, Philip decided to pick up his quill and write what he dubbed his 'toyfull booke', which he called *Arcadia*. It was an epic romance in five books with ancillary songs and poems, which he had started some years earlier. In 1579, he retired to his sister, Mary, Countess of Pembroke's home at Wilton, to complete it. A year later, perhaps in response to the marriage of Penelope Devereux, once earmarked by Sir Henry as a suitable match for his son, Philip composed *Astrophil and Stella*, a sequence of 108 sonnets and eleven songs. It tells the story of the unhappy love of Astrophil ('star-lover') for the married Stella ('star'). The language of Tudor courtship is replete with images of the heavens, of stars, moons and suns.

Underneath his untroubled surface, however, Philip began to despair for lack of an official position and money. What he needed to do was wed a wealthy woman and, in September 1583, he chose Frances, the fifteen-year-old daughter of Sir Francis Walsingham. While the marriage partly alleviated his financial woes, Philip was not destined for a settled domestic life. Wanderlust struck again after a mission to Europe in 1584 had to be abandoned. This time, Philip dreamed of making a fortune in the New World. He invested in Sir Humphrey Gilbert's voyage to North America and, in return, was granted three million acres of undiscovered lands there (one can only imagine the value of such a landholding today). He also sought to join Sir Francis Drake's voyage to the West Indies in September 1585. But his monarch had different designs for him: he was ordered to go to the Low Countries to fight with Leicester, in what turned out to be a fairly fruitless battle, against the Spanish.

On 22 September 1586, at the Battle of Zutphen, Philip was wounded. He was not wearing thigh armour and a musket ball struck him just above his left knee, shattering the bone. His friend, Greville, would later tell the story of how, injured on the battle-field, Philip declined a drink of water and offered it instead to a wounded common soldier. Twenty-five days later, he died of gangrene in the wound. His father-in-law, Walsingham, arranged a splendid state funeral for him – he was the last commoner to have a state funeral until Nelson in 1806. His funerary helm (a special helmet marking his reputation as a warrior) remains at Penshurst. With accolades to his heroism, youth and courtly poetry abound-ing, in death he managed to achieve the status he had not been accorded in life. We can perhaps think of Sidney as a forerunner of the nineteenth-century Romantic poets, who also travelled, lived impecuniously, dreamed large and died untimely deaths.

Other Tudor treasures to see: look out for the portraits of Philip's brother, Robert, first Earl of Leicester (after Leicester's death) and his wife, Barbara Gamage; a black sixteenth-century lute by Padova Vienderville; a sixteenth-century harpsichord, gilded in rococo style; a cast-lead bust of the head of Elizabeth I from the effigy on her tomb in Westminster Abbey (from 1605); an alleged fragment of Sir Philip Sidney's shaving mirror; and Robert Dudley, Earl of Leicester's sword of state.

THE EARLY TUDOR GREAT HALL

Every great Tudor house displays its individuality, but nearly every grand house had, as its centrepiece, a Great Hall. The Great Hall was the centre of activity. Traditionally, it had been the place where the King or nobleman would dine alongside their retainers and servants on a daily basis but, by the sixteenth century, the hall was instead generally used for servants' dining, as a common room and entrance hall, and on special occasions for feast days, plays and entertainments. A year after Elizabeth I's death, Shakespeare's company, the King's Men, performed *A Midsummer Night's Dream* in the Great Hall at Hampton Court. It was also conventional to feed hoards of guests at Christmas and on other great feast days, as when Thomas Howard, Duke of Norfolk, offered meals to 235 'strangers' at Framlingham Castle at Christmas 1526.

Great Halls vary dramatically in size. The Barons' Hall at Penshurst, for example, is sixty-two feet by thirty-nine feet, which was enormous in fourteenth-century England, when it was built. The Great Hall at Guildhall is a much larger 151 feet by 48 feet. Nevertheless, they do all have similar, recognisable features: every hall has a raised dais at one end, generally lit by a large bay window, which is where the great man of the house would sit. The other end is the service end, partitioned off by ornately carved wooden screens that helped prevent draughts. In the sixteenth century, it became fashionable to build a minstrels' gallery over the screens' passage (there is an example of this at Penshurst), as a place for musicians to entertain.

Underneath the Great Hall you would probably find a vaulted, cave-like room, known as the undercroft, which was ostensibly a cellar or storeroom. Some of them are so fine, however, as to suggest they had other uses as well. Every house had a chapel, and most royal palaces also had private closets for worship.

As the nobility and monarchy withdrew – for comfort and privacy – from dining in the Great Hall, they moved into other rooms: the Great Chamber, and beyond it, the Privy Chamber. By the end of the sixteenth century, the lord of the manor would likely have slept in the Privy Chamber, named after its position between the Great Chamber and the privy.

The privy, also known as the garderobe (after the Old French for 'wardrobe', like our use of the word 'cloakroom'), or more colloquially, the jakes, was generally a wooden seat over a hole dropping down a shaft into a pit or even, quite commonly, straight into the moat. At Hampton Court in 1536, a 'Great House of Easement': a twenty-eight-seater latrine on two floors, was built over the moat, though the waste was directed into a nearby river.

Rochester Castle
Kent

*'Say what they will, she is nothing as fair
as she hath been reported.'*

R ochester is a forbidding, medieval stone castle, situated in an impressive and strategically important position on the banks of the River Medway. There has been a castle on this site (as so often is the case) since soon after the Norman Conquest, but the ragstone keep that still stands was built around 1127 by the then Archbishop of Canterbury, William of Corbeil. It is one of the finest and oldest surviving twelfth-century castles in England. Although besieged twice in the thirteenth century, and captured and ransacked during the Peasants' Revolt of 1381, it remains, albeit in partial ruin, fundamentally intact. It was already ancient when Henry VIII surprised his fourth wife-to-be, Anne of Cleves, here on New Year's Day 1540 – and it was her behaviour at Rochester that determined not only the course of their marriage, but her entire future.

By 1539, Henry VIII had been mourning Jane Seymour's death for a couple of years and his advisers urged him to marry again in order to secure the succession with a bevy of boys. A number of European women were considered (including Christina, Duchess of Denmark, whose legendary response was that if she had two heads, 'one of them would be at the King of England's disposal'). In an effort to bolster Henry's alliances in Europe, his first minister Thomas Cromwell urged Henry to marry one of the daughters of the German Duke of Cleves. Soon after, reports of the beauty of the eldest, the twenty-four-year-old Anne, reached Henry's ears. English ambassador Christopher Mont claimed that 'everyone praiseth the beauty of the said Lady, as well for the face, as for the whole body, above all other ladies excellent', and added that in looks she surpassed the Duchess of Denmark 'as the golden sun excelleth the silver moon'. Hans Holbein was dispatched to the Continent to paint images of Anne and her sister Amelia for the King's consideration. Henry found the picture of Anne so appealing that he retained it in his royal collection long after he had dispensed with the flesh-and-blood version.

On the strength of Holbein's portrait, the King decided to marry her. Anne set out in November 1539 to travel the slow land-route to the English territory of Calais, and thence on to the mainland. By New Year's Eve, she had arrived at Rochester Castle, where it was intended that she would spend the New Year holiday, before travelling on to meet her groom-to-be at Blackheath on 3 January. Entertainment was provided for the young lady to pass the time while she waited for her bridegroom: entertainment such as the blood sports so favoured by the Tudors.

On New Year's Day, Anne was standing by a window watching bull-baiting on the grass beside the keep when six gentlemen burst into her room unannounced, all hooded and disguised in identical gowns. One of the men stepped forward to present her with a gift from the King. He started kissing her and made advances. Disconcerted, but not flustered, the demure Anne seems to have tried to ignore this break with courtesy by 'regard[ing] him little but always look[ing] out of the window on the bull-baiting'. The man swept out of the room and returned moments later in a gown of purple velvet. It was, of course, Henry VIII himself.

The King had hoped that by surprising Anne he would 'nourish love', because it was a widely known chivalric notion that true lovers could recognise each other through a disguise. He also probably hoped that his sheer royal bearing and dashing good looks would win her attention. Her lack of response was deeply humiliating. The lesson Henry took was that she was unschooled and lacked the cosmopolitan wit of the courtly lady that he sought. There was some truth to that: Anne was very parochial in her education and accomplishments, and she barely spoke English, let alone Latin or French. But what was more painfully obvious was that at forty-eight, and with a waist of nearly fifty-four inches, Henry was no longer the Adonis he had once been.

According to his close servant, Sir Anthony Browne, Henry spoke barely twenty words to Anne and left quickly. The next day he told Browne that he saw, 'nothing in this woman as men report of her', and to Cromwell, that he liked her, 'nothing so well as she was spoken of'. As time went on, he became more emphatic, telling Cromwell, 'Say what they will, she is nothing as fair as she hath been reported' and on the day of their delayed marriage, 6 January 1540, muttered, 'If it were not to satisfy the world and my realm, I would not do that I must do this day for none earthly thing.' Hardly what one hopes the groom will say before he walks down the aisle.

Anne has been slandered throughout history as an ugly 'Flanders' Mare' (a phrase invented in the seventeenth century), but Henry only made passing mention of her looks, and other people continued to praise her beauty. On their wedding day, the chronicler Edward Hall reported that Anne was 'so fair a Lady of so goodly a Stature & so womanly a countenance' and her hair, 'fair, yellow and long'.

The real problem was Henry's sense of shame and humiliation. This meant that when he came to consummate the marriage, and touched her belly and breasts, he quickly convinced himself that 'she should be no maid... which struck me so to the heart when I felt them that I had neither will nor courage to proceed any further in other matters'. It had to be her fault and not his.

On 9 July, Anne was informed that the court had decided her unconsummated marriage had been annulled. Although initially distraught, she gathered her wits and played her hand well. Agreeing to being honoured as the King's 'sister', she earned Henry's gratitude, and with it an income of £4,000 a year and the palaces of Richmond and Bletchingley, to which were later added Hever, Kemsing and Seal: not a bad haul for six months of benign companionship.

Of all Henry's wives, Anne was the one who truly survived. She lived the longest and, when she died in 1558, Mary I buried her in a prominent tomb in Westminster Abbey. Anne's fate rested on that serendipitous moment at Rochester when she found baited bulls more compelling than a bullheaded old man.

Allington Castle

If you've time, it's worth driving past nearby Allington Castle. It's not open to the public (if you must see its interiors, you will have to get married there), but this thirteenth-century stone-moated castle has an important role in Tudor history as the home of the Wyatts. Sir Henry Wyatt entertained Henry VIII here in the summer of 1527 but, more importantly, it was the birthplace of his son, Sir Thomas Wyatt the Elder, famed poet of Henry VIII's court. In the 1520s, Wyatt was probably in love with Anne Boleyn, who lived down the road at Hever, but he was prevented from courting her by his existing unhappy marriage. It is suggested that he is alluding to Anne and Henry's love for her in his sonnet 'Whoso list to hunt' – in which the hunter abandons his vain pursuit of a deer after seeing that her collar indicates that she belongs to Caesar. Perhaps as a result of this flirtation, in 1536 Wyatt was accused of committing adultery with Anne and was imprisoned in the Tower, from where he watched the execution of the other accused men, but miraculously escaped the chop. He retired to Allington to lick his wounds. Allington was also the birthplace of his son, Sir Thomas Wyatt the Younger, who led a vast rebellion against Mary I in 1554 [see WINCHESTER CATHEDRAL]. Unlike his father, he could not escape execution, and was beheaded for treason at the Tower.

Christ Church
Oxford, Oxfordshire

*'I would all the world knew that I have
nothing but it is the King's of right, for by him,
and of him I have received all that I have.'*

Christ Church is Oxford's largest and arguably most impressive college. As well as a seat of learning, it is, or has been, a priory, cathedral, royal court and, more recently, a double for Hogwarts in the *Harry Potter* films. Its chapel, which is also the City of Oxford's Cathedral, dates from the twelfth century when it was part of an Augustinian priory dedicated to St Frideswide, Oxford's patron saint. The college itself was originally called Cardinal College and was founded in 1524 by Thomas Wolsey, Lord Chancellor of England and Henry VIII's right-hand man.

Wolsey was famously born – as his Tudor biographer and gentleman-servant, George Cavendish, described – 'an honest poor man's son' in 1470. His father, Robert, was an Ipswich butcher and cattle-farmer, but Wolsey rose from these humble origins with the help of a degree from Magdalen College, Oxford, and a clerical benefice from the Marquess of Dorset. Under Henry VII, he became a royal chaplain and the Dean of Lincoln Cathedral.

But it was in Henry VIII's reign that his rise became truly me-
teoric. Starting off as the royal almoner and member of the King's
Council, Wolsey's list of promotions in a few short years reads
like a panoply of church hierarchy: in 1513, he was made Dean of
York and Bishop of London; in 1514, Bishop of Lincoln and
Archbishop of York; in 1515, Cardinal. These appointments
brought him great wealth, but his real power was derived from
the King's increasing dependence upon him as Lord Chancellor
of England from 1515. Before long, the Venetian ambassador
would observe that Henry, 'leaves everything in charge of Cardinal Wolsey', while Erasmus noted that he governed 'more really
than the King himself'.

Cavendish attributed Wolsey's success to his charisma and
'special gift of natural eloquence... with a filed [polished] tongue...
he was able... to persuade and allure all men to his purpose'.
Wolsey was indispensable to Henry because he took the burden of
state affairs off the young King's shoulders, 'putting the King in
comfort that he shall not need to spare any time of his pleasure for
any business'. Wolsey also worked tremendously hard. His servant
recalls one occasion when he rose at 4 a.m. and worked straight
through until 4 p.m., during which time 'my Lord never rose once
to piss, nor yet to eat any meat but continually wrote his letters
with his own hands, having all that time his night cap and kever-
chief on his head'.

Wolsey's greatest achievements were in the realm of foreign
diplomacy. He negotiated the marriage of Henry's younger sister,
Mary [see St Mary's, Bury St Edmunds] to the French King,
Louis XII, and managed to position the relatively puny England as
a peace broker between the great kingdoms of France and the Holy
Roman Empire. His Treaty of Universal Peace in 1518 was his stel-
lar accomplishment and was celebrated in glorious, spectacular
fashion at the Field of Cloth of Gold [see Leeds Castle], in a

masterly display of organisation that epitomised his consummate skill as a civil servant, politician and diplomat.

Wolsey, the butcher's son, lived as befitted his status as a Prince of the Church and was known for the splendour and richness of his court. At his death, he owned over 600 tapestries of incalculable value; when he received the King, or ambassadors, he served up courses of 100 dishes and entertained with 'masques and mummeries in so gorgeous a sort and costly manner that it was an heaven to behold'. He travelled in the sort of pomp that might seem absurd today, processing astride a mule trapped in crimson velvet and gilt stirrups, dressed all in red and swathed in sable fur, behind men carrying aloft two silver crosses, two silver pillars, the Great Seal of England and his red Cardinal's hat. Christ Church's badge still features Wolsey's hat, and his very hat is preserved in the college library.

Like his house at Hampton Court, Wolsey intended Cardinal College to proclaim his magnificence, as well as his cultural patronage of, and commitment to, learning. He did it, however, by getting permission from the Pope to suppress St Frideswide's Monastery in 1524 (well before Henry's later dissolution), and use the land and funds to build his new college. Parts of the original monastery do still exist, however, and form the oldest parts of the college: the Chapter House, cloisters and refectory.

The rest of the monastery was demolished to make way for Wolsey's grand new project. He completed three sides of the enormous Tom Quad (named after the Great Tom bell in Sir Christopher Wren's later Tom Tower), which at 264 by 261 feet is the largest quadrangle in Oxford. Wolsey also had the kitchens and the Great Hall built. The hall's original hammer-beam ceiling was replaced in the eighteenth century after a fire. The college was so impressive that Thomas Cromwell proclaimed in 1528 that, 'every man thinks the like was never seen for the largeness, beauty, sumptuous, curious and substantial building'.

Not every scheme that Wolsey spearheaded for the King was successful, but Wolsey had always managed to find a gracious way out of trouble until, that is, Henry sought to annul his marriage to Katherine of Aragon. Despite the Cardinal's best efforts, after the Pope was taken captive by Katherine's nephew, the Holy Roman Emperor, Charles V, and with Katherine's refusal to accept the authority of the 1529 court at Blackfriars, even the great Wolsey could not figure out a way to secure Henry's 'Great Matter' through the proper papal channels. It is a huge injustice that for one so devoted to furthering his master's interests, Wolsey became the scapegoat for the incident.

On 9 October 1529, he was indicted on a charge of *praemunire* (allegiance to a foreign power), deprived of his position and required to surrender all his properties and possessions, among them, Cardinal College. According to one observer he did this willingly, saying: 'I would all the world knew that I have nothing but it is his [Henry's] of right, for by him, and of him I have received all that I have: therefore it is of convenience and reason, that I render unto his Majesty the same again with all my heart.'

In the following months, though banished from court, there still seemed a chance of his reinstatement. But his rivals, nobles who had resented Wolsey as an ambitious upstart, agitated for his removal. Wolsey was urged to visit his diocese at York, and finally travelled north in April 1530. Events took a turn for the worse in November with a rumour that Wolsey had opened negotiations to acquire a papal order to force Henry and Anne Boleyn to separate. William Walsh, gentleman of the Privy Chamber, was sent to arrest Wolsey on a charge of high treason. But he would never face a trial or punishment. On the journey south to the Tower of London, Wolsey fell ill of dysentery, and died at Leicester Abbey on 30 November 1530. According to Cavendish, in these last days he mused ruefully, 'If I had served God as diligently as I have done the King, he would not have given me over in my grey hairs.'

Known for some years as 'King Henry VIII's College', Cardinal was refounded by Henry as Christ Church in 1546. During the Civil War, it became a royalist stronghold and was briefly Charles I's court. Wolsey's great quadrangle was completed in gratitude after the restoration of the monarchy.

Among Christ Church's alumni are thirteen prime ministers and the great and good of literature and art, philosophy, theology (John and Charles Wesley founded Methodism as students here) and science. In the end, Wolsey achieved his goal of creating a famous place of learning and enduring splendour, even if he himself did not live long to see it.

Broad Street
Oxford, Oxfordshire

'We shall this day light such a candle, by God's grace,
in England, as I trust shall never be put out.'

In the centre of Broad Street in Oxford, outside Balliol College, an unceremonious small cross of cobblestones set in the middle of the tarmac road marks the site of the 1555 and 1556 burnings of the 'Oxford martyrs': Hugh Latimer, Nicholas Ridley and Thomas Cranmer, formerly the bishops of Worcester and London, and the Archbishop of Canterbury. This inconspicuous reminder, together with the doors of Balliol College that were scorched by the fire and that now hang between the front and garden quadrangles, testify to the ugly side of the revival of Roman Catholicism in England when Mary I came to the throne.

During Mary's reign, from 1553 to 1558, 312 people were either burned as the penalty for heresy, or died in prison after being charged with heresy. This scale of punishment for heretics was unprecedented, and 'Bloody' Mary's reign remains the most intense period of Christian persecution in English history.

Mary aimed to eliminate all religious dissidents, but it is worth noting that she was not alone in believing that there could only be one true faith. Religious tolerance was not considered a virtue in the sixteenth century. All right-thinking Christians believed that it was necessary to purge the world from the polluting influence of heresy or else the spread of these diabolical errors would, they thought, incur divine wrath and threaten to overturn the social and moral order; Protestants and Catholics just differed in their understanding of what heresy was. In the Tudor period, what one believed about what happened during the Eucharist or how one was made right with God could therefore be, literally, life and death issues.

In Oxford, unlike the big burning towns of London, Canterbury and Colchester, only three Protestants were martyred. But these three were the most important leaders of the Protestant movement and, among them, Thomas Cranmer was pre-eminent. Together, they symbolised everything Mary's Catholic government thought had gone wrong in England since the break with Rome.

Cranmer was a reforming cleric, who was constantly mired in the murky world of Tudor politics. He had risen to prominence when he acted for Henry VIII to produce the academic case for the annulment of Henry's marriage to Katherine of Aragon, Mary's mother. It was he who, as Archbishop of Canterbury from 1533, declared the marriage to Katherine null and void, and played an important role in the coronation of Anne Boleyn. He also had the unpleasant duty of alerting Henry VIII to Katherine Howard's infidelity in 1541 [see PONTEFRACT CASTLE]. But his really important work, and lasting legacy, was writing the Book of Common Prayer, the first English prayer book, published in 1549. Modified only marginally since, Cranmer's words are still spoken in Anglican churches every Sunday.

When Mary became Queen, he was, understandably, her number one target. His support for the Protestant Queen Jane

(Lady Jane Grey) meant that he was tried and found guilty of treason at the London Guildhall in late 1553, but although this came with a death penalty, Mary wanted more: she wanted Cranmer to be officially deprived of his position and declared not only a traitor, but a heretic.

At first, Cranmer was imprisoned with Ridley, Bishop of London, and Latimer, Bishop of Worcester, in the Tower of London, and then in Bocardo, the Oxford town prison (near present-day St Michael's Northgate on Cornmarket), although the three were later separated.

Each of the three faced a disputation (a sort of religious cross-examination) with Cambridge theologians in the Oxford University Church of St Mary the Virgin in April 1554, followed by a trial for heresy in September 1555. In the first, they were interrogated on the question of transubstantiation: did they believe that the bread and the wine actually became the body and blood of Christ after words spoken by a priest? In the second, their entire lives were on trial. They were, of course, found guilty.

On 16 October 1555, Ridley and Latimer accused of the same crime as Cranmer, were burned in a ditch outside the city gate, in what is now Broad Street. Latimer's last words were moving and memorable: 'Be of good comfort, Master Ridley, and play the man. We shall this day light such a candle, by God's grace, in England, as I trust shall never be put out.'

Latimer perished quickly, but poor Ridley suffered in protracted agony. Cranmer was made to watch, and was traumatised by the sight.

The deaths of his friends, his prolonged isolation from family and supporters and the terror of his own impending death began to tell on Cranmer. He wrote several statements, each varying in their degree of capitulation to the Catholic Church, and most followed by retractions. Finally, when after more than two years of imprisonment, on 24 February 1556, the writ was issued for his burning, Cranmer collapsed and signed a full recantation of his Protestant faith.

Under normal canon law, his repentance should have saved his life, but Mary was unyielding and the burning was ordered to proceed. To celebrate his reconversion, on the day of his execution, the authorities paraded Cranmer in University Church and permitted him to pray aloud to demonstrate his repentance. Halfway through, though, he started to deviate from his text. Over the resulting commotion, he just managed to make his key message heard: 'And as for the Pope, I refuse him, as Christ's enemy, an antichrist with all his false doctrine.'

He was pulled from the stage and hurried through the rain and streets of Oxford to the stake. To punish the hand that had signed the recantation, Cranmer stretched out his arm into the heart of the fire, repeating, 'This hand hath offended,' and then 'Lord Jesus, receive my spirit... I see the heavens open and Jesus standing at the right hand of God.' Cranmer had turned his death, which could have been a great victory for the Catholic Church, into a huge coup for the Protestant cause.

The blood of the martyrs remained fixed in the English Protestant imagination for centuries. The Victorians built a memorial to the Oxford martyrs sixty-five feet away on St Giles, but it is the door licked by the flames of these human pyres, and the simple stone cross in the ground, that most evoke the terrible sacrifice of these men for the cause in which they so fervently believed.

Loseley Park
Surrey

'Invidiae claudor, pateo sed semper amico.'
'I am shut to envy, but always open to a friend.'
(Motto over inner door at Loseley.)

J ust outside Guildford, at the centre of miles of picturesque parkland, is a beautiful Elizabethan mansion belonging to the More-Molyneux family. It is a lovely house with many treasures but, above all, it offers a glimpse into one of Henry VIII's missing palaces.

An ancestor of the More-Molyneuxes, Sir William More built Loseley House in the 1560s using 860-year-old stone from the ruins of nearby Waverley Abbey. Elizabeth I visited the house on at least three occasions (1577, 1583 and 1591) and the house is suitably elegant inside as well as out.

It has some gems of Tudor portraiture and craftsmanship. The Great Hall has many important portraits, including those of Mary, Queen of Scots, and Edward VI (wearing the gold collar also worn by Henry VIII in his picture at the WALKER ART GALLERY). Look out, too, for the painted coats of arms on the windows, which are original, from the sixteenth century. In the wood-panelled library, there is an ornately decorated overmantle bearing the arms and initials of Elizabeth I, while the chimneypiece in the Great Chamber (or drawing room) was elaborately sculpted by French carvers in 1565 from one solid block of chalk. Elizabeth I herself is believed to have sewn the needlework cushions that you can see on the low Elizabethan 'maid-of-honour' chairs either side of the fireplace. Also in the Great Chamber, there are portraits of Sir William More, and his relative by marriage, the Lord Chancellor Sir Thomas More, and an eighteenth-century image of Anne Boleyn.

But the real treasures at Loseley Park come from one of the most celebrated English buildings of the sixteenth century, the greatest of all Henry's palaces: Nonsuch. Henry VIII spent over £24,000 (today, roughly £7.4 million) and nine years building Nonsuch Palace at Cuddington in Surrey, and it was still unfinished when he died. This lavishly decorated hunting lodge was built, as its name suggests, to be a palace nonpareil: a house without equal. As construction started on 22 April 1538, thirty years to the day after Henry VIII's accession, it was almost certainly intended to be a celebration of his rule, and of his recently born son and heir, Edward.

It also had another purpose. By this stage, Henry VIII, as he was described in 1548, had 'waxed heavy with sickness, age and corpulences of body and might not so readily travel abroad, [so] was constrained to seek to have his game and pleasure ready at hand': because of his painful, weeping ulcer and great weight, the King could not go hunting on long progresses far from London. So he enclosed the chase of Hampton Court, and built Nonsuch within it, to provide such entertainment nearer to home. For Henry, hunting now meant sitting on a horse while his minions scared deer directly into his path!

Nonsuch was unlike any palace before it. Unusually, Henry did not build onto an existing structure; in fact, he swept away the manor house and village at Cuddington to create an ornate palace that was one of the finest examples of Renaissance architecture in

England. Rather than build a medieval-style Great Hall, as at Hampton Court, Henry ordered a long gallery – one of the first in England. In addition, while the outer courtyard had a normal turreted gatehouse in brick and stone, the inner court was timber-framed, and those timbers, hidden by plaques of carved slate, held *stucco duro* or fine plasterwork panels that created a dazzlingly ornamented display. William Camden in his *Britannia* of 1586 wrote that Nonsuch was, 'built with so great sumptuousness and rare workmanship, that it aspireth to the very top of ostentation for shew, so as a man may think, that all the skill of Architecture is in this one piece of work bestowed, and heaped up together'.

Loseley possesses some of the very few remaining panels from Nonsuch. In the Great Hall, you can see that some are painted: decorated with the initials of Henry VIII (HR for '*Henricus Rex*') and his last queen, Kateryn Parr, or with the portcullis badge. Others, in the Minstrels' Gallery and in the corridor upstairs, depict classical gods and mythical characters in a fanciful grotesque style. There are also some splendid inlaid *trompe d'œil* panels that create the illusion of arched passages stretching away into the distance. Finally, there is even a marble-on-alabaster table decorated with a Tudor rose and Scottish thistle in the entrance hall, said to come from Nonsuch.

Despite its pedigree and later becoming one of Elizabeth I's favourite houses, Nonsuch was unaccountably demolished in 1682–3 by Charles II's mistress, Barbara Villiers, Duchess of Cleveland: an ignoble end for what was ostensibly the finest palace in the realm. The site was lost until excavations in Nonsuch Park in 1959 unearthed it, and the area is now marked only with stones. The pieces at Loseley matter so much because they are practically all that survive from this legendary palace.

Arundel Castle
West Sussex

'Beware of high degree. To a vainglorious, proud stomach,
it seemeth as the first sweet. Look into all the chronicles and
you shall find that, in the end, it brings heaps of cares...
and, most commonly, in the end, utter overthrow.'

Arundel Castle is a magnificent stately home and hard to beat for a cultural day out. In truth, it is more Norman and Victorian than Tudor: many of its jaw-dropping interiors are reproductions. On the other hand, it is one of the only surviving homes (Framlingham and Charterhouse are the others) of the Howards, arguably the most ambitious, egotistical and powerful of all the Tudor families, and so it must be included in a visit to Tudor England. The other Howard estates at Kenninghall in Norfolk, Norfolk House in London and Surrey House in Norwich have all reverted to dust.

Arundel Castle is still the home of the dukes of Norfolk, and has been so ever since it passed into the hands of Philip Howard, Earl of Arundel, in 1580, following the marriage of his mother Lady Mary Fitzalan to Thomas Howard, fourth Duke of Norfolk. The Howard family was ambitious, but far from always successful. Consider their fortunes: this is a family in which every Tudor duke was attainted as a traitor and one was beheaded; two nieces became English queens and both were executed; one heir to the dukedom was beheaded; and another died in prison. Surely the most remarkable feature of this dynasty was its ability to rise constantly phoenix-like from the ashes.

Arundel itself has a long and illustrious history. There has been a castle here since soon after the Battle of Hastings, as the gatehouse, dating from around 1070, testifies. The stone keep and parts of the curtain wall you see now were built by William de Albini in the early twelfth century out of Caen stone from Normandy, as well as the local Pulborough stone and flint. Queen Matilda would have seen this when she visited the castle in 1139. The Barbican – the squared towers either side of the entrance gate – and the Bevis Tower date from the late fourteenth century. There was also once a thirteenth-century Great Hall and lodgings around the South Bailey, but they were demolished in the Civil War and it is on their remains that the present Victorian house is built.

The house itself is an exceptional example of the revival of Gothic architecture in the nineteenth century. The chapel mimics the thirteenth-century style of Westminster Abbey or Lincoln Cathedral almost perfectly, while the Barons' Hall is Gothic style reinvented on a mammoth scale: it is 131 feet long! The house is so stunning that it is no wonder that Queen Victoria and Prince Albert came to stay here in 1846. Yet, it is only the medieval castle, and the Fitzalan Chapel in the grounds, that would have been familiar to the Tudor visitor.

The Howards are commemorated here in a series of portraits in the Picture Gallery. You can see Thomas Howard, third Duke of Norfolk, born 1473, in a portrait by Daniel Mytens, after Hans Holbein. It fits a description of the Duke by the Venetian ambassador Ludovico Falieri in 1531 – he was 'small and spare in person, and his hair black' – but Norfolk's slender frame is masked by his rich silk, velvet and ermine clothes, and eclipsed by the symbols of his powerful status and prestigious office: the Earl Marshal's baton and Lord Treasurer's stave, and the ostentatious collar of the Order of the Garter. In many ways, it is a successful portrait in that it sums up this driven, proud man.

Norfolk could be charming, but was also something of an egoistic bully and a sycophant, with a quick, violent temper and a tendency to whine. He longed to be a Wolsey or a Cromwell: the King's right-hand man. Falieri noted that he 'aspires to greater elevation'.

In early life, he married Anne Plantagenet, daughter of Edward IV, and he is buried with her at Framlingham. Two years after she died in 1511, when he was nearly forty years old, he married Elizabeth, the fifteen-year-old daughter of Edward Stafford, third Duke of Buckingham. Their marriage became one of the greatest scandals of the age when, in 1527, Norfolk took a mistress, Bess Holland, whom Elizabeth described as a 'washer-woman of her nursery'. The Duke and Duchess separated in 1534, and Elizabeth complained miserably to Thomas Cromwell about her mistreatment and poverty, even alleging that the ladies of Norfolk's household had attacked her 'until I spat blood'.

Norfolk was central to Henry VIII's reign: he fought at Flodden, was ambassador to the French and did the King's dirty work in the aftermath of the Pilgrimage of Grace [see PONTEFRACT CASTLE]. But loyalty to a mercurial king comes at a price, and frequently required the abandonment of scruples in other areas. For example, though Anne Boleyn was his niece, Norfolk himself presided over her trial, only to encourage another niece, Katherine Howard, to take her place in the King's bed several years later. In 1546, he finally fell foul of the King and was attainted on account of his son's – Henry Howard, Earl of Surrey – actions.

Surrey, who was born in 1513, can be seen in a large six feet by six feet painting in the Gallery facing the foot of the stairs. As a teenager, Surrey had been close friends with the King's illegitimate son, Henry Fitzroy, Duke of Richmond and Somerset, to whom his sister Mary Howard (also seen in a portrait here) was married in 1533. Surrey was an exuberant and intemperate young man, once sent to Fleet Prison for breaking the Lenten fast and 'as of a lewd and unseemly manner walking in the night... and breaking with stonebows of certain windows'. He was also a candid and innovative poet, who reflected indiscreetly on the perils of serving under a tyrant. He was to discover these dangers for himself.

With lofty ambitions and treason in his blood on both sides of the family, in December 1546 Surrey was arrested for quartering the royal arms with his own: literally, adding the royal insignia on a small portion of his own coat of arms. Heraldry was a serious business in the Tudor age, and Henry VIII feared that Surrey planned 'himself to govern the realm'. This grandiose portrait (a copy from 1610 of the original by William Scrots) displays Surrey's avaricious pomp, leaning on a broken pillar (a symbol of endurance), with the baffling motto, '*Sat super est*' ('Enough remains'). Surrey was found guilty of treason and beheaded on 19 January 1547. It was scheduled that his father should also die on the morning of 28 January. Norfolk had been a master survivor, but it seemed nothing could save him now. Until, that is, Henry VIII died in the night, mere hours before Norfolk's planned beheading. Instead, he lived on the grand old age of eighty when, in 1554, he died in his bed.

Aged eighteen, Norfolk's grandson and Surrey's son, Thomas (the Tudor historian's job is complicated by a dearth of Christian names in the period), became the fourth Duke of Norfolk. He is depicted at Arundel, wearing his collar of the Garter, in a portrait by Hans Eworth. He married three times, first to Mary Fitzalan, portrayed nearby. His greatest claim to fame is that in 1572, he followed his father to the block for treacherously supporting the Ridolfi plot to free Mary, Queen of Scots. He had also hoped to make the beautiful Scottish Queen [see TUTBURY CASTLE] his fourth wife. In the Tower, Norfolk wrote a lesson to his teenage son, Philip, which would have served well for all the Howards:

> Beware of high degree. To a vainglorious, proud stomach, it seemeth as the first sweet. Look into all the chronicles and you shall find that, in the end, it brings heaps of cares... and, most commonly, in the end, utter overthrow.

In the library, you can see a facsimile of Norfolk's death warrant. The Roman Catholic cause for which he died is also commemorated at Arundel: in the dining room you will find the gold and enamel rosary beads carried by Mary, Queen of Scots to her execution at Fotheringhay Castle.

Not the first, or the last, teenager in history to do so, Philip disregarded his father's advice, preferring to enjoy the lavish life of Elizabeth I's court. But in the 1580s, after his wife Anne Dacre's conversion, and having heard the persuasive religious defence of the Jesuit Edmund Campion, Philip attested that walking one day in the gallery of his castle at Arundel, he 'lift[ed] up his eyes and hands to Heaven... [and] firmly resolved to become a member of God's church and frame his life accordingly'. The decision to convert to Roman Catholicism was one fraught with danger, and in April 1585, the Earl sought to flee the country, but was trapped as he crossed the Channel by men in Sir Francis Walsingham's spy-ring. 'For being reconciled to the Pope' he was declared a traitor, and imprisoned in the Beauchamp Tower, where his graffiti remains [see THE TOWER OF LONDON]. He lived under the threat of death for ten and a half years, finally dying of dysentery in October 1595, having never seen his son and heir, from whom the present dukes of Norfolk, and the keepers of Arundel Castle, are descended.

Other Tudor sights to see at Arundel: in the Armoury, there are four composite sixteenth-century suits of armour, while in the gallery, you can see a chest that Mary I gave to Henry Fitzalan, twelfth Earl of Arundel. There is also a 'Nonsuch chest' from 1682, with a picture of the façade of Nonsuch Palace.

South West

Pendennis and St Mawes Castles
Cornwall

'Semper vivet anima Regis Henrici Octavi
qui anno 34 sui regni hoc fecit fieri.'
('May the soul of King Henry VIII, who had this
built in the 34th year of his reign, live ever.')

Pendennis and St Mawes castles stand on headlands proudly facing each other across the mouth of the River Fal on the south-western tip of the Cornish coast. Guarding the estuary and anchorage known as Carrick Roads, near to Falmouth, they are perfect surviving examples of the scheme of coastal fortification constructed on Henry VIII's orders after 1539. They were intended to be, quite literally, the last bastion of defence in the event of an invasion by the Catholic powers of Europe.

Henry VIII's decision to break from the Roman Catholic Church and establish himself as Supreme Head of the new Church of England had meant not only schism, but that he was seen by the Pope and Catholic monarchs as an 'impious and heretical tyrant'. As such, they came to believe that it was their Christian duty to fight a holy war against the heretic and restore Catholic authority in England. In 1538, this situation became pressing. The French King, Francis I, and the Holy Roman Emperor, Charles V, signed a ten-year truce and, in December, the Pope published a decree excommunicating Henry VIII, freeing English subjects from any allegiance to him and authorising an attack on England. Invasion seemed not only unavoidable, but imminent.

In response, Henry VIII's commissioners put together an ambitious programme, known as the 'Device of the King', to build a chain of new forts, castles, embankments, ditches and bulwarks to protect the vulnerable ports and landing points along the southern and eastern coasts. These coastal artillery forts were the last castles built in England. Much of the money to finance them came directly from the dissolution of the monasteries [see FOUNTAINS ABBEY], while monastic bells were melted down in bulk to provide gunmetal.

As the first safe place to land for ships heading up from the Mediterranean and an ideal springboard for an invasion by England's enemies because of its wide, deep estuary, Carrick Roads was judged a soft target. Henry's advisers, therefore, decided to build two forts, one on either side of the river, so that any advancing ships would be caught in the crossfire of their guns.

Pendennis Castle is one of these structures. The circular gun tower was built in the early 1540s, although the gatehouse, ramparts and forebuilding (with its elegant oriel window) are all Elizabethan additions. The central tower was designed to be fifty-seven feet in diameter, with octagonal rooms over several floors featuring gun ports from which heavy artillery could be fired. The recreation of such a room here, with replica guns, suggests just how cramped, noisy and smoky the rooms would have been if they were ever used. The tower is surrounded by a chemise, or gun platform, with embrasures for another fourteen guns and there is also a high lookout tower. The guns that the Tudors used were smooth-bore and front-loading, mounted on wheeled truck carriages, each of which took four strong and skilled men to aim and fire. Completed by 1545, Pendennis Castle cost £5,614 to build: over £1.5 million today.

Across the water, St Mawes Castle (also completed by 1545 at a cost of £5,018) is an even finer example of Henry's fortifications. It has a graceful geometry, with a forty-six-foot circular central tower and three lower semicircular bastions arranged around it in a cloverleaf pattern. It has survived remarkably well: all the buildings, including the gatehouse, are original.

St Mawes is particularly special because of its Latin and English inscriptions, which praise Henry VIII and his son. Over the gatehouse window is a carving of the Tudor royal arms and an inscription composed by John Leland (who wrote an itinerary of all the buildings in England in the 1540s), which reads, '*Semper honos Henrice tuus laudesque manebunt*' ('Henry, by honour and praises will remain forever'). On the second floor of the central tower, each room has an English inscription in the door spandrels that states, 'God save King Henry VIII' and 'God save Prince Edward'. The door from the forward bastion into the central tower is also carved, this time with sea creatures and another Latin inscription: '*Semper vivet anima Regis Henrici Octavi qui anno 34 sui regni hoc fecit fieri*' ('May the soul of King Henry VIII, who had this built in the 34th year of his reign, live ever'). Perhaps the inscriptions were intended to rouse the men defending the fort to daring acts of patriotism (though not all soldiers would have been able to read – even the English!).

St Mawes also houses an original Tudor bronze Alberghetti gun, one of the great range of Tudor guns and munitions including culverins, falcons, demi-cannon, slings and minions that were used at these castles. Both Pendennis and St Mawes also have small blockhouses or gun towers close to the water's edge, which were probably built before the main castles had been constructed.

Pendennis and St Mawes are two of the best examples of the circular castles that were part of the 1539 device programme. Others still standing include Walmer, Deal, Portland and Calshot. Reflecting new ideas about fortification, there were more angular castles built in the late 1540s at Southsea, Sandown and Yarmouth. In fact, as has often been the case throughout the history of grand defensive military schemes, by the time the castles were completed, the risk of invasion had passed.

They were not built in vain, however. Under Elizabeth, the threat arose again, and both castles were garrisoned and provided with guns. Sir Walter Ralegh mustered 500 men at Pendennis in 1596, when a Spanish fleet attempted to land and use Carrick Roads as a bridgehead from which to launch an invasion.

Buckland Abbey
Devon

'Sic parvis magna'
'Great achievements from small beginnings'

The converted Cistercian abbey at Buckland in Devon is chiefly remembered as the home of England's most famous seaman, privateer and adventurer, Sir Francis Drake (which explains the bizarre decision to turn the top floor into a replica ship). Drake, rightly, remains a legendary hero of British history, but the story of Buckland Abbey reveals how much of his fame and success was a question of luck and timing, as well as of character and courage.

Born around 1540 of humble yeoman stock, Francis Drake's life at sea began when he was apprenticed to the master of a small coasting ship. He was the eldest of the eleven children of Edmund Drake, a lay preacher whose fervent Protestant faith helped to shape Drake's sense of personal destiny. Another crucial ingredient in Drake's formation occurred on a slaving voyage with John Hawkins in 1568: the English captains were tricked, ambushed and defeated by the Spanish at the Battle of San Juan d'Ulua off the coast of Mexico, inciting Drake's life-long hatred of Catholic Spain and his determination to avenge England at sea.

Stocky and strong, Drake was of middling height, with reddish brown curls and the ubiquitous sixteenth-century beard. He was cheerful, gregarious and direct, with an intrepid and impressive ability to inspire and lead. He made three bold and successful raids on the Spanish Main in the early 1570s, operating as a privateer (a private man-of-war licensed by the government, with a share of the spoils going to the Crown), although his first expedition – the first raid by any Englishman – was carried out without authorisation, which technically made it piracy. On his third voyage, he captured the Spanish treasure town of Nombre de Dios. His haul of 300,000 pesos' worth of gold made him a rich man at home and a feared man abroad.

Drake was most famous, however, for his circumnavigation of the globe in 1577–1580. Surviving violent encounters with natives, threats of mutiny, relentless storms and attacks by the Spanish, he and his crew sailed through the Strait of Magellan, up the coast of Peru, across the Pacific and home via the Cape of Good Hope. He discovered Cape Horn, claimed England's first overseas possessions during Elizabeth's reign – Elizabeth Island and Nova Albion in California – and on his return was knighted on board his own ship, now renamed the *Golden Hind* (Sir Christopher Hatton part-financed the voyage, and the hind was his crest [see KIRBY HALL]). For Drake's flagrant intrusion into Spanish waters, the Spanish christened him '*El Draco*' ('the Dragon'). Compare this with the so-called achievements of Sir Walter Ralegh [see SHERBORNE CASTLE] and you may conclude that it's a wonder the two are ever mentioned in the same breath.

After circling the globe, Drake, with his first wife, Mary Newman, acquired Buckland Abbey, and other nearby manors at Yarcombe, Sherford and Sampford Spiney. Buckland had been the last Cistercian abbey to be founded in England, in 1278, and had passed into the hands of the Grenville family after the dissolution of the monasteries in 1541. Sir Richard Grenville and his son Roger started converting the Abbey into a family house but after Roger, as captain of the *Mary Rose*, sank on board his ship in July 1545 [see the MARY ROSE], Buckland was inherited by his infant son, the younger Richard Grenville.

The lives of Richard Grenville and Frances Drake are rather uncannily similar, and if circumstances had been slightly different, it could be Grenville we remember as a Tudor hero and Drake who is largely forgotten. Grenville, like Drake, was a staunch and committed Protestant, who loved to sail and also wanted to defy the Spanish. In 1573, Grenville had proposed a voyage to explore the South Seas, to seek new lands in Terra Australis, and search for the Northwest Passage. Elizabeth, then trying to please the King of Spain, had refused. However, when Drake had suggested the same scheme four years later, during a very different diplomatic environment, Elizabeth had eagerly signed up. So Drake set off around the world on the voyage that would make him famous, while Grenville stayed at home converting Buckland into a pleasant modern dwelling. He pulled down one of the wings to streamline the building and let in more light, built a two-floored east wing for the kitchens and domestic servants and put three floors into the church, creating a Great Hall out of the nave.

Grenville also put in the Great Hall's stunning wood panelling, plasterwork ceiling, overmantle and frieze (see if you can spot the spy holes: a small staircase running behind this wall allowed servants to spy on guests), granite fireplace with herringbone slate and pink and white triangular patterned tiled floor. The room remains unchanged and, unlike much of the rest of the house, which has been altered over the centuries, is a picture-perfect example of Tudor domestic style.

The irony is that when, after all this work, Grenville could no longer afford to keep the house, it was the newly returned, knighted and wealthy Sir Francis Drake whose agents bought Buckland from Grenville for £3,400. Drake moved in during 1581, and lived here for nearly fifteen years. He made practically no changes to the fabric of the house, keeping it instead as Grenville had left it.

Drake's life here was not entirely untroubled. His wife, Mary, died childless after thirteen years of marriage in January 1583, and although Drake married again to the beautiful heiress Elizabeth Sydenham (her portrait of 1585 by George Gower can be seen at Buckland), she too did not bear him an heir.

In terms of career and reputation, however, Drake's star was still in the ascendancy. In 1587, Drake 'singed the beard of the King of Spain' with his raid against Cadiz, when he destroyed and captured, by his own account, thirty-nine Spanish ships, including a galleon belonging to the intended commander of the Armada, the Marquis of Santa Cruz. When the Spanish Armada itself finally attacked in July 1588, it was Drake's daring, if maverick, capture of the prize *Rosario* and its 50,000 Spanish ducats that won acclaim (Drake was lucky again: terrible weather and delays among the Spanish army in the Netherlands played a pivotal role in the victory). Some of Buckland's treasures – the Armada badges, the portrait of Drake from 1590 by Marcus Gheeraerts the Younger, a set of Elizabethan armour – allude to the Spanish defeat. Poor Richard Grenville also played an efficient, but far less fêted, role in dispatching the Armada, while even the Admiral of the Fleet, Lord Howard of Effingham, didn't get the credit lauded on Drake.

Drake set out from Buckland for his last voyage in August 1595. Unfortunately, he had finally run out of luck and this expedition, with its 27 ships, 1,500 sailors and 1,000 soldiers, would see tragedy. First, Drake's old friend, Sir John Hawkins, fell sick and died as the fleet sighted their old place of defeat, San Juan. Then, off the coast of Panama, and on his ship, the aptly named *Defiance*,

Drake himself died of dysentery on 28 January 1596. His body was sealed in a lead coffin and buried at sea.

Drake's adopted motto, '*Sic parvis magna*' ('Great achievements from small beginnings'), can be seen on the coat of arms at Buckland. It perfectly encapsulates the life story of this bluff, courageous and ever-so-slightly lucky man.

❈

Other sights to look out for at Buckland: there are portraits of Charles Brandon, Duke of Suffolk, and a lady said to be Elizabeth I, from the circle of Marcus Gheeraerts the Younger. Also try to spot the internal remains of the original Abbey, including a carved ox of St Luke in the corner of the Georgian dining room. Of interest, too, is the Roman Catholic chapel built in 1917 on the site of the original Abbey's high altar (the fiercely Protestant Grenville and Drake would be turning in their graves if they knew!)

THE SPANISH ARMADA

Twice during the Tudor period, the incumbent Pope authorised an attack on England. In 1538, after the break with Rome, Pope Paul III excommunicated Henry VIII and declared that English subjects no longer owed allegiance to their King. As a result, an invasion by France or the Holy Roman Empire was felt to be a very real threat. Then, in 1570, Pope Pius V issued a similar decree regarding Elizabeth I. He declared her to be a heretic, excommunicated her and released her subjects from loyalty to her. In the eyes of Catholic Europe, she was not really Queen. In some ways, then, it was only a matter of time before a foreign Catholic power attempted an invasion, and that moment came in July 1588.

The 'invincible' Spanish Armada of 134 ships and 30,000 men was ready to set sail by mid-May 1588. Everyone involved had been granted a remission of punishment for sin by Pope Sixtus V for sailing against England's heretical Queen, and their standard, which read, 'Arise, O God, and defend your cause!' proclaimed their agenda of Catholic restoration.

They were immediately unlucky. The weather in May was so bad that the fleet was forced to wait three long weeks to set sail. When it finally did, the Spanish ended up sailing directly into the wind, so that it took them another two weeks to reach Cape Finisterre, 160 miles away from their point of departure. After such a delay, it was necessary to stop off at Corunna for supplies. Here, they were hit by a fierce south-westerly gale. The storm lasted two days and in that time, two galleasses and twenty-eight other warships went missing. All this, and they had not even left Spanish waters. The situation was so grim that the Spanish commander, Don Alonso Pérez de Guzmán, Duke of Medina Sidonia (the Marquis of Santa Cruz had died a few months before the Armada was ready to set sail), wrote to Philip II, suggesting that they abandon the expedition. Philip instead urged them on.

On 21 July, the Spanish took to sea again and, blessed with calm waters and a south-easterly breeze, they caught sight of England eight days later.

Once the Spanish ships were spotted, a series of beacons were lit to pass the news swiftly along the coast. The English, under the command of the Lord High Admiral, Lord Howard of Effingham, and his second-in-command, Sir Francis Drake, had more ships than the Spanish – 177 – but fewer guns. The real worry was that the Spanish might manage to land and invade: the English could not beat them on the ground.

Lord Howard took fifty-four ships out of Plymouth harbour and managed to zigzag behind the Spanish, giving the English the advantage of the wind but, despite a few skirmishes, the Spanish continued unopposed. The Spanish plan was to pick up a huge army under the Duke of Parma in the Netherlands but, here, the English had their first piece of luck: Parma's troops were not ready. Therefore, the Armada needed to anchor near Calais to await Parma's word and, as such, they were sitting ducks. The English sent fireships – warships packed with explosives and set afire – to drift towards the middle of the Armada, forcing the fleet to scatter.

Nevertheless, the Spanish were soon able to regroup, and withstood the English in a nine-hour battle at Gravelines. When the Spanish eventually sought to flee the bombardment, they had their own luck: the wind shifted to west-south-west, allowing them an opportunity to escape the English fleet and head north-west.

Meanwhile, Elizabeth I met her army, which had assembled at Tilbury under the command of Robert Dudley, Earl of Leicester and, on 9 August 1588, delivered her famous address to rally the troops: 'I know I have the body of a weak and feeble woman. But I have the heart and stomach of a king, and a king of England too.'

In fact, the worst of the danger had already passed. Heading up into the North Sea, Medina Sidonia had sailed away from Parma's army and now, because of the winds, could not easily get back.

At this point, the weather dealt the Spanish another cruel blow. They met a frontal mass of cold Arctic air and 'a most extreme wind and cruel storm, the like whereof hath not been seen or heard a long time'. The storms were accompanied by freezing fog and poor visibility. One account said that, in the height of summer, 'the days [were] so dark, the fogs so weird, that all our senses were obliterated'. It was also punishingly cold, and the Spanish were running very short on rations. As if this weren't enough, as they headed around the coast of Scotland and back south past Ireland, they were hit by the tail end of a tropical hurricane (something that has only happened at this latitude once since, in 1961).

In search of relief, seventeen ships headed for the Irish coast, but only two ships sailed away again: local inhabitants murdered the crews of the rest.

When the remnants of the fleet finally returned to Spain, only sixty-seven out of the original 134 ships had survived. Two-thirds of the men – 20,000 – had died of starvation, cold, disease, murder or shipwreck. Except for the fireships, not one English ship had been lost.

Philip II remarked, 'I sent my ships to fight against men and not against the winds and waves of God.' The unseasonable British weather had kept the Catholic threat at bay.

Sherborne Castle
Dorset

'He hath been as a star at which the world
has gazed; but stars may fall.'

The biscuit-coloured Sherborne Castle was the Tudor home of Sir Walter Ralegh (he preferred this spelling, and contemporary sources suggest it was pronounced 'Rawley'). He built the four-storey square building between 1594 and 1600; Sir John Digby, Earl of Bristol added the H-shape wings in 1630.

For someone who failed at almost everything he did, it is remarkable that we remember Ralegh as a great hero. Although he tried his hand at many things: chemistry, poetry, exploration, history and war, he did little to deserve his extravagant posthumous reputation. Any schoolboy knows that Ralegh introduced potatoes and tobacco to England: but he didn't – according to the latest research – although he did make smoking fashionable in England (at Sherborne, there is a pipe of Virginian maplewood said to have been smoked by Ralegh on the scaffold in 1618). And the fable that he spread his cloak over a 'plashy place' so that Elizabeth could cross it is unreliable gossip. Worse still, he was said to be 'damnably proud', with an 'awfulness and ascendancy in his aspect over other mortals' that won him few friends. Or perhaps he was simply a terribly ill-fated man, disproportionately punished in life for his pride and vanity.

Although the castle is now a memorial to the generations of Wingfield-Digbys who lived here after him – filling the house with their Georgian and Victorian furnishings – rather than a monument to Ralegh, the vigilant can spot Tudor elements in the original central house.

For a start, although the original house was smaller (comprising only the central square, not the H-shape wings), the exterior lime-rendered walls match the house's original appearance. We can be sure of this because maintenance work in 2002 exposed part of the outside wall of Ralegh's house, which you can see at the corner of the Green Drawing Room, formerly Ralegh's Great Chamber. The Solarium ('sun room'), Ralegh's parlour, has the original plaster-work ceiling adorned with Tudor roses, and there are Tudor ceilings in the Green Drawing Room, featuring acorns and fleurs-de lis, and in Lady Bristol's Bedroom, once Ralegh's Great Bedroom, which bears his badge of a buck. Also, the fireplace in the Green Drawing Room has a gilt mantelpiece and overmantle showing Ralegh's coat of arms and his motto, '*Nul q'un*' ('None but one'). More obviously Tudor are the small dining room, kitchens, bakehouse and Hall, which was the original entrance to the house. The floor here has since been raised (the Tudors were, on average, a few inches shorter than us, but not hobbit-sized!)

In fact, Ralegh was known for his height: at six feet tall, he was dark-haired and handsome, with a light curling moustache and fine clothing. As you might be able to see in the portrait of him by Zucchero hanging in the Hall, Ralegh was thought to be devastatingly attractive. This was crucial to his success at court because, as the antiquary John Aubrey put it, 'Queen Elizabeth loved to have all the servants of her court proper men.' You can see her surrounded by some of her 'proper men' in the *Procession of Queen Elizabeth I* painting, by Robert Peake the Elder, in the Red Drawing Room.

Before coming to court, Ralegh had had a chequered career. Born around 1552–1554, he had served in France with the Huguenot armies, studied at Oriel College, Oxford (but not stayed long enough to gain a degree) and sailed with Sir Humphrey Gilbert's colonising enterprise to the New World as the luckless captain of the *Falcon* (his ship disappeared for six months and probably didn't get further than Cape Verde before turning round and coming home). His introduction to court may have come through his aunt Kat Astley, Elizabeth's former governess; in 1580, he was given the privileged position of Esquire of the Body Extraordinary (part of a group of affable young men available, unpaid, for minor duties at court). His first mission for the Queen was to transport 100 soldiers to Ireland to tackle the Irish 'rebellions'; in Ireland, he is still remembered as the perpetrator of the Smerwick massacre in which 600 people died.

Nevertheless, he had gained the Queen's favour – according to an account fifty years later, Elizabeth 'took him for a kind of oracle' – and his rise was rapid. In 1585, Ralegh was knighted and appointed both Vice Admiral of the West and Lord Lieutenant of Cornwall, and when Sir Christopher Hatton died in 1591 [see KIRBY HALL], Ralegh became Captain of the Guard: a high status position that made Ralegh effectively Elizabeth's bodyguard. The Queen granted him Durham Place in London (where Katherine of Aragon lived before her marriage to Henry VIII) and in January 1592, sub-let him estates near Sherborne, including Sherborne Old Castle, now in ruins.

Ralegh's actual achievements range from the exaggerated to the downright false. Although he secured the patent for colonisation and sent two expeditions to Virginia (he never went himself), they were not successful. The colonists failed to consider the resolve of the Algonquin whose lands they were settling. The secret to the mystery of what happened to Ralegh's lost colony at Roanoke Island may simply have been a massacre by the Indians.

He may yet have been successful, but for his secret marriage to Bess Throckmorton, one of the Queen's maids-of-honour in 1591, which was discovered after Bess gave birth in March 1592. Elizabeth was furious – the monarch had to grant permission when her maids or courtiers wanted to wed – and both husband and wife were sent to the Tower of London. They were soon released but banished from court. Ralegh spent the next five years renovating the Old Castle at Sherborne, and built himself a smaller, more modern house next door: the present Sherborne Castle.

Ralegh's second misstep was his failure to court Elizabeth's other courtiers. As a result, Robert Cecil almost certainly blackened Ralegh's name with Elizabeth's successor, James I, so that when Ralegh was, probably unjustly, implicated in a plot to kill the King and put Lady Arbella Stuart, granddaughter of Bess of Hardwick [see HARDWICK HALL] on the throne, he was inevitably found guilty. Although initially spared the death sentence, he was imprisoned in the Tower of London for thirteen years. During this time, his wife was allowed to visit (and bore him a son) and Ralegh passed his days dabbling in chemistry and writing his *History of the World* – a monumental work of some one million words.

Ralegh bargained for release on the grounds that he would go to South America – as he had done unsuccessfully once before – and find El Dorado, the fabled hidden city of gold deep in the jungles of Guiana. Sickly, old and paralysed in one leg, he was released in March 1616 and set sail the next year. On arrival, contrary to the terms of their licence, the English sacked the Spanish town of San Thomé. Ralegh's son died in the mêlée, and despite going 300 miles inland, the expedition found neither gold nor silver. The crew grew mutinous and, in his grief, Ralegh was forced to return to England empty-handed, to face a charge of treason for fomenting war between England and Spain.

After a moving speech, and having quipped to the sheriff that the axe was 'sharp medicine... a physician for all diseases', Ralegh was executed on 29 October 1618. Bess carried away his head in a red leather bag and kept it with her until her death. Ralegh had already surrendered Sherborne to the Crown. On his death, the attorney general declared, 'He hath been as a star at which the world has gazed; but stars may fall.'

Sandford Orcas Manor House

If Ralegh's castle isn't Tudor enough for you, just down the road is the golden-coloured Sandford Orcas Manor House. This virtually unknown gem is a wonderful sixteenth-century house that you can tour, for a small fee, with owner Sir Mervyn Medlycott. The current family has owned the house since 1736, and it was restored in 1978. The Great Hall dates from around 1550: the fireplace and splendid eighteen mullion windows are original, though the furniture and panelling are Jacobean. There is a 'solar room' above the Hall with the same mullion windows and a Jacobean four-poster bed from 1620. Note the spiral staircases, indoor porches, gatehouse and garderobe. Look out for the leather Tudor children's shoes, found behind a cabinet where they had probably been put to ward off evil, and some fine examples of Elizabethan blackwork (decorative embroidery), including a bodice and coif (linen cap), embroidered with gold thread.

Hailes Abbey
Gloucestershire

'But a duck's blood'

The ruined abbey of Hailes in Gloucestershire is a desolate reminder of a world that vanished in the 1530s. For Hailes was once one of the most famous abbeys in England, attracting pilgrims from far and wide to visit its precious holy relic: the Blood of Hailes, a silver and crystal phial said to contain Christ's blood.

Established in 1246 as a Cistercian abbey, Hailes was founded by King Henry III's brother, Richard, Earl of Cornwall. We can imagine that it looked a little like a small version of Westminster Abbey: it was built at the same time and had the same 'chevet' design, or coronet of chapels, at its east end. This is where the shrine containing the holy blood was housed.

Earl Richard's son, Edmund, had given the blood to the monks at Hailes in 1270. He came by it in Flanders, and the Patriarch of Jerusalem, later Pope Urban IV, had guaranteed its authenticity. For centuries the masses flocked to Hailes to behold this most sacred of relics, in hope of absolution from their sins.

In 1538, the Blood of Hailes became the centre of a scandal. On 24 February 1538, John Hilsey, Bishop of Rochester preached at St Paul's Cross in London against the idolatry and deception of Hailes and its sister abbey of Boxley in Kent. The Rood of Grace from Boxley, carved with figures thought to move by supernatural intervention, was exposed as an automaton. As Hilsey explained, 'It was made to move the eyes and lips by strings of hair... whereby they had gotten great riches in deceiving the people.' When Hilsey stopped speaking, the rood screen was unceremoniously broken up into little pieces by the crowd. Then Hilsey turned his attention to the Blood of Hailes. He said that he had been told twenty years earlier, in a confession by the abbot's mistress, that it was 'but a duck's blood'.

Hilsey could get away with this claim because, having made himself Supreme Head of the Church of England in 1534, Henry VIII liked to think of himself as an Old Testament king, like David or Josiah, who had a special mandate from God to bring down idols and reform religious abuses. The royal injunctions of 1536, part of the first wave of doctrinal statements by the new Church of England, bemoaned the fact that, 'superstitions and hypocrisy [had] crept into divers men's hearts'. With the Blood of Hailes, Henry VIII had a chance to prove his reforming credentials.

The Bishop of Worcester, Hugh Latimer, led a commission to Gloucestershire to examine the relic in October 1538. He concluded it was not drake's blood, but 'unctuous gum [that had been] coloured' and seized the phial. On 24 November 1538, Hilsey preached again at St Paul's, saying that the blood was merely 'honey clarified and coloured with saffron, as had been evidently proved before the King and his Council'. Whether duck's blood, saffron honey or coloured gum, what was certain to the examiners was that it was no holy relic. It may be that Abbot Sagar, whom Latimer nicknamed 'the bluddy abbott', told the truth when he swore that he had inherited the relic and displayed it in good faith, but to Henry VIII, it was further proof of the greed and dishonesty of the Catholic Church, and provided a great opportunity to seize the wealthy abbey.

On Christmas Eve, 1539, Sagar surrendered his abbey to the King's commissioners. Over subsequent years the Abbey was gradually demolished, leaving only an outline today, where many pilgrims' feet had sought an encounter with the divine.

Hailes Abbey is emblematic of the end of popular medieval devotion, and marks the beginnings of an age whose population would be less ready to accept the pronouncements of the clergy on trust alone.

Sudeley Castle
Gloucestershire

*'As truly as God is God, my mind was
fully bent the other time I was at liberty
to marry you before any man I know.'*

The graceful honey-coloured Sudeley Castle, in the heart of the
Gloucestershire countryside, is mostly Elizabethan, with beau-
tiful late medieval ruins, exquisite gardens and a separate chapel.
Now owned, and still inhabited, by the Dent-Brocklehurst and
Ashcombe family, there has been a castle at Sudeley since before the
Norman Conquest of 1066. Sudeley has a rich Tudor history:
Henry VIII and Anne Boleyn stayed here in 1535, and Elizabeth I
held a party here to celebrate the defeat of the Armada (there is a
stained-glass window of her in the stairwell of the house to mark
this). Sudeley's chief distinction, however, is as the final resting place
of one of England's most under-appreciated queens, Henry VIII's
sixth wife, Kateryn Parr.

Kateryn Parr has generally been dismissed as a dowdy old
widow whom Henry VIII married solely to have a nursemaid, but
this sorry analysis overlooks the evidence of her considerable

beauty, vitality and intelligence, and her life of great hardship, adventure, passion and peril.

For a start, she may have been a widow when she made her royal marriage, but she was anything but dowdy. A lock of her pretty strawberry-blonde hair at Sudeley confirms the loveliness seen in her recently identified portrait at the National Portrait Gallery, where she is youthful, with delicate features, a tiny waist and evident sartorial flair.

Her unlined face does not bear the marks of her tumultuous life. Left without a father at the age of five, Kateryn – who had, extraordinarily enough, been named after her godmother Katherine of Aragon – had to leave the carefree, encouraging and scholarly environment of her mother's house when she was married off at sixteen to a frail young husband, Edward Borough. For the first two years of their marriage, she made her uncomfortable home with her bullying new father-in-law at Gainsborough Old Hall. When Edward died, Kateryn was still only twenty, and now an orphan: her mother had died two years earlier.

Her uncertain future was secured by marriage to John Neville, Lord Latimer of Snape Castle in Yorkshire, in 1534. Though just twenty-one years old to his forty, Kateryn served Latimer well as a stepmother to his two teenage children. Latimer's daughter, Margaret Neville, would later become Kateryn's maid-of-honour. Though their nine-year marriage was happy enough, all was not peaceful. In 1536, during the Pilgrimage of Grace rebellion [see PONTEFRACT CASTLE], an armed mob of rebels took Lord Latimer prisoner. Two months later, Kateryn herself faced great danger when an armed mob ransacked Snape Castle, seizing her and the children as hostages. It is little wonder that after this Kateryn was keen to move south!

In the winter of 1542–3, Kateryn was in London and, with the help of her sister, Anne Herbert, had taken up a position as one of

Mary Tudor's ladies-in-waiting. This brought her into contact with the high-fliers of Henry VIII's court, including Sir Thomas Seymour, brother to the late Queen, Jane. Seymour was handsome, charming and recklessly ambitious. When Latimer died in February 1543, Seymour began to court Kateryn, and the twice-widowed Kateryn fell, for the first time, wildly in love. As she later wrote to Seymour, in a love letter that can be seen at Sudeley Castle:

> I would not have you to think that this mine honest good-will towards you to proceed of any sudden motion or passion for as truly as God is God, my mind was fully bent the other time I was at liberty to marry you before any man I know.

But marry him she could not, because she had caught the King's eye and, no matter what her heart preferred, a proposal from Henry VIII could not be turned down. Henry VIII married his sixth wife on 12 July 1543 in the Queen's private chapel at Hampton Court Palace before a small crowd of nineteen close friends and family.

A capable, accomplished and energetic queen, Kateryn was an important patron of the clergy, arts and education. She guided the rising stars of the Church, Matthew Parker (later Elizabeth I's Archbishop of Canterbury), Miles Coverdale and Nicholas Ridley [see BROAD STREET]. It was she who sponsored the artists William Scrots, Master John, Lucas and Susanna Horenbout, the Bassano family of court musicians and the playwright Nicholas Udall. She founded Well Grammar School in Clare, Suffolk. She even excelled in scholarship herself: Kateryn was both the first Queen of England to publish her own book, and the first English woman to publish a work of prose in the sixteenth century. You can see her signed, beautiful 1546 copy of her *Prayers and Meditations*, bound in red silk and embroidered with gold and silver thread, in the exhibitions at Sudeley.

As stepmother to the future Queen Elizabeth, Kateryn was an important role model. Entrusted with the position of Regent-General when Henry went to war in France in 1544, Kateryn demonstrated strong female rule to the young Elizabeth: England's greatest monarch undoubtedly learnt the skills of queenship at Kateryn Parr's side.

When Henry VIII died in January 1547, Kateryn's years of duty finally seemed behind her. She impetuously rushed ahead with a marriage to Thomas Seymour in May, well before the usual two years of mourning were up, and by Christmas (which they spent with Edward VI at Hampton Court), the now four times married Kateryn was finally pregnant by the man she loved.

In the summer of 1548, Kateryn and Thomas moved to his beautiful country house at Sudeley in advance of the birth, with Lady Jane Grey in attendance. In preparation, Seymour had spent £1,000 (around £340,000 today) adding to the ancient castle, which already included a magnificent Banqueting Hall with fine oriel windows (now in ruins).

On the eve of her labour, both princesses wrote to encourage her: Elizabeth thanking her for writing despite 'being so great with child', and Mary hoping 'to hear good success of your Grace's good belly'. Heralded by these well-wishers, on 30 August 1548, the thirty-six-year-old Kateryn gave birth to her first child, a healthy girl, whom she named Mary after her eldest stepdaughter. Thomas could boast joyfully of his little daughter's prettiness.

But their happiness was short-lived. Within days, Kateryn had developed the fever that comes from puerperal sepsis, a bacterial infection caused by a doctor's lack of hygiene. She died on the morning of 5 September 1548. Wrapped in a waxed cloth and encased in lead, she was buried in the chapel at Sudeley (later ruined in the Civil War). Her chief mourner was the ill-fated Lady Jane Grey [see GUILDHALL]. Crazed with grief, Seymour's subsequent foolish acts led to his execution on Tower Hill, while their daughter, Mary, does not seem to have lived past the age of two.

Kateryn Parr remains at Sudeley. In 1782, her tomb was discovered by a group of Georgian ladies. When they broke open the lead casing, they were astonished to see Kateryn's perfectly preserved face gazing back at them. However, their vandalism began her body's decay and, though grave-robbers managed to remove a few locks of hair and teeth, Kateryn was eventually reburied under a marble effigy in St Mary's Church, in the castle gardens.

Although Kateryn is chiefly remembered today in the popular rhyme as Henry VIII's wife who 'survived', it is Sudeley Castle, where she spent her happiest months, pregnant with Sir Thomas Seymour's child, that stands as a more poignant memorial to this Queen of England, whose talents far exceeded her modern reputation.

Other Tudor treasures to spot at Sudeley: if you go on a tour of the private family apartments, you can see portraits of Edward Seymour, Duke of Somerset; an early sixteenth-century court lady with a French hood (possibly Mary Boleyn); and Mary Tudor, Duchess of Suffolk by Johannes Corvus. Also in the apartments, look out for the extraordinarily well-preserved sixteenth-century Sheldon Tapestry and eighteenth-century copies of Hans Holbein the Younger's court sketches by George Vertue.

Thornbury Castle
Gloucestershire

*'Alas the while that ever ambition should be the loss of so
noble a man, and so much in the King's favour.'*

Thornbury Castle is a story of what might have been. It is also
the only Tudor castle in England in which you can stay as a
hotel guest.

Edward Stafford, the third Duke of Buckingham, built Thornbury Castle. Buckingham, like the Tudors, was descended from
Edward III through the Beauforts and, additionally, through the
Plantagenet prince Thomas of Woodstock. When Buckingham began
his ambitious building project around 1511, a year after receiving a
licence to castellate his manor and enclose a park of 1,000 acres, he
evidently aspired to create a semi-regal castle-palace for himself.

Thornbury was built to resemble a medieval fortress. The main
gate had a portcullis, and the outer of its two courtyards has no
windows on the ground floor except crossbow loopholes and two
gun ports beside the entrance. The north range of the outer court
was designed like a barracks, to house Buckingham's men and
horses, while a high crenulated wall surrounded the inner court.
This raises a question: did Buckingham intend Thornbury to be a
defensive stronghold, either in the event of an uprising by his

unhappy Welsh tenants or, more ambitiously, as a place from which to launch an attempted coup against Henry VIII? Henry evidently thought the latter. The King was suspicious enough of Buckingham's intentions to have him killed, even though historians today question the defensibility of the castle, and despite the fact that in 1518, Henry VIII called Buckingham his 'right trusty and right entirely well-beloved cousin'.

There is no doubt, however, that Thornbury was intended to be seriously impressive: an appropriately lavish dwelling for the most prominent nobleman in the land. The outer courtyard, Base Court, was to be nearly two and a half acres: bigger even than the imposing Base Court at Hampton Court Palace. You can see the west range of lodgings beyond the vineyard, and wander through the overgrown remains of the north range of lodgings, where fireplaces in the walls (the large joist holes show that the original floor would have been at head height) sit forlornly, still unused. What at first glance looks like Tudor ruins is in fact a Tudor building site, for the castle was never finished.

The gatehouse leading into the inner court is decorated with coats of arms and family badges, including the golden knot of the Staffords, the swan and antelope of the Bohuns, the fiery wheel hub of Woodstock and the mantle of Brecknock, all of which testify to Buckingham's royal ancestry. The gatehouse is also inscribed:

Thys Gate was begon in the yere of our Lorde Gode MCCC-CCXI, the ii yere of the reyne of Kynge Henri the viii by me Edw. Duc. of Bukkyngha' Erlle of Herforde Stafforde ande Northampto': Dorenesavant.

The motto '*Dorenesavant*' translates from Old French as 'From now on, henceforth or hereafter' and further suggested, to the suspicious at least, Buckingham's regal pretensions.

The main castle was to have four great towers, only one of which is complete: the others remain only two storeys high. The Duke and Duchess's living quarters were in this completed tower, to the right side of the inner court. Here, beautifully elaborate oriel windows overlook the privy garden, and the original and ornate brick chimneystacks rival any of the Victorian recreations at Hampton Court.

On the left side of the court were all the kitchens needed to provide for Buckingham's household of 125 people: a wet and dry larder, an enormous bakehouse, the great kitchen and a privy kitchen. You can even see where the spits would have roasted. Opposite the gatehouse was Buckingham's Great Hall. It was knocked down in the eighteenth century, but a recent excavation discovered tiles from its floor (a photograph of which can be seen at the castle). Their elaborate decoration – each was inscribed with the emblem, '*Honi soit qui mal y pense*' ('Shamed be he who thinks evil of it': the motto of the Order of the Garter) – suggests that they would have been finer and more costly than the floor tiles at Hampton Court or Buckland Abbey. They are another indication that had it been completed, Thornbury would have been one of the largest and finest palaces in England.

All this grandeur befitted a man who valued his noble status highly. Buckingham's first public role had been at Henry VII's coronation when he was only eight years old. In adulthood, he was known for the gorgeous splendour of his clothing: in 1501, at the wedding of Prince Arthur to Katherine of Aragon, he wore a gown valued at a staggering £1,500 (around £730,000 today). He maintained a quasi-kingly court including, in 1508, such entertainers as two minstrels, two harpists, six trumpeters, two wrestlers, four players, a bear and a fool. He also did his bit for the monarch, supplying men for the French war of 1513–14, hosting Henry VIII with 'excellent cheer' at his house at Penshurst and accompanying the King to the Field of Cloth of Gold.

At times, Buckingham's finery and grandstanding were taken for arrogance. Contemptuous of their lowly station, he treated his servants harshly, even suing eleven of them when they failed to meet his arbitrary expectations. Such behaviour ultimately cost him his life. Nor was he deferential to those with more power: he foolishly criticised Wolsey and the King's pro-French foreign policy and, in November 1520, fell out of favour with Henry for retaining a royal servant named Sir William Bulmer. When, subsequently, Buckingham asked the King for permission to raise an armed bodyguard to suppress the riots among his tenants in Wales, Henry refused, no doubt aware that Buckingham's father had mustered an armed guard in Wales shortly before rebelling against Richard III.

Nonetheless, Buckingham's summons to court from Thornbury in April 1521, and arrest as he approached London, came suddenly and without warning. According to his indictment, he was accused of high treason for having 'traitorously... conspired and imagined... to shorten the life of our sovereign Lord King'. The charges against him included listening to predictions (a dangerous hobby in Tudor times) by the Carthusian monk Nicholas Hopkins that the King would have no male heir, and that Buckingham would succeed him. Buckingham had also told his son-in-law, Ralph, Earl of Westmorland, that if anything but good should happen to the King, he was next in the line of succession, and these comments were repeated to the Lord High Steward's court by three of his servants, who crucially appeared as witnesses against him. On the other hand, Buckingham was merely voicing a common sentiment; the Venetian ambassador, Sebastian Giustinian, had written in September 1519 that the Duke was 'very popular' and 'were the King to die without heirs male, he might easily obtain the Crown'. By the early 1520s, however, Katherine of Aragon's failure to produce a male heir made this a very sensitive point, and case law, if not statute, recognised imagining the King's death in words as treason. These musings by an over-mighty subject who vaunted his royal blood were enough to assure his early death. As the chronicler Edward Hall remarked: 'Alas the while that ever ambition should be the loss of so noble a man.'

Buckingham was executed on Tower Hill on 17 May 1521. In 1523, his lands were confiscated by the Crown and Thornbury became a royal demesne. As well as Henry VIII and Anne Boleyn, the future Queen Mary I stayed here briefly as a child.

Building at Thornbury ceased after Buckingham's execution. The contrast between the magnificent completed apartments at Thornbury, and the abandoned and unfinished north range, speaks poignantly of a glittering life cut short.

Today, Thornbury is reborn as an upmarket boutique hotel where you can stay in the sumptuous bedchamber where Henry VIII and Anne Boleyn stayed for ten days in 1535, in a room with arrow loops in the stone walls (for the full castle experience), or in a bedroom in which you have to tilt a cross to enter the bathroom.

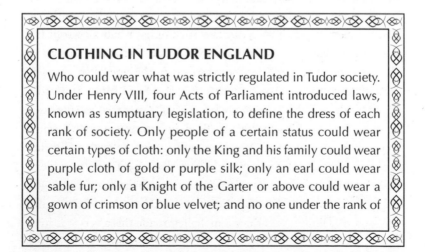

CLOTHING IN TUDOR ENGLAND

Who could wear what was strictly regulated in Tudor society. Under Henry VIII, four Acts of Parliament introduced laws, known as sumptuary legislation, to define the dress of each rank of society. Only people of a certain status could wear certain types of cloth: only the King and his family could wear purple cloth of gold or purple silk; only an earl could wear sable fur; only a Knight of the Garter or above could wear a gown of crimson or blue velvet; and no one under the rank of gentleman – except graduates, yeomen, grooms and pages of the King's and Queen's households, and those with land to the value of £100 a year (about £40,000 today) – could wear velvet doublets or satin or damask gowns or coats. Clothes were meant to represent the natural social hierarchy.

Men's clothes

The basic male outfit in Henry VIII's day was a gown, doublet and hose. The gown was a loose-fitting garment, which hung to between mid-thigh and knee, with sleeves and a large collar that folded back over the shoulders. A voluminous gown exaggerated the shoulders to make a man look big, muscular and powerful, and would be made of the most expensive material an individual was allowed and could afford.

Underneath the gown was the doublet, which fitted to the upper body, fastened at the front with buttons and often had skirts. The finest doublets were made of velvet or satin, and could be richly decorated with gold cords, or slashed to show a layer of silk peeping through the slashes.

Below the doublet, a man wore breeches or upper stocks, which covered the waist to the thigh, and gathered at the knee. These again were often slashed to show off a silk lining. The codpiece was a separate item that laced to the hose and doublet. In the early Tudor period, it became so heavily padded that it appeared grotesquely inflated, and was a powerful symbol of virility. Men's legs were shown off in clinging nether stocks or hose of silk, wool or taffeta, held up with garters.

These fashions and fine fabrics were for the elite, but ordinary men also wore a more simple version of this dress. Those lower down the social scale wore homespun coarse woollen cloth, and might exchange the doublet for a loose-fitting tunic or leather jerkin (short jacket). But every man, regardless of status, would wear a linen shift beneath his outer clothes. This layer, in contact with the skin, was the garment that was most often washed. Rich men had the collar and cuffs decorated with embroidery, known as blackwork. All men, too, wore a cap or bonnet of some sort.

Fashion evolved at Elizabeth I's court. Men's gowns got shorter, and the codpiece became outmoded. The male doublet was now padded at the stomach, and a short flared cloak or cape replaced the gown. Clothing became more elaborately decorated with embroidery, lace, slashing, braiding or pinking. Elizabeth loved her courtiers to dress finely, but compared to the masculinity-accentuating styles of the early sixteenth century, the Elizabethan trend was for a more effeminate style of dress. In fact, the narrow waists and swelling hips of men's clothing at the end of the century appeared to echo the feminine figure of the monarch.

Women's clothes

In the first half of the century, the basic item of female dress was a kirtle – a sleeveless dress with a square décolletage that fitted to the body and then fell to the ground. In the second half of the century, a 'kirtle' came to mean the skirt alone, with the bodice (meaning a 'pair of bodies', as front and back were two parts) made separately. The bodice was reinforced with boning and made of rich fabric.

On top of this was worn a gown or overdress. It opened at the front and was laced or pinned together. Sleeves were made separately and tied onto the bodice. In the early sixteenth century, it was fashionable to have large oversleeves on top of quilted undersleeves, which (having tried them myself) seriously restricted the movement of the arms.

Women's undergarments included their own version of the linen shift or smock, a padded bum roll to pad out the skirt at the hips and multiple petticoats. From the 1550s, the farthingale came into fashion, although Katherine of Aragon had introduced it to England as far back as 1501. It was a hooped underskirt that gave a bell-shape to skirts (a little like a Victorian crinoline). Tudor women did not wear knickers.

The early sixteenth century headdress was an English gable hood, shaped like a little birdhouse and displaying the centre parting of the hair. Anne Boleyn introduced the French hood, a more flattering semi-circular hood worn further back on the head. Under the hood, women wore a linen cap or coif.

During Elizabeth I's reign, especially after the introduction of starch to England in 1564, female dress became stiffer. The ruff – originally a frill on the collar of the linen smock (which had developed a high collar by mid-century) – became increasingly large and elaborate, until it had to be supported by a wire frame. The bodice extended to a point, often with the help of a stomacher, an inverted triangle of material reinforced with whalebone busks (strips inserted into the casing). Sleeves too were propped up with wires and whalebones, and became exaggeratedly puffed and padded. Finally, in the 1590s, the farthingale changed into a drum or wheel shape that carried the skirts out at right angles from the waist before then falling to the ground. All these fashions emphasised a desirable tiny waist.

Glastonbury Tor and Abbey
Somerset

'Great, goodly, and so princely
that we have not seen the like.'

Perhaps most famous now as the site of Britain's biggest music festival, Glastonbury has an ancient and deeply spiritual history. Legend has it that Joseph of Arimathea travelled to Glastonbury bearing the Holy Grail, and the hawthorn bush you can see here is said to be an offshoot of his staff where he planted it in the ground. It is reputed to be the fabled Isle of Avalon where King Arthur was buried: in 1191, a coffin of a man and a woman with golden hair was unearthed under Glastonbury Abbey on the site where Arthur and Guinevere were said to be entombed. Glastonbury is also well known for its tor – a natural, 518-foot-high conical hill visible for miles – that many hold to be an uncommonly mystical place, but in Tudor times, it became notorious for one particularly gruesome event.

In the early sixteenth century, Glastonbury Abbey was a vast and famous Benedictine monastery; the church at the Abbey, at

580 feet long, was the longest monastic church in the country. The central towers rose to 216 feet, two or three times the height of the remaining ruins of the Lady Chapel. It was important enough for Henry VII and his retinue to visit in 1497.

Like all the abbeys, Glastonbury would suffer as a result of the dissolution of the monasteries [see FOUNTAINS ABBEY]. Unlike most, however, not only the Abbey, but its abbot, too, would perish in the process.

When Henry VIII's commissioners visited Glastonbury in September 1539, they reported that the Abbey was so 'great, goodly, and so princely that we have not seen the like', 'a house meet for the King's Majesty'. It held enormous wealth for the King's coffers, but Henry was not going to get it without a fight: the abbot, Richard Whiting, refused to surrender the monastery.

The King's commissioners set about building the case against him. They cross-examined the abbot, allegedly finding evidence of his 'cankered and traitorous heart and mind'. They ransacked his study and discovered a book that opposed the King's divorce from Katherine of Aragon. Finally, they came across a gold chalice, and other plate and ornaments that had been hidden from the commissioners 'in walls, vaults, and other secret places'. They considered this embezzlement and 'manifest robbery'. In all, Whiting's crimes amounted to high treason. Though a 'very weak man and sickly', the abbot was confined to the Tower of London, and on 14 November he was tried and condemned.

If these deeds seem insufficient to qualify as treason, it is probably because they were: they were the pretext that Thomas Cromwell needed to get rid of Whiting because he was an obstacle to the King's plans. A note in Cromwell's files makes this clear. It reads, 'Item the Abbot of Glastonbury to be tried at Glastonbury and also executed there with his accomplices.' Not only does it order Whiting's arraignment, it also assumes his guilt and decides his punishment before he had even been tried.

On 15 November 1539, after being dragged behind a horse through Glastonbury on a hurdle, Whiting was executed on the tor with two of his monks. The place was well chosen to magnify his misery. Standing on the blustery top of the tor, near the fourteenth-century St Michael's Church tower, you can imagine that Whiting's last sight would have been the turrets of his doomed abbey. He was hanged, quartered and beheaded: the quarters were displayed at Wells, Bath, Ilchester and Bridgwater, and his head was mounted on the gates at Glastonbury Abbey. An observer said that he and his monks 'took their deaths patiently'.

Whiting's real crime was to decline Henry VIII's invitation to donate his monastery to the Crown, and he wasn't the only one – Hugh Cooke, Abbot of Reading and Thomas Beche, Abbot of Colchester did so too. Beche expressly voiced his opposition to the dissolution and denied the King's position as Supreme Head of the Church of England, allegedly saying 'that those who made the King so were heretics'.

It is astonishing that from more than 800 religious houses, only three abbots stood up to defend the centuries-old monastic life from royal usurpation. Sadly, most surrendered their abbeys without a whimper. After the deaths of the Carthusian monks [see CHARTERHOUSE], of Thomas More and Bishop John Fisher, and of the Pilgrimage of Grace rebels of 1536, including many monks [see PONTEFRACT CASTLE], few dared to join Beche in calling the King and his advisers 'wretched tyrants and bloodsuckers'.

As a result, by 1540, not a single monastery remained in all of England. Richard Whiting on Glastonbury Tor was one of the valiant few who refused to go gently, and he paid the price.

Montacute House
Somerset

*'The magnificent house of my most worthy and right
Worshipful neighbour...Sir Edward Phillippes... so stately
adorned with the statues of the nine Worthies.'*
Traveller Thomas Coryate, 1611

Named after the nearby pointed hill (*'mons acutus'* in Latin),
for many, Montacute is one of the most enchanting and
endearing of all the Elizabethan mansions. It is a spectacularly
beautiful house. Wrought out of the local tawny-coloured Ham
Hill stone, it is grand and symmetrical, but neither too ostentatious
nor too severe. Today it is an outpost of the National Portrait
Gallery, displaying a wonderful selection of must-see Tudor
portraits: the greatest collection you can find in one place outside
the National Portrait Gallery itself.

The man responsible for building Montacute was Sir Edward
Phelips, a Somerset lawyer and MP, who eventually became Speaker
of the House of Commons and Master of the Rolls. He worked
with a master mason called William Arnold, who also designed and
built Wadham College, Oxford. Between them, they constructed a
house that encapsulated the design values of the Elizabethans.

As the building records do not survive, we don't know the
exact dates of construction. The house is mentioned in William

Camden's *Britannia* of 1607, and there are three clues at Montacute itself to date it further: '1601' is carved above the entrance on the west front, '1599' features in the plasterwork overmantle in the dining room and a panel of heraldic stained glass in the Great Hall is dated '1599'. The date of completion is probably 1601, so the house must have been started by 1596 at the latest, and possibly as early as 1590.

Built on the usual 'E' pattern (for Elizabeth I), Montacute deliberately eschews the 'quaint' higgledy-piggledy style of houses like Little Moreton Hall for a symmetrical squareness. At the same time, with the addition of the curved gables, balustrade and statues of the Nine Worthies (historical, biblical and legendary heroes) on the upper floor of the east front, the result is a softened version of the more angular lines of Hardwick Hall.

Like Hardwick Hall, Montacute also has desirable, and expensive, acres of glass to light up the interior and provide gorgeous views over the surrounding countryside. Seen from a distance, the contrast between dark, glittering glass and honey-coloured stone is visually arresting, although it is this very combination of too much glass and easily eroded ham limestone that makes the structure of Montacute weak today.

The house was designed to be approached from the east front through a gatehouse that once stood between the two domed pavilions at the corners of the forecourt. These pavilions are decorative follies, intended for no use except to look pretty. Now, you'll enter from the west and, when you do, you'll find yourself inside a house that has barely changed since it was built.

The first room you encounter is the Great Hall, which retains its original oak panelling, chimneypiece and unusual stone screen with classical columns. Spot the arms of Elizabeth I in the centre of the heraldic stained-glass windows, which are also original. At the far end of the hall is a rather surprising inclusion: a plaster panel depicting a 'stang ride'. This shows the story of a man who secretly helps himself to beer, only to be caught and hit on the head with a shoe by his wife. A neighbour spots them and the hen-pecked husband is humiliatingly paraded around the village 'riding the stang' (a wooden bar or pole), because he has allowed gender norms to be turned upside down. It says much about social relations under the Tudors: the man's crime is not taking the beer, it is that his wife has authority over him. Hierarchy was everything, and that included men's rule over women. Men who fell short in this respect would be shamed.

Four portraits on the ground floor are must-sees: one of Robert Dudley, Earl of Leicester; one, in the dining room, of Mary, Queen of Scots (probably derived from a miniature of her by Nicholas Hilliard in 1578); one of Jane Seymour (after Hans Holbein) in the library ante-room; and the last, of Montacute's builder, Sir Edward Phelips himself, in the Great Hall.

On the floor above, the Great Chamber – now the library – is another impressive room with its original panelling, plaster frieze and forty-two shields of heraldic stained glass. The most striking feature is the magnificent chimneypiece with Corinthian columns made of Portland stone. Only the ceiling is Victorian.

Perhaps the most remarkable room in the house is the Long Gallery, on the second floor, which stretches the entire length of the house. It is the longest of its kind to survive – 176 feet long – with semicircular oriel windows at each end that act as viewing bays. Here is where you'll find the great collection of portraits.

In the first room, you'll find notables from the reign of Henry VIII, including Sir Thomas Wyatt, the poet, painted around 1540, by an unknown artist. There is a picture of Kateryn Parr, from around 1545, looking severe and sporting the high-necked fashion of the period, but wearing a man's bonnet. Thomas More's portrait, after Holbein, shows him as Lord Chancellor, and here you can also see Sir William Petre, Secretary of State from 1544 to 1557. We also have Sir William Butts, one of Henry VIII's over-worked physicians, and his jowly-cheeked patient, seen here in later life. Finally, we see Henry's son in a regal profile picture of Edward VI from the studio of William Scrots.

Another room displays pictures of Elizabeth I and her court. Here is Elizabeth in a glorious painting known as the Armada Portrait, attributed to George Gower. Elizabeth, in her moment of triumph, drips in pearls (which was the Tudor symbol of virginity) and precious stones, and her rich attire is covered with gold stars. The cropped scenes behind her show fireships being sent to attack the Armada and the sinking of the fleet off the Irish coast. Nearby, note particularly portraits of Robert Dudley, Earl of Leicester from around 1575, the time of his last bid for Elizabeth's hand [see KENILWORTH CASTLE]; Sir Christopher Hatton [see KIRBY HALL]; Sir Nicholas Throckmorton and Elizabeth Talbot, Countess of Shrewsbury or 'Bess of Hardwick' [see HARDWICK HALL]. There is also a portrait of Sir Walter Ralegh replete with symbolism. Ralegh is decorated with pearls – symbolising his allegiance and devotion to the Virgin Queen – and wears a cloak that depicts the rays of the moon. There is a small crescent moon in one corner and the inscription in Latin reads 'Love and virtue'. Ralegh is suggesting that Elizabeth is Cynthia, the moon goddess, endowed with supernatural powers.

Finally, the Long Gallery itself has two portraits you must see: William Cecil, Lord Burghley who holds the white rod of the Lord High Treasurer and displays a cameo of Elizabeth on his hat [see BURGHLEY HOUSE]; and Robert Devereux, second Earl of Essex (the last man to whom Elizabeth lost her heart) by Marcus Gheeraerts.

Montacute, perhaps unusually for a great house of its time, may not have a richly storied past replete with love, betrayal, fortune and tragedy, but it is no less worth visiting for that. Come for the collection of portraits, its tasteful Elizabethan style and its beautiful surroundings in the Somerset hills.

West
Midlands

Ludlow Castle
Shropshire

*'He had never felt so much joy in his life
as when he beheld the sweet face of his bride.'*

In the eleventh century, a number of Norman castles were erected in the Welsh Marches to control the borderlands of the still fragile kingdom of England. Ludlow Castle was one of them, and parts of the original castle survive. At the turn of the fourteenth century, Peter de Geneville and Roger Mortimer – who helped depose Edward II in 1326 – transformed the castle into an outstanding palace-fortress. In 1461, Ludlow Castle became Crown property and, soon after, Edward IV sent his son Edward to be brought up here. Henry VII did likewise in 1492 with his heir apparent, Arthur, and it was in this rugged fortress on a hilltop above the River Teme that history was made, and the course of the Tudors decided.

At the centre of Ludlow, a pretty town with many a Tudor timber-framed building, the castle remains an impressive sight. Although ruined and uninhabitable, its walls are well preserved, and it is a strangely evocative place to explore. It has a sense of significance and serenity, perhaps partly because it is the place where Arthur, Prince of Wales, eldest son of Henry VII and Elizabeth of York, died in 1502.

Arthur was born on 19 September 1486, and christened at Winchester Cathedral with a name that evoked the glory days of Camelot. As the son of a king, his titles and responsibilities came quickly. In November 1489, when he had just turned three, he was created a Knight of the Bath, Prince of Wales and Earl of Chester; a year later, he was made warden over the Scottish Marches, and in 1492, while his father was in France, Arthur nominally became Lord Keeper of the Great Seal of England and the King's lieutenant.

He was already betrothed. At the age of two, his father had promised him in marriage to Katherine of Aragon, the daughter of Ferdinand of Aragon and Isabella of Castile. It was quite a coup for Henry VII, representing a diplomatic vote of confidence for the brand new Tudor dynasty.

In the interim years, between engagement and marriage, Arthur was in intensive training to become king. In 1492, at the age of six, he arrived at Ludlow Castle to learn his craft. He received an excellent education: by the time he married, the studious Arthur was particularly accomplished at Latin.

His wedding to Katherine took place on Sunday 14 November 1501 in sumptuous style at St Paul's Cathedral. Arthur must have been astonished to see his bride as she processed towards him in a white silk veil and a stunning white satin dress that billowed out under the waist in a bell-shape, caused by the farthingale (hooped skirt) she worn beneath her dress, as the fashion was entirely new to English onlookers. Certainly, a fortnight later, Arthur would write to Katherine's parents that he 'had never felt so much joy in his life as when he beheld the sweet face of his bride. No woman in the world could be more agreeable to him.' He promised to be a 'true and loving husband' to her. He was just fifteen.

Just how loving would become a question that would rock Christendom. Katherine would later swear, when her marriage to Arthur's brother, Henry, was contested, that her first marriage had never been consummated, but an English witness maintained that the morning after the wedding, Prince Arthur swaggered, with a teenage boy's typical braggadocio: 'I have this night been in the midst of Spain.'

In late December, the couple moved back to Ludlow Castle. They lodged in the Solar Wing, to the east of the Great Hall, living on the top floor of the three-storey building. The wooden floors have long crumbled away but you can see where they would have been, and spot the fireplace that Arthur and Katherine would have sat before in the chill of winter, along with the arched windows that gave them a magnificent view over the town. The Great Chamber, on the other side of the Great Hall, retains its hooded fireplace with carved heads that, though now eroding away, must have been a fine decorative feature when Arthur and his teenage bride lived in the castle. They would have also worshipped in the Norman chapel of St Mary Magdalene: its circular nave, with carved arches of alternate designs, remains a beautiful piece of architecture. Did they climb the steep spiral stairs of the Great Tower or explore the dark nooks and crannies of the castle? One dark corner they must have visited is the Garderobe Tower (lavatories): with its unglazed windows, it must have been perilously cold in the midst of January.

Their stay was brief, for Tudor lives were never long without tragedy. Less than five months after the wedding, on Easter Day, Arthur fell sick. Within a week, he was dead. The cause of his death is unknown: it was perhaps pneumonia, the deadly sweating sickness that scourged England in the early sixteenth century, or consumption (pulmonary tuberculosis). Arthur's body was disembowelled, embalmed and filled with spices, and laid out in his chamber at Ludlow for three weeks before being buried at Worcester Cathedral.

The death of this young lad was extraordinarily significant in the course of history, as it made his younger brother, Henry, heir to the English throne.

It was not the last time the Tudors were to use Ludlow Castle: Mary I spent three winters here between 1525 and 1528 as the head of the Council of the Marches, and the castle's role as the council's home – and therefore effectively the capital of Wales – meant that there was much building here during the 1550s and 1580s. The current shop is in what used to be the porter's lodge, built in 1552; the Judges' Lodgings were built by Sir Henry Sidney in 1581 (his arms can be seen on the outside); and the Tudor Lodgings give away their date of construction by the red-brick, star-shaped chimneys on their roof, similar to ones at Thornbury and Framlingham castles.

Castle Lodge

Next to Ludlow Castle is Castle Lodge, probably constructed in the late fifteenth century. Although much of the authenticity of the interiors is uncertain, it is worth visiting. It has extraordinary linenfold panelling, intricately carved fireplaces (with the Prince of Wales's heraldic badge of three white feathers bound by a gold coronet) and a plasterwork ceiling of fleurs-de-lis, rams and Tudor roses, said to date from the sixteenth century. Perhaps because it dearly needs some care and restoration, there is something ineffably sad about it.

Tutbury Castle
Staffordshire

'Exposed to all the winds and injuries of heaven…'

The forbidding ruined Tutbury Castle, high on a windswept hill at Tutbury in Staffordshire, is a suitably dramatic place to remember the tragic tale of Mary, Queen of Scots. She was confined here most miserably during her eighteen years of imprisonment in England, before her execution in 1587. If you're lucky, you might also catch the curator, Lesley Smith, who has leased the castle from the Crown (as the Earl of Shrewsbury did in Mary's day), magnificently portraying the Queen in historic dress.

The story of Mary Stewart (Mary would later adopt the French spelling 'Stuart'), who became Queen of the Scots only six days after her birth on 8 December 1542, is the stuff of romantic novels. Scottish born, she moved to France at the age of six after her engagement to the Dauphin, later Francis II, and became almost wholly French including, crucially, converting to Roman Catholicism. She ruled next to her husband as Queen of France from April 1558 until his premature death just eighteen months later. The young widowed Queen returned to Scotland, already famous for her unusual beauty, her great height (she was six feet tall) and her gregarious and charismatic demeanour. Unsurprisingly, many men fell for her.

She made a rather foolish choice of second husband, marrying Henry, Lord Darnley in July 1561. It was a troublesome union from the start, and Mary soon became involved in a close liaison with her secretary, David Riccio. Darnley was suspicious enough of Riccio's influence on Mary to arrange to have him murdered in her presence. Less than a year later, in 1567, Darnley himself was also assassinated. Within three months, Mary married the Earl of Bothwell, the prime suspect for Darnley's murder. As a result, the Scottish nobles fomented a rebellion, and Mary was imprisoned at Lochleven Castle. On the evidence of the 'Casket Letters' (which historians now mostly believe to have been damning forged pages inserted into genuine letters), Mary was linked to her former husband's murder. Her illegitimate half-brother, the Earl of Moray, secured her abdication in favour of her one-year-old son, James VI, and, escaping her prison in May 1568, Mary fled to England.

It was out of the frying pan and into the fire. Mary had not endeared herself to Elizabeth in her claims for the English throne (she had argued that, as an illegitimate Protestant, Elizabeth I had no right to reign), and Elizabeth's councillors feared that Mary would become the focus of discontent for English Catholics. Unable to send her back to Scotland, unwilling to send her to France, Elizabeth decided that Mary should be imprisoned – with all the luxury befitting her status as a queen. The Earl of Shrewsbury, husband of Bess of Hardwick [see HARDWICK HALL], was soon made her custodian.

In early 1568, Mary was moved to the hunting lodge within the grounds of Tutbury. Chosen mainly for its secure fortifications and its location far from northern Catholics and from London, it was dark, dank, dismal and dilapidated. In a letter to the French ambassador, Mary described it as: 'exposed to all the winds and injuries of heaven... situated so low... that the sun can never shine upon it... nor any fresh air come into it... In short the greater part of it is rather like a dungeon for base and abject criminals.' The timber-framed lodge is no longer standing, but its position can be clearly seen. Before long, Mary was complaining of rheumatism, fever and of the bitter cold, and was moved elsewhere in April 1568.

Unfortunately, she was returned to the loathed Tutbury after an uprising by northern Catholic nobles in late 1569. By May, she was petitioning again to move, protesting that the drains at Tutbury smelt dreadful. She stayed at Chatsworth and Sheffield, before again being transferred back to Tutbury for the spring and summer of 1571.

After years of being moved from one prison to another, and a couple of botched plots to rescue her, it was decided in 1584 that she would be removed from the care of Shrewsbury, who, it was thought, had grown slightly too fond of the beautiful Queen. Like many others, he was alleged to have fallen prey to what the Queen's servant, Nicholas White, described as Mary's 'alluring grace, pretty Scottish accent and searching wit'. Furthermore, Shrewsbury had been almost bankrupted by the costs of housing the Scottish Queen.

Under the custody of Sir Amias Paulet, in January 1585 Mary was confined again to the damp and smelly Tutbury. It was only at the end of 1585, when the dung heaps of Tutbury had become so rank and noxious that they were unsanitary, that Paulet allowed Mary to relocate to Chartley Castle in Staffordshire. Alas, Mary's health had already declined as a result of the conditions at Tutbury and when she arrived at Chartley, she was bedridden for two months.

Elizabeth's councillors, especially William Cecil, Lord Burghley had long fretted about the constant threat that Mary's very existence posed to England. In 1586, Elizabeth's spymaster, Sir Francis Walsingham, found a way to catch Mary red-handed. Mary had devised a system of smuggling letters out of the castle in small, watertight containers placed into beer barrels. The local brewer (who had also supplied Mary at Tutbury) received the letters and sent them on. But he was a double agent working for Walsingham, passing the letters to a code-breaker, who deciphered and copied them before dispatching them, so that Mary suspected nothing. The letters confirmed Walsingham's worst fears: Anthony Babington, an English Catholic, was weaving an elaborate plot involving a Catholic rebellion aided by the Spanish to assassinate Elizabeth and rescue Mary, the so-called Babington Plot.

Fatally, on 17 July 1586, Mary wrote to Babington that she accepted the plan. It was the evidence that Walsingham and Burghley needed to secure her execution. Babington and the other conspirators were arrested and died horrific deaths: first hanged, they were cut down while still alive in order to watch while their 'privies' were cut off. They were then disembowelled, before finally being quartered. Even the inured London spectators were aghast at this cruelty.

Mary, meanwhile, was sent to Fotheringhay Castle. To Elizabeth, Mary was still a queen, and so it was only with great reluctance that she signed her death warrant in February 1587. Mary was beheaded for treason and buried at Peterborough, only later being moved to Westminster Abbey.

While imprisoned, Mary had adopted her mother, Mary of Guise's motto, 'In my end is my beginning', and her badge, the phoenix rising from the ashes. Mary was right: she died, but her son lived on to claim the English throne. Along with its dreaded buildings, at Tutbury you can see replicas of her embroidery depicting this subversive message to the world.

Kenilworth Castle
Warwickshire

'An "ambrosial banquet" of 300 sweet dishes,
"very strange and sundry kinds of fireworks" including
one that "burnt unquenchably beneath the water"... thirteen
bears baited with mastiffs... and water spectacles including
a twenty-four-foot dolphin that emerged from the
lake with six musicians in its belly.'

The vast, magnificent ochre ruins of Kenilworth Castle have a baleful and crestfallen air. How the mighty have fallen. At its height, in 1575, mercer Robert Laneham extolled 'the stately seat of Kenilworth Castle, the rare beauty of building... every room so spacious, so well belighted, and so high roofed within'. These walls have seen many great persons and wondrous events over the centuries.

There was first a castle at Kenilworth in the 1120s, but its glory days began when King John built a defensive dam and withstood a great siege here in 1266. John of Gaunt built the Great Hall in the 1370s, which was unchanged when Elizabeth I visited 200 years later. Henry V erected a luxury manor house retreat, 'the Pleasance in the Marsh', here in 1415–20, while Henry VII had a tennis court built in the early 1490s. Under Henry VIII, the castle was surveyed and maintained. During the Civil War, Kenilworth was slighted (partially destroyed) and, in the early nineteenth century, Sir Walter Scott made Kenilworth famous in his novel of the same name.

The story Scott told – if in a highly fictionalised version – is the one that remains most associated with the castle: Robert Dudley, Earl of Leicester entertaining Queen Elizabeth I here on a grand scale in 1575.

In 1563, Kenilworth had been granted to Dudley, who was made the Earl of Leicester in 1564. His father, John Dudley, Duke of Northumberland, had also briefly held the castle, but as the man who had put Lady Jane Grey on the throne, he had been executed as a traitor in 1553 (Leicester would never entirely shrug off his father's disgrace).

Nevertheless, very soon after Elizabeth became Queen, Leicester had become her greatest favourite. His position as Master of the Horse, one of the most senior royal posts, gave him a highly coveted physical proximity to the Queen and, on 23 April 1559, Elizabeth created Leicester a Knight of the Garter, a singular and prestigious honour.

The conspicuous affection displayed between Leicester and Elizabeth caused much comment at court. The Venetian ambassador, Paulo Tiepolo, noted that Leicester was 'in great favour and very intimate with her Majesty', while the Spanish ambassador the Count de Feria wrote scandalously that 'during the last few days, Lord Robert has come so much into favour that he does whatever he likes with affairs and it is even said that her Majesty visits him in his chamber day and night'. The tanned and dark-eyed Robert, whose looks earned him the nickname 'the Gypsy', disported himself as the Queen's consort in all but name.

To marry Leicester would have provoked the opprobrium of the nobility, and would have demeaned the Crown, especially as Leicester was the lowly son of a traitor. The real problem, though, was that Leicester was already married. So, when on 8 September 1560, Leicester's wife, Lady Amy Dudley, was found dead at the base of a staircase with a broken neck, the worst was suspected, and the scandal was enough to make any marriage impossible. Yet, Elizabeth continued to tease and taunt Leicester, and to deploy him as a shield when the diplomatic courtships she was required to consider came her way.

It was in this context that Leicester entertained Elizabeth at Kenilworth four times, in 1566, 1568, 1572 and, most remarkably, for nineteen days in the summer of 1575: the longest stay at any courtier's house during any progress.

In preparation, Leicester had building works done at the castle to make it fit for Elizabeth. He constructed what is now called Leicester's Building in 1571 to provide private apartments for the Queen and her close servants. This sumptuous house included a dancing chamber. He also built the gatehouse to provide an impressive new entrance to the castle. Converted in the 1640s by Colonel Joseph Hawkesworth into a private house, this building features some of the only surviving pieces of the lavish interiors created by Leicester, which were moved here in the 1650s from Leicester's Building. The fine alabaster fireplace with its ornately carved overmantle in the Oak Room probably came from Elizabeth's Privy Chamber. It is inscribed with Leicester's initials, the year 1571, his ragged staff badge and his motto '*Droit et loyal*' ('Just and loyal').

An elaborate temporary garden was also designed and installed for Elizabeth's visit in 1575. It featured two 'fine arbours [made] redolent by sweet trees and flowers'; an aviary decorated with gems; obelisks, spheres and white bears carved from stone; fragrant herbs; and apple, pear and cherry trees. Described in detail in Laneham's contemporary account, it has now been very successfully recreated by English Heritage, with the planting designed to peak each July, the month of the Queen's visit.

Elizabeth arrived on horseback on 9 July. At this time, Kenilworth was surrounded by a 100-acre lake and, as Elizabeth crossed it via the 600-foot bridge, she was met by a moving island carrying the Lady of the Lake and two nymphs. Such pageantry was a sign of things to come. Over the next two and a half weeks, Elizabeth was entertained with all manner of gorgeous spectacle: every detail recorded in a long letter by Laneham and an account by author George Gascoigne.

The festivities included music, dancing, hunting, boating, an 'ambrosial banquet' of 300 sweet dishes, 'very strange and sundry kinds of fireworks' including one that 'burnt unquenchably beneath the water', an Italian acrobat performing feats of agility, Morris dancers, thirteen bears baited with mastiffs, jousting, ceremonial gunfire, skirmishes or mock battles, a 'Savage Man' who appeared from the forest 'himself for grown all in Moss and Ivy', and water spectacles including a twenty-four-foot dolphin that emerged from the lake with six musicians in its belly – one can only imagine what on earth such a thing would have looked like. All the pageants and plays shared the same theme: marriage.

Was this Leicester's last lavish attempt to win Elizabeth's hand in marriage: a final extravaganza to win her round? Or was it instead an ultimatum – marry me or release me – with this extraordinary, unsurpassed revelry a parting gift? Certainly, the enormous cost half-crippled Leicester's finances. But was it all in vain?

In December 1575, Leicester revived an old flirtation with Lettice Knollys, Countess of Essex, the Queen's cousin. When Elizabeth discovered that they had secretly married in September 1578, she was incandescent with rage. She had regarded Leicester as her own possession, and it took him five long years to claw his way back into her affections, while his wife was never welcome at court in his lifetime.

In 1588, Leicester died, aged fifty-six, on his way to Kenilworth. In his will, he left the Queen a string of 600 pearls with a great diamond and emerald jewel as a 'token of an humble faithful heart and the last gift that ever I can send her'. According to the Spanish ambassador, on hearing the news of his death, Elizabeth locked herself away and refused to come out for several days, until William Cecil, Lord Burghley ordered the doors to be broken down. Two months later, it was reported that the Queen was 'much aged and spent, and very melancholy'.

Elizabeth outlived Leicester by fifteen years. He was buried in St Mary's Church, Warwick with his elder brother Ambrose, and Kenilworth was left to Leicester's illegitimate son, also named Robert Dudley (1574–1619). The castle would never see such magnificence again.

Shakespeare's birthplace
Stratford-upon-Avon, Warwickshire

'An upstart crow, beautified with our feathers...
with his tiger's heart wrapped in a player's hide.'

On William Shakespeare's death, his cantankerous rival, Ben Jonson, paid the bard a compliment that continues to define our attitude to Shakespeare: 'He was not of an age, but for all time.' Shakespeare was such a rare talent that his creativity still permeates the cultural fabric of society, and his works have never been more performed, adapted or imitated than they are today. So it is easy to think of him as a man out of time. But, in fact, he was born in a rural market town in the early years of Elizabeth I's reign, and was formed by the social, religious and political world-view of the period. His plays were written to meet the commercial demands of the flourishing theatre culture of London in the 1590s, and his heyday straddled the last days of Gloriana and the early years of James I's reign.

You can experience Shakespeare anywhere you can see or read his plays but, as the thriving tourist industry attests, the best place to remember the man himself is in his hometown of Stratford-upon-Avon. (The controversy over whether the man from Stratford actually wrote the plays, or whether it was someone else, is an old one that flares up from time to time, including during the time of writing. Until otherwise proven, let's assume the man from Avon and the Bard are one and the same.)

Between 20 and 25 April 1564, William was born to John Shakespeare and Mary Arden in part of the house in Henley Street, Stratford now known as 'Shakespeare's birthplace'. The house, built in 1530, is a timber-framed building made of wattle-and-daub. Inside, it is recreated to look as it may have done in Shakespeare's day, and the parlour retains its original sixteenth-century floor of blue limestone across which, as a child, William might have crawled and tottered.

William's family on both sides came from the Forest of Arden: the derivation of his mother's maiden name. His father, John, practised the highly skilled trade of glove making – which is recreated here today – and was respected in the town: four years after William's birth, he became bailiff (mayor) of Stratford.

William survived the devastating outbreak of plague in 1564 and lived in the Henley Street house – which was probably extended to its current size in 1575 – until the age of fourteen. He attended the excellent local grammar school, King's New School, where he was trained in Latin literature including Ovid, Virgil, Seneca, Livy and Cicero, and was taught his Bible and Book of Common Prayer. During these years, he almost certainly saw one of the fifteen companies of players who called on Stratford between 1568 and 1582, and his love of theatre must have started here.

In the summer of 1582, as an eighteen-year-old, he started to pay visits to the cottage of orphaned siblings Anne and Bartholomew Hathaway, in the nearby village of Shottery. This fifteenth-century thatched cottage survives with the basic medieval 'cruck' or A-frame design [see THE TYPICAL TUDOR HOUSE]. It had been extended from a simple two-room abode in the 1560s, exchanging the central hearth for a fireplace with a smoke hood and adding a second storey. It also had two 'joyned' (four-poster) beds (two from the 1580s are there now).

William certainly enjoyed his visits, for on 27 November 1582, in a rush to beat the ban on marriages in Advent, a marriage licence was issued for William and Anne. His twenty-six-year-old bride was pregnant, and their daughter, Susanna, was born six months later.

The couple returned to Henley Street to live with William's parents and, in 1585, Anne gave birth to twins, Hamnet and Judith, named after old Catholic friends of the family. Twins, of course, frequently feature in Shakespeare's plays. But no more children were born to the Shakespeares, which might suggest that William had already left for London, for apart from his children's baptisms and a court case in 1587, Shakespeare disappears from the records for a decade after his marriage, only re-emerging in a pamphlet in 1592 that indicates he had achieved some fame (or infamy) as a writer in London.

How Shakespeare moved from glover's son to acclaimed London playwright we may never know, and this fuels much of the speculation concerning his authorship. All we know is that by April 1592, his *Henry VI Part 1* was being performed at the Rose Theatre in London, and attracting crowds of 2,000 to 3,000 people a performance, for fifteen shows.

Many of his early plays, such as *Titus Andronicus*, *The Two Gentleman of Verona* and *The Taming of the Shrew*, adapted existing plots, and it was for this that Robert Greene attacked Shakespeare in his 1592 pamphlet, which plays on a line from *Henry VI Part 3*:

> There is an upstart crow, beautified with our feathers, that with *his tiger's heart wrapped in a player's hide* supposes he is as well able to bombast out a blank verse as the best of you, and being an absolute *Johannes Factotum* (Jack of all trades), is in his own conceit the only Shake-scene in a country.

Despite this criticism, it was Shakespeare's verse that won him not only acclaim, but patronage. In 1593, he dedicated his erotic poem 'Venus and Adonis' to his new patron Henry Wriothesley, the Earl of Southampton. Another epic poem, 'The Rape of Lucrece', followed the next year. In theatrical terms, too, he had found a patron: in May 1594, Shakespeare and Richard Burbage joined with the newly formed Lord Chamberlain's Men, under the patronage of Lord Hunsdon. What followed was an extraordinary outpouring of creativity as Shakespeare produced a series of plays including *Romeo and Juliet* and *A Midsummer Night's Dream.*

His family continued to live at the Henley Street house, with William returning perhaps only annually. In August 1597, William received some devastating news from Stratford: his only son, Hamnet, had died at the age of eleven. Psychoanalysts may find some link between this tragedy and Shakespeare's apparent crisis, seen in the sonnets he produced around this time. After being married for fifteen years and living mostly apart from his wife, William wrote a string of sonnets to a beautiful young aristocrat, and then a number of impassioned love poems to a married woman, his dark mistress [see GAWSWORTH HALL]. 'Shall I Compare Thee To a Summer's Day' was written to a man, tentatively identified as William Herbert, later Earl of Pembroke, and described in the lines:

A woman's face, with nature's own hand painted,
Hast thou, the master-mistress of my passion.

In 1597, Shakespeare decided to invest in some property. He returned to Stratford to buy New Place, the second biggest house in town. It no longer stands, having been demolished in the eighteenth century (something that to modern sensibilities would seem unconscionable), but has recently been excavated, and was described by antiquary John Leland as a 'pretty house of brick and timber'. You can visit the site, next to Nash's House, later owned by Shakespeare's grandchild, Elizabeth, and her husband, Thomas Nash. As you walk around Stratford with its many wonderful Tudor houses, you'll find it isn't difficult to imagine what sort of house New Place was.

Over the next year, Shakespeare wrote *The Merchant of Venice* and created his beloved character, Falstaff, in *Henry IV Part 2*. These were followed by four famed plays examining the inner life: *Henry V*, *As You Like It*, *Julius Caesar* and *Hamlet*, his first tragedy, with its character whose name was so reminiscent of his son's. *Julius Caesar* was probably the first play to be performed in the Chamberlain's Men's new theatre on the south of the Thames, the Globe, which could hold an astonishing 3,300 people.

In 1601, Shakespeare again returned to Stratford, this time to bury his father, in Holy Trinity Church. Back in London, he lodged with a French Huguenot family in Silver Street (a few streets away from Nicholas Hilliard in Gutter Lane) and wrote his great *Othello*. On 2 February 1603, Shakespeare's company performed before Elizabeth I for the last time. After forty-five years of rule, she died a month later and, on James I's command, the Lord Chamberlain's Men were reborn as the King's Men. Over the next four years, with this royal patronage, Shakespeare was again productive, writing *Measure for Measure*, *All's Well That Ends Well*, *Antony and Cleopatra* and his great plays, *King Lear* and *Macbeth*. In total, between 1599 and 1606 he completed fourteen plays, including some of the most celebrated works in English literature.

During 1608–10, plague closed the London theatres, and Shakespeare probably returned to Stratford, where he buried his mother and, at New Place, possibly wrote *The Winter's Tale*, *Pericles* and *The Tempest*. As his last solo play, *The Tempest*, with its talk of 'heavenly music', is often seen as a valediction.

The original Globe Theatre only lasted fourteen years. It burnt down in June 1613 during a performance of *Henry the Eighth, or, All is True* after a stray cannon ball set fire to the thatched roof. It was rebuilt a year later and this second iteration lasted until the Civil War. In 1997, a modern reconstruction was completed, 750 feet from the original theatre. Although not an exact reproduction of the Elizabethan venue, it is as faithful to the original as modern ideas of safety and comfort allow – it holds only half the original audience – and has already outlived the theatre that Shakespeare knew.

Three years later, on almost exactly his fifty-second birthday, William Shakespeare passed away. To his long-suffering Stratford wife he left 'his second best bed'. At Holy Trinity Church in Stratford you can visit his grave, which was left unscathed during a 2008 restoration of the church, thereby respecting the lines on his gravestone which read:

'Blessed be the man that spares these stones, and cursed be he who moves my bones.'

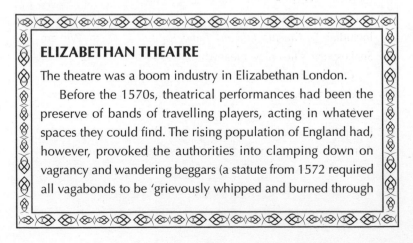

ELIZABETHAN THEATRE

The theatre was a boom industry in Elizabethan London.

Before the 1570s, theatrical performances had been the preserve of bands of travelling players, acting in whatever spaces they could find. The rising population of England had, however, provoked the authorities into clamping down on vagrancy and wandering beggars (a statute from 1572 required all vagabonds to be 'grievously whipped and burned through the gristle of the right ear with a hot iron' an inch in diameter). Touring companies of actors needed a new, fixed home.

At first, they started to perform in the courtyards of inns, such as the Bull in Bishopsgate, the Bell and the Cross Keys in Gracechurch Street and the Bel Savage outside Ludgate. But in 1576, under the patronage of Robert Dudley, Earl of Leicester, carpenter-turned-actor James Burbage built 'The Theatre', the country's first purpose-built professional theatre. It seems to have been wooden and polygonal, with three storeys of galleried seating, and a central pit open to the sky. The following year 'The Curtain' was built 200 yards away. Shoreditch, a mile north of the walls of the City of London, had become London's first theatre district.

One of the earliest plays to be a popular success with the new mass audience was Thomas Kyd's revenge tragedy *The Spanish Tragedy* or *Hieronimo is Mad Again*. It was quickly followed in 1587 by another hit, Christopher Marlowe's *Tamburlaine*, the story of an oriental emperor, told in the new form of blank verse (unrhymed verse). Before Marlowe was murdered in a lodging in Deptford in 1593, he had produced several other successes, including *Dr Faustus*, *Edward II* and *The Jew of Malta*. William Shakespeare's first play, meanwhile, was staged in 1592.

One of the reasons that Shakespeare would go on to produce so many plays was commercial pressure. The Elizabethan theatre had a quick turnover. Theatrical entrepreneur Philip Henslowe kept a diary that reveals that his players, the Admiral's Men, performed as many as fifteen different plays in a month. New scripts were urgently demanded to satisfy returning spectators.

Theatre attendance became a mass phenomenon. When, in 1599, Shakespeare's troupe, the Lord Chamberlain's Men, headed south of the river to build their new theatre, the Globe, they constructed an amphitheatre that could house an audience of 3,000. Other grand theatres, including the Swan and the Rose, soon joined them in Southwark. The Fortune was built in the north of the city.

Designed for audiences used to the cruelty of bearbaiting, theatrical performances were full of gore, ribald humour and slapstick comedy. There was no scenery or stage painting, but the actors used a great variety of props. Performances were always during daylight, as there was no possibility of lighting an outdoor theatre sufficiently at night. Although women had always acted in court masques, no women performed in public plays until after 1660, and instead, their parts were played by boys.

The theatre still retained associations with theft (pickpockets were rife), riot and licentiousness, were accused of staging 'lewd jigs, songs and dances' and were thought to attract 'lewd and ill-disposed persons'. However, one person who attended some of Shakespeare's plays was Queen Elizabeth I herself.

Harvington Hall
Worcestershire

'He was so skiful both to devise and frame the [hides]
in the best manner… that I verily think no man
can be said to have done more good of all those
that laboured in the English vineyard.'
Father John Gerard, Catholic priest, describing Nicholas Owen

There is more than meets the eye to the red-brick Elizabethan
mansion of Harvington Hall, located a mile outside the quaint
village of Chaddesley Corbett on a moated island. At its core is a
fourteenth-century timber-framed building, but the majority of
the house is Tudor, built from 1578 onwards by Humphrey Packington. It was uninhabited and stripped of some of its original
furnishings in the nineteenth century, but this benign neglect
ensured Harvington's survival until the early twentieth century,
when it was restored. It features some beautiful and unique decorative remains, but its chief distinction is that concealed in its
walls is the finest surviving set of priest holes in the country.

There are many fascinating details of architecture and design to
spot at Harvington Hall. The medieval house is now the restaurant,
with a beamed ceiling from 1500. The Great Kitchen retains its two
huge fireplaces and a separate bread oven. The best bedchamber,

now Lady Yate's Room, has Elizabethan panelling from floor to ceiling, with an ornate overmantle and ensuite garderobe, dropping to the moat. The simple sixteenth-century panelling continues onto the fourteenth-century walls of the Withdrawing Room, but it is the Great Chamber that would have had the most striking panelling, richly painted in red, black and yellow to imitate inlay. Fragments survive in two corners, and the ornately decorated door into Mermaid's Passage gives some sense of the overall effect.

If you were suddenly transported back in time, you'd probably find the house surprisingly garish, but wealthy Tudor houses were distinguished by their use of bold, extravagant colour and elaborate ornamentation. You can see this in the rare examples of Elizabethan wall painting at Harvington. Mermaid's Passage features exquisite arabesque paintings of scrolls, shells, flowers, birds, animals and the eponymous mermaids, in an Italianate style reminiscent of the panels from Nonsuch Palace [see LOSELEY PARK]. The Nine Worthies Passage is adorned with almost life-size images of the Nine Worthies (legendary and biblical heroes) and the Great Staircase features shadow painting from 1600. The small chapel also has walls emblazoned with rather lurid rows of red and white drops to represent the blood and water that flowed from Christ's side. Also, don't miss the glorious carved Elizabethan four-poster bed, from 1590, in the Priest's Room, and a more recent example of craftsmanship: the chimneypiece in the Great Chamber, which was made in Elizabethan style in 1996 following descriptions from 1600.

As attractive as it is, Harvington also throws light on a less becoming feature of Elizabethan society. Elizabeth I has gained an anachronistic reputation as a religiously tolerant monarch who, famously, did not seek 'to make windows into men's souls'. It is true that in the first twenty years of her reign, the regime realised the limits of its power to enforce the Anglican faith and was, in comparison to governments on the Continent, relatively lenient towards members of the dissident faith, insisting only on outward conformity through attendance at church every Sunday and holy day (with fines to punish recusants). However, in 1570, the zealous new Pope Pius V issued a papal bull entitled *Regnans in Excelsis*, excommunicating 'Elizabeth, pretended queen of England'; releasing English Catholics from their duty of allegiance; and encouraging them to overthrow their Queen. From 1574, a Catholic seminary in Douai in northern France started training English Catholics as priests and sending them home to reconvert England and provoke Catholics into open rebellion. After 1580, their numbers were bolstered by Jesuit missionaries, and the Elizabethan state had to react.

A series of draconian new laws from 1571 to 1593 clamped down on this potential fifth column. In 1585, it became treason for any Catholic priest, ordained by the Pope's authority, to enter England, and for any person to give him aid or shelter. Yet, Catholicism remained strong in some quarters, especially among sections of the nobility and gentry who had the resources and wherewithal to hide priests from the eyes of the authorities. Humphrey Packington was one such man.

Like many others, Packington engaged the services of the master craftsman and Oxford carpenter Nicholas Owen to construct an elaborate series of concealed hiding places, or priest's holes, to provide safe haven during raids by priest hunters, known as the Pursuivants. The first hide you'll see at Harvington is to the left of the fireplace in the Withdrawing Room. It retains its original ladder (now in the alcove on the other side of the fireplace) and creates a hide above the bread oven in the kitchen. In the Great Chamber, there is a primitive hiding place above the ceiling to the north-west corner of the chamber, accessed from the Great Staircase. Two of the five stairs that lead down from the Nine

Worthies Passage to the staircase can be raised (they're very heavy!) to reveal the large inner hiding place, with a spyhole into the Great Chamber itself.

One of Owen's most ingenious hides is in Dr Dodd's library: so ingenious, it remained hidden for centuries and was only discovered in 1894. Five feet from the floor, once behind a book cupboard, it is hidden behind a beam that hangs on a pivot: once the lower end is pressed, the beam releases to swing up revealing a hole big enough – eight feet long, two feet wide and six feet high – to conceal several priests. The bottom of the beam could then be bolted from the inside and the books replaced, concealing the hiders in the very walls of the building.

In the chapel, used from 1590, you can pick up the floorboards to reveal a 'secret corner': not big enough for a man but sufficient to hide the 'Massing stuff' of the forbidden Catholic Mass, while in the Marble Room, the entire fireplace is fake – even to the point of smoke-blackened bricks – and designed as a bolt-hole up into a large hiding place in the roof.

We don't know whether Owen's handicraft was ever needed; there is no evidence of a raid at Harvington, but elsewhere the hides were lifesavers. Baddesley Clinton in Warwickshire was searched in 1591 when priests John Gerard, Robert Southwell and Henry Garnet were concealed there. The Pursuivants left unsatisfied, and John Gerard, who later made a daring escape from the Tower of London, lived to tell the tale.

This was not, however, always the case. Edmund Campion and two other priests were at the home of the Yate family at Lyford Grange near Wantage when it was raided in July 1581. They hid but, by chance, one among the searchers 'espied a chink in the wall of boards' above the stairwell, and when it was found to be hollow, the Pursuivants broke in. Campion was escorted to the Tower, where he was repeatedly racked and had all his nails pulled out. In

November 1581, he was hanged, drawn and quartered before the crowds at Tyburn.

Campion was not the only one to be caught, as carvings in the Tower of London make clear. In fact, 129 priests and 36 laymen were executed for treason between 1577 and 1603. Nicholas Owen himself would later be arrested and tortured to death in the Tower. In light of this, Elizabeth's reputation for religious toleration must be considered an exaggeration.

East
Midlands

Bosworth Battlefield
Leicestershire

'A horse! A horse! My kingdom for a horse!'

It all began on 22 August 1485: the day the Tudor dynasty was founded (although for political reasons – so that those who fought against him could be declared traitors – Henry VII would later date the commencement of his reign to 21 August). But it was on 22 August that Richard III was killed in battle, and Henry Tudor became Henry VII, the first Tudor monarch.

Historians have argued over the exact location of the battlefield, which was somewhere in the vicinity of Ambion Hill, less than two miles south of Market Bosworth in Leicestershire. In 2009, the Heritage Lottery Fund funded a metal detection project to unearth the site. The results of this work suggested it was near Fenn Hill Farm on private land, about two miles away from the previously identified spot. Sadly, it is also therefore two miles away from the Bosworth Battlefield Heritage Centre and not accessible to the public. Yet one field can look very much like another and this award-winning, child-friendly museum and heritage trail best commemorate the event, telling the story and, most importantly, displaying objects found on the battlefield from the day that Henry Tudor ended 331 years of Plantagenet rule.

Our impression of Bosworth, and the events leading up to it, has been significantly shaped by Shakespeare's *Richard III*, a version of events written to please the victorious Tudor dynasty. In it, Richard III emerges as a 'deformed' villain, whose last, lamenting speech – 'A horse! A horse! My kingdom for a horse!' – is renowned. The truth is that Henry Tudor had only the feeblest of claims to the throne, and was certainly no more entitled to the throne than Richard himself.

Henry Tudor was born in Wales to Edmund Tudor, first Earl of Richmond (son of Owen Tudor and Catherine de Valois) and Margaret Beaufort. It is through his mother that Henry derived his claim to the Crown: she was the great-great-granddaughter of Edward III. The Beauforts had been legitimised by Act of Parliament under Richard II, but both this act and Henry VI's declaration of 1407 made it clear that this legitimisation did not extend to inheriting the throne – a fact that Henry Tudor conveniently ignored when the time was right.

We know of Henry's early life only in fragments. He never met his father, who died three months before his birth at Pembroke Castle on 28 January 1457. He spent the first four years of his life at Pembroke, before his mother married again, at which point Henry went to Raglan Castle, in Wales, as the ward of William, Lord Herbert. In 1470, Henry made one visit to England before his fight for its Crown, and had an audience with Henry VI. When Edward IV won back the throne in 1471 in the Wars of the Roses, Henry Tudor fled the country with his uncle, Jasper Tudor, Earl of Pembroke. They landed in the duchy of Brittany, where they remained for thirteen years, first as asylum seekers and later under virtual house arrest. So far, so inauspicious, for a future king of England.

Meanwhile, in April 1483, Edward IV died suddenly. His eldest son and heir – Edward V – was still a child, and his uncle, Richard, Duke of Gloucester, quickly acted to put the young King and his brother, Richard, Duke of York, in the Tower of London. (For years their fate was unknown, until the bones of young boys were found in the Tower in 1674.) Gloucester, in a transparent display of self-aggrandisement, declared that the boys were illegitimate and that therefore he was the rightful heir to the Crown. He was crowned on 6 July.

Richard's actions provoked an outcry from various quarters, especially after the young boys mysteriously failed to be seen in public. In an atmosphere of near-open rebellion, Henry Tudor sensed his moment. Inspired by his resourceful mother (whose own claims to the Crown were overlooked), with support in England and with Francis, Duke of Brittany's help, Henry declared that he would fight Richard for the throne. He also swore, in Rennes Cathedral on Christmas Day 1483, that as soon as he became king, he would marry Elizabeth, Edward IV's eldest daughter, thereby uniting the Wars of the Roses' two feuding families.

In April 1484, Richard III's son and heir, Prince Edward, died at the age of seven. Knowing that this put him in greater danger, and capitalising on the illness of the Duke of Brittany, Richard reached an agreement with Peter Landois, the treasurer of Brittany, in which Landois would surrender Henry Tudor to him. But Henry caught wind of the plot and managed to escape, using the classic ploy of dressing as a servant. He assembled his English followers and on 1 August 1485, having raised an army of some 4,000 men, he set sail from the Seine, bound for Milford Haven. Once he had landed, he marched east, collecting rebel troops along the way. The King mustered an army of at least 10,000, and by Sunday 21 August both sides had set up camp near Ambion Hill, ready for the battle that would follow.

The story of the clash is told to dramatic effect at Bosworth today. King Richard, with his superior numbers and cannon, looked set to conquer the rebel forces under the leadership of the Earl of Oxford. But a combination of Henry's superior strategic formation, and the reluctance of Richard's men (namely the Earl of Northumberland and the Stanley family) to commit to his cause, thwarted Richard's assured victory.

With divine confidence, Richard decided to take matters into his own hands, and bravely charged across the battlefield to engage directly with Henry's own vanguard. He cut down and killed Henry's standard-bearer, to come within feet of Henry himself. Henry's saviour came in the form of Sir William Stanley, who at that moment traitorously threw in his lot with the rebels and raced into the battlefield with his men to engage Richard's troops. In doing so, he rescued Henry from sure defeat and disaster.

Fighting boldly to the last, Richard was cornered, unhorsed and swiftly demolished. Henry was proclaimed king: legend has it that Reginald Bray, finding Richard's gold circlet in a nearby thorn bush, crowned Henry on the battlefield. In a little less than two hours, the fight was over; the Tudor had won. To this day, Richard remains the last English king to have died in battle, and the only one to do so on English soil since Harold was (or was not) shot through the eye by William the Conqueror's archers at Hastings.

At Bosworth's Heritage Centre, they have a collection of objects found at the battlefield, which together evocatively conjure up that eventful day: from shot to belt buckles, coins to horse harness pendants. The crucial object, however, is a silver gilt badge depicting a boar: Richard III's badge, lost for years under the soil where he met his unhappy end.

This was the decisive day. Henry Tudor had become King Henry VII. When, towards the end of his life, he built his chapel at Westminster Abbey, Henry envisaged that the moment would be forever commemorated atop the shrine of Edward the Confessor by a gold-plated statue of him kneeling in full armour and holding aloft the crown he had received that day. The statue was never made, but the dynasty that Henry established that Monday in August 1485 has never been forgotten.

Hardwick Hall
Derbyshire

'There is no Lady in this land that I better love and like.'

Sitting atop a hill, stunning in its symmetry and glinting in the sun, Hardwick Hall is one of the most spectacular buildings of the Elizabethan age. It was built by the most remarkable non-royal woman of the long Tudor century: Bess of Hardwick.

Bess was born in a manor farmhouse at the Old Hall at Hardwick in 1527, her humble origins as the daughter of minor gentry not betraying the fact that she would one day become the richest and most powerful woman in England after the Queen. Her father died before she was seven months old and, aged twelve, Bess was sent to learn noble ways from the Zouche family of Codnor Castle in Derbyshire. Here, before she turned sixteen, she had met and married Robert Barlow, the first of her four husbands. However, before the couple had 'bedded together', Barlow died and the young Bess began the first of many fights for her rights – in this case, her widow's dower of £30 a year.

Next, Bess became a waiting woman in the house of Lord and Lady Dorset, the Grey family. Her attachment to the Grey girls was considerable: she kept a picture of Lady Jane Grey on her bedside table for the rest of her life. In 1547, Bess married Sir William Cavendish. He was more than twice her age (forty to her nineteen), and had made his fortune as a commissioner during the dissolution of the monasteries. Bess bore him eight children in ten years, six of whom survived infancy.

When Cavendish died in October 1557, he left everything to Bess – an unusual thing to do at the time – with their house and land at Chatsworth entailed on their eldest son only after Bess's death. He also left her a debt to the tune of £5,000 (equivalent to £850,000 today). A less feisty woman would have sold off the properties to pay the debt, but Bess instead contested it and it was eventually reduced, in 1563, to an amount of only £1,000 (today equivalent to £170,000). The earliest portrait that we have of Bess dates from about this time and hangs at Hardwick. She is red-haired, blue-eyed and desirably pale, but not excessively beautiful.

Following Elizabeth I's accession, Bess became one of the Queen's Ladies of the Bedchamber. This was the start of a long friendship between the women: Elizabeth would later say of Bess, 'There is no Lady in this land that I better love and like.'

Elizabeth's Master of the Horse at that time, and the captain of her personal guard, was Sir William St Loe. In August 1559, he and Bess married. A recent biography suggests this relationship was the passionate love of Bess's life, but it did not last long. In February 1565, St Loe died suddenly: foul play by his brother Edward was suspected. Edward didn't know that St Loe had changed his will to leave everything to Bess and 'to her heirs forever'. This extraordinary act – even Cavendish had entailed the estate on his son after Bess's death – tarnished her reputation in some quarters, as detractors held Bess responsible for the impoverishment of the St Loes.

It did not, however, prevent George Talbot, Earl of Shrewsbury's interest in Bess. Shrewsbury was one of the richest men in the country, a virtual 'Prince of the North'. The couple married in February 1568, and sealed their union by simultaneously marrying Bess's seventeen-year-old son, Henry, to Shrewsbury's eight-year-old daughter, Grace, and Shrewsbury's fifteen-year-old son, Gilbert, to Bess's twelve-year-old daughter Mary! The eglantine table of inlaid marquetry in the High Great Chamber at Hardwick, decorated with the sixteenth-century pursuits of cards, backgammon and music, was probably commissioned to mark this triple marriage.

The marriage made Bess one of the most prominent and important women at court. It started happily enough, with Shrewsbury writing to Bess as 'My None' (a contraction of 'mine own') and 'my sweetheart'. But in December 1568, Shrewsbury was put in charge of the imprisonment of Mary, Queen of Scots [see TUTBURY CASTLE], and, over the next fifteen years, the draining costs of this guardianship, the wiles of the beautiful Scottish queen (remember, nearly every red-blooded male who met this extraordinarily enthralling Queen ended up falling for her) and Bess's absences from Shrewsbury's own place of virtual imprisonment took their toll. By 1580, the marriage was falling apart. Shrewsbury wanted to be rid of Bess, but to hold on to the lands she had brought into their union. He sent men to terrorise Bess's sons and dependants, and at one point broke into their house at Chatsworth with a force of forty armed men. The situation became so inflamed that the Queen herself ordered a six-month investigation into their marital breakdown, and wrote to Shrewsbury, helpfully, 'We do not suffer in our realm to persons of your degree and quality to live in such a kind of discord.'

Throughout this difficult period, Bess played her hand expertly. When Shrewsbury died in 1590, he left Bess a very wealthy woman: wealthy enough to build, from scratch, a house to be envied.

In previous years, Bess had invested in Chatsworth and doubled the size of the Old Hall at Hardwick. Now, in her old age, she wanted to build at Hardwick a state-of-the-art house in which she could entertain the Queen.

She turned to premier master mason Robert Smythson for the design. Smythson had designed a lookout tower in Chatsworth's park wall – still standing and now known as the Hunting Tower – as well as Bess's fourth husband's house at Worksop. Famously, he also designed the great houses of Longleat and Wollaton. But, despite Smythson's input, Hardwick Hall was very much Bess's own: the building accounts show her watchful eye on every expense and design decision. The exterior of the house remains exactly as Bess intended it.

The watchword of the design was 'symmetry', which was the height of innovative architectural fashion. The house spoke not only of taste, but of wealth and status: glass was still very expensive, and Smythson's design called for lavish acres of glass, even creating false windows in order to maintain the house's extravagant symmetry. Robert Cecil quipped that Hardwick Hall was 'more window than wall' (which is now remembered in the ditty, 'Hardwick Hall, more glass than wall').

What really distinguishes Hardwick, though, are the six towers. These ingenious turrets give a romantic and endlessly varied silhouette, and made Hardwick unusually and impressively high by Tudor standards. Each is surmounted by the giant stone initials, 'ES', for Elizabeth Shrouesbury (as Bess signed herself), under her countess's coronet, thereby proclaiming her name, in a piece of shameless self-aggrandisement, to onlookers for miles around.

Inside, there are forty-six rooms, three of particular note. Firstly, there is the extraordinarily long stone staircase now hung with tapestries galore (with all these stairs, it's strange to think that Bess probably moved here to celebrate her seventieth birthday). This stately approach leads to the show floor, and the second astonishing room: the High Great Chamber. This enormous room was designed to be bigger than the Great Chamber at Theobalds (belonging to Lord Burghley and at that time the grandest house in England) and is a riot of colourful decoration, with the large and crudely cut plasterwork frieze of Diana above the ubiquitous tapestries and canopy of estate (a rich fabric canopy mounted above a throne). This is a room intended for royalty. Not only did Bess anticipate that Elizabeth I would visit, but she hoped that her grand-daughter, Arbella, daughter of Charles Stuart and Bess's daughter Elizabeth, would one day succeed to the English throne. Arbella, because of her English birth, was thought by some to be Elizabeth's obvious successor, instead of the Scottish-born James VI; Elizabeth herself once told the French ambassador's wife, 'Look to her well. She will one day be even as I am.'

The third remarkable room is the Long Gallery, which at 167 feet long, 26 feet high and 39 feet wide could practically fit within it a whole street of Victorian terraced houses. The Gideon Tapes-tries on display here are immensely valuable, and the largest set of tapestries you'll ever see; Bess bought them from Sir Christopher Hatton's heir [see KIRBY HALL] at a knockdown price in 1592. It is because of these tapestries that these rooms, which would have been flooded with light from the many windows, are now shaded. Sadly, the conservation imperative dictates that the eyes of the house are closed, as if in mourning for its lost patron.

Bess died at Hardwick on the morning of 14 February 1608, a stone's throw away from the place of her birth. The house has remained, Miss Havisham-style, effectively unchanged since.

Other Tudor treasures not to miss at Hardwick: two portraits of Bess; portraits of Bess's four husbands; two portraits of Arbella; and two portraits of Elizabeth, one of which is a remarkable full-length portrait from the studio of Nicholas Hilliard, 1599.

Commissioned by Bess when Elizabeth was sixty-six, she shows no signs of age, and her skirt is embroidered with dragons, flowers, sea-serpents, fish and birds. There are also portraits of Lord Burghley; Stephen Gardiner; Edward Seymour; Robert Dudley; Reginald Pole; Robert Cecil; Philip II; James V; and Mary, Queen of Scots, with Lord Darnley. Also look out for the painted cloth wall hangings in the chapel and the embroidery worked by Bess and Mary, Queen of Scots. Finally, don't forget to visit the Old Hall next door: it was extended by Bess between 1587 and 1596, and partly dismantled in the mid-eighteenth century.

SOCIAL CLIMBING THE TUDOR WAY

Tudor England was characterised by an inherent and profound sense of the importance of social hierarchy and its direct correlation to the maintenance of order in the cosmos. Yet it was possible to achieve a surprising degree of social mobility.

For those seeking social advancement, there were three possible routes: the Church, the law and service. Cardinal Thomas Wolsey became Henry VIII's closest and most trusted adviser through his position in the Church, though he was the lowly son of a butcher and cattle farmer from Ipswich. Thomas Cranmer, though 'gentleman-born', owed his post as Archbishop of Canterbury to the Church, and would later remind Bishop Stephen Gardiner, 'I pray God that we, being called to the name of lords, have not forgotten our own baser estates, that once we were simple esquires.'

For Sir Thomas More and Sir Christopher Hatton, their training as lawyers helped them rise to favour, while the lives of Sir John Thynne and Bess of Hardwick illustrate the importance of service in noble households as a means of bettering oneself. Sir John Thynne's role as steward to the Duke of Somerset enabled him to enrich himself to the point of being able to build a great 'prodigy' house at Longleat, while Bess's service in the households of the Zouches and the Greys brought her into marriages that led to her becoming a countess, one of the richest women in England and the builder of Hardwick Hall.

While service could advance you, it was, paradoxically, a great social faux pas to attempt to do this by marriage. When the widowed Frances Brandon, Duchess of Suffolk (and niece to Henry VIII) married her Master of the Horse, Adrian Stokes, in 1555, the match was thought ignominious. Elizabeth I's response on hearing the news was: 'Has the woman so far forgotten herself as to marry a common groom?'

Many of the Tudors who were knighted or ennobled were self-made. Thomas Cromwell, Earl of Essex and one of Henry VIII's right-hand men was, famously, the son of a blacksmith. Sir Francis Drake was born into humble yeoman stock and his father was a lay preacher but, in time, through his intrepid skills as a sailor and his natural talent as a leader, he was knighted and was able to buy Buckland Abbey.

Other families were raised to power by the Tudor dynasty, including the Dudleys, the Cecils and the Sidneys. William Cecil was born to a gentleman and a gentleman's daughter, but became Elizabeth's first minister, Lord Burghley, the builder of the palaces of Theobalds and Burghley House and was able to pass his position to his son, Robert. Penshurst Place had belonged to a duke, but was given to a mere knight, Sir William Sidney, in 1552.

In fact, this was an age of frustration for many of the great nobles: men such as Edward Stafford, Duke of Buckingham or Thomas Howard, Duke of Norfolk who didn't feel they were receiving the degree of honour and share of power that would have been accorded to their ancestors. Henry Howard, Earl of Surrey was executed by Henry VIII for the crime of adding the royal insignia to his own coat of arms, while it was Robert Devereux, Earl of Essex's great desire for political power that almost certainly led to his foolish rebellion in 1601. He was declared a traitor and executed as a result. There were right ways and wrong ways to advance oneself in Tudor England.

𝕭urghley 𝕳ouse
𝕷incolnshire

'More like a town than a house... the towers and pinnacles like so many distant country churches.'

The first thing that strikes you about Burghley House is its extraordinary skyline of cupolas, turrets, chimneys and the one central obelisk. Daniel Defoe said it looked 'more like a town than a house... the towers and pinnacles like so many distant country churches'. It is certainly an incredible and impressive spectacle: a palatial testament to one of the most accomplished and important men of the Elizabethan age.

Sir William Cecil (pronounced 'Sissil'), Lord Burghley dominated Elizabethan politics for forty years, first as Secretary of State (1558–72), then as Lord Treasurer (1572–98). He was not only Elizabeth I's most trusted councillor; he was also arguably the greatest builder of her reign. He built three fabulous houses: Cecil House in Westminster; the grand Theobalds in Hertfordshire that he spent nearly £10,000 (today equivalent to £1.7 million) transforming and which Elizabeth visited eight times; and the house he referred to as his 'principal house', Burghley, which is the only one of his properties still standing.

Burghley (as William Cecil was known after he was made Baron Burghley in 1571) was born in 1520, and rose as a politician under

Edward VI. Shrewd and diplomatic, he survived favouring Lady Jane Grey in the succession crisis of 1553, and was the first of Edward's council to kiss Queen Mary's hand. Crucially, however, he was also at Elizabeth's side at Hatfield on the day Mary died, and was soon sworn in as a member of her Privy Council and Secretary of State.

Before long, the confident, clever and controlled Burghley had become the pre-eminent statesman in Elizabeth's England, a position he maintained until his death in 1598. As Secretary, he managed all of the Queen's correspondence and chaired meetings of the Privy Council; he was at the centre of state business and commanded the machinery of power. In 1570, Elizabeth even gave him permission to stamp her signature on routine documents of state.

Burghley believed ardently in England's 'true religion'. He may even have been one of the patrons of John Foxe, the author of *Acts and Monuments*, popularly known as 'Foxe's Book of Martyrs', a collection of tales of the deaths of Protestant English martyrs first produced in 1563. The central objective in all Burghley's work under Elizabeth was, therefore, to fight for the survival of Protestant England against the attacks of Catholic Europe. Believing that the only way to secure England against Catholic invasion was through a clear succession, Burghley constantly urged the Queen to marry.

His other great preoccupation was the elimination of Mary, Queen of Scots whom he saw as a deadly threat to Elizabeth's throne. Following the Babington Plot [see TUTBURY CASTLE], it was Burghley who convinced Elizabeth to sign the death warrant that he had conveniently prepared earlier, although his subsequent decision to dispatch the warrant and have Mary executed without Elizabeth's express command so infuriated the Queen that Burghley was banished from her presence for four months.

Burghley worked tirelessly until his death at seventy-seven years of age. His last surviving letter to his son, Robert, instructed him to 'serve God by serving of the Queen, for all other service is indeed bondage to the Devil'. Burghley had dedicated his all to Queen and country, working exceptionally long hours and frequently suffering from ill health. He once said to his brother-in-law, Sir Nicholas Bacon, that he had 'forborne wife [Lady Mildred Cecil], children, friends, house, yea all mine own to serve, which I know not that any other hath done in this time'. In return, he had been elevated to the peerage, created a Knight of the Garter in 1572 and made enormously wealthy.

In Tudor times, wealth needed to be displayed through magnificence. And what could be more magnificent than Burghley's flamboyant 'prodigy house' near Stamford? Altering an existing house that had been built by his father, Richard Cecil, in the 1540s, Burghley had begun rebuilding Burghley House in 1555 and continued until 1587. He acted as his own architect, as at Theobalds, but employed master mason John Symonds to oversee the work, as the demands of court life meant his visits to Lincolnshire were rare. He spent a fortune to create a spectacular and imposing classical house that corresponded to, and evoked, his noble, privileged status.

The grand exterior remains substantially as Burghley intended it. The only changes are that in the 1760s, the north-west wing was demolished at the suggestion of Capability Brown to improve views of the parkland, and the south front roof line was raised.

Internally, much has been altered since Burghley's day, and very little remains inside of the Elizabethan house. The interiors are stunning baroque, created in the late seventeenth century by John Cecil, the fifth Earl of Exeter. This means that Burghley's original Elizabethan Long Gallery (124 feet) is now five separate rooms, and what would have been Burghley's Great Chamber is now the Heaven and Hell Chambers, named after their incredible ceilings, painted by Antonio Verrio (who also worked on the baroque palace at Hampton Court).

Still, some traces of the original Tudor interiors survive for those who are willing to search for them. The Old Kitchen with its elaborate rib-vaulted ceiling and lantern is unchanged, as is the Roman staircase – a wonderful example of Tudor classicism – which is ornately carved with the arms and badges of Tudor families. In the alcoves of the Pagoda Room, there are the remains of Elizabethan linenfold panelling, while you can see Tudor plasterwork high up near the last window on the right before entering the Great Hall. The Great Hall itself also has an original and magnificent hammer-beam ceiling and Tudor fireplace (everything else is nineteenth century). If you ask the room guides, they might also be able to show you pictures of the Elizabethan fresco recently found behind the panelling in the Third and Fourth George Rooms.

In particular, there is a stunning view of the inner courtyard from the windows of the antechapel. Here, Burghley, who loved heraldry, featured roundels of the Emperor Charles V and Suleiman the Magnificent of the Ottoman Empire, and others of Paris and Aeneas (whom Tudor genealogy thought to be the ancestors of both Elizabeth and Burghley). The obelisk clock tower dates from 1585 and still has one of its original hands.

The other great sixteenth-century treasures are in the immense portrait collection. There are two portraits of Burghley; one by Marcus Gheeraerts of Elizabeth at an advanced age; another of one of Elizabeth's favourites, Robert Devereux, Earl of Essex; and an idealised portrait of Henry VIII from 1535 by Joos van Cleve.

Eighteen generations of Burghley's descendants have lived at Burghley House since his death. With time, there will always be change, but this building remains a monument to its indefatigable and talented creator, Elizabeth I's right-hand man: even if he is only one of the characters in the house's long history.

Kirby Hall
Northamptonshire

'To lack you is more than hell's torment...
Would God I were with you but for one hour.'

Elizabeth I's reign was an age of great brinkmanship in architecture, as nobles hoping to entice their monarch into a royal visit competed with each other to produce some of the finest houses ever seen. Kirby Hall was one of the best. It was built by Sir Humphrey Stafford in 1570, but was lavishly completed by Sir Christopher Hatton in the hopes of receiving a visit from the Queen.

Hatton belonged to a circle of men who were Elizabeth's 'favourites', and rivalled Robert Dudley, Earl of Leicester; Edward de Vere, Earl of Oxford; and Sir Walter Ralegh for her affections. He was also a man of many talents and over his lifetime held many positions of power, such as Captain of the Queen's Guard, Gentleman of the Privy Chamber, Knight of the Garter, Privy Councillor and Lord High Chancellor of England.

Kirby was only one of his houses: his large house at Holdenby was built in 1570–83 (some of it survives), while London's diamond and jewellery district, Hatton Garden, was named after him as Elizabeth granted him the Bishop of Ely's residence here in 1581. Kirby, however, gives a much greater sense of the exceptional grandeur and innovative beauty for which Hatton's homes became famous.

Hatton, who was born in 1540, was probably first spotted by Elizabeth in 1562 acting in a play at Inner Temple, where he was Master of the Games. He was young, attractive and, by all accounts, a fabulous dancer. Sir John Perrot remarked cynically that Hatton had come to court 'by the galliard' (a popular Eliza-bethan dance in which the men leap and strut), and the antiquarian William Camden ascribed Hatton's favour to the fact he was 'young and of a comely tallness of body and amiable countenance'.

By 1565, Hatton was regularly appearing in court jousts, wear-ing Elizabeth's Tudor rose engraved on his armour. He entered Parliament in 1571 and, through his proximity to the Queen, soon became her spokesman. He also represented her in Scotland at the baptism of the future James VI and then at the trial of the Duke of Norfolk in 1572. In 1574 he was given a title to match his status, succeeding Sir Francis Knollys as Captain of the Queen's Guard. He was knighted in 1577 and soon after made Vice Chamberlain of the Royal Household and a member of the Privy Council. As Vice Chamberlain, it was Hatton who made the arrangements for Elizabeth's yearly progresses. In a great many ways, Hatton had become indispensable to Elizabeth well before he was given his highest accolade of Lord Chancellor of England in April 1587.

There was, however, more between Hatton and Elizabeth than merely a professional relationship. Nearly all of Elizabeth I's courtiers considered themselves possible suitors, but Hatton seems to have genuinely been in love. His letters to her are extraordinarily ardent, filled with melodramatic, almost ineloquent, passion. In June 1573, he wrote to her:

> to lack you is more than hell's torment... My heart is full of woe... Would God I were with you but for one hour...

Passion overcometh me. I can write no more. Love me; for
I love you.... Ten thousand thousand farewells...

They had been separated for two days.

He was also a jealous lover, and was upset by the Queen's atten-
tions to other men. In 1572, he wrote to his friend Edward Dyer
for advice on how to manage the Queen's fickle attachments. Dyer
sensibly instructed him to refrain from chastisement, and instead
'joyfully to commend such things as should be in her, as though
they were in her indeed', and wait and see 'whether the Queen will
make an apple or a crab of you'.

Tudor courtship, Hatton's bold letters notwithstanding, could
also be highly cryptic and was governed by the complex laws of
courtly love. Elizabeth affectionately dubbed Hatton 'Lidds',
perhaps because of his sultry, hooded eyes, so he sometimes signed
his letters with two dotted triangles. Her other name for him was
'Sheep', while Oxford was known by his crest of a boar and Ralegh
by a corrupted version of his first name. These sobriquets explain
both Hatton's letter to Elizabeth urging her to reserve her favour
'to the Sheep, he hath no tooth to bite; where[as] the Boar's tusk
may both rase and tear', and Elizabeth's message to him in 1582
to remember 'she was a Shepherd, and then you might think how
dear her sheep was unto her'. Once, she sent him a dove, a symbol
of the receding floodwaters in Genesis, as an indication that
'Water' was no threat to him either. Theirs was a tender relationship, and Elizabeth was right to prefer him: unlike Oxford or
Ralegh, Hatton never married and stayed loyal to Elizabeth until
his death.

It was in the hope of playing host to Elizabeth that Hatton
bought Kirby, and later built Holdenby. He chose well. Kirby
embodied cutting-edge Renaissance architectural ideas of symmetry and balance, and classical features including a loggia and giant

pilasters (flattened columns) across the north façade of the inner courtyard. It is also ornately decorated and designed to impress.

Kirby is a grand affair, with an outer forecourt, graced by two flamboyant gateways added by Hatton, and a large inner courtyard that housed the Great Hall, the courtiers' lodgings and the Long Gallery. As you enter the gatehouse and walk through the loggia, you'll see ahead of you the south wing with the Great Hall to the right, and the buttery and service rooms to the left. Notice that the two sides are intended to look identical, even though the long window on the left is entirely superfluous. At the centre is the porch, which is elaborately carved, with nine small columns across the gable. Built by Stafford, it bears the date 1572, and his knot and motto, '*Je seray loyal*', 'I will be loyal': it could have been Hatton's own. Inside, the plaster ceiling displays Hatton's crest: the hind. Other doorframes around the court are carved with foliage and other emblems of the Staffords.

The Great Hall is one of the parts of Kirby to retain its ceiling, which helps conjure up its original state. Blue panels with unpainted oak beams recreate its original appearance. Stairs lead up from the hall to what was once the Long Gallery: a small section of the plaster decoration of the original ceiling of the gallery survives. Hatton's real legacy at Kirby is, however, the state suite, with the Great Withdrawing Chamber and Best Bedchamber built in hope of that all-important visitor. It was here that James I stayed when he visited in 1619. Although the interiors were significantly altered in the eighteenth century, the original double bay windows remain one of Kirby's most stunning features, and must be seen from the gardens to be appreciated. They were a magnificent state-ment of intent, but Hatton had little opportunity to enjoy them. In a letter of 1583 he planned his first visit to Kirby and added 'leaving my other shrine, I mean Holdenby, still unseen, until that holy saint may sit in it to whom it is dedicated'.

Sadly, Hatton's 'holy saint' never made it to either Kirby or Holdenby. The cost of building these abandoned palaces was ruinous; on Hatton's small salary as Vice Chamberlain of the Royal Household, he could not afford them. When he died, he left an enormous debt of £42,139 5s (today equivalent to £6.3 million). Elizabeth had ultimately made a 'crab' of him. Ironically, however, she did visit him four times at his London house, staying with him for five days and nursing him herself during his last illness in November 1591. He had given everything he had to serve her. It is poignant that his portrait [see NATIONAL PORTRAIT GALLERY] pictures him clutching her image in his fingers, devoted in perpetuity. Kirby is symbolic, therefore, of the whole of Hatton's life: a whimsical offering to a monarch, which was ultimately in vain.

Holdenby House

Sir Christopher Hatton's principal house was at Holdenby, where he built a vast and gorgeous palace between 1570 and 1583. It was elegantly symmetrical and had two grand courts, with mullioned windows, Doric columns and onion domes. Courtier Thomas Heneage described it in Hatton's day:

> For my own opinion, Holdenby is altogether the best house that hath been built in this age; and it more showeth the good judgement and honour of the builder than all the charge that hath been bestowed upon stones by the greatest persons and the best purses that hath been in my time.

Two archways from the Green or Base Court dated 1583, and very much like those at Kirby, survive. Hatton's debts meant that his descendants had to sell the house to the Crown, and much of the rest of Holdenby was demolished in 1650. The house that remains on the site is variously described as the kitchen wing of the original palace that was restored in the nineteenth century, or as being built in the nineteenth century in a style reminiscent of the old. Either way, the interiors are entirely nineteenth century, and this pretty house occupies only a small portion of the original great house.

THE ELIZABETHAN 'PRODIGY' HOUSES

Architectural fashion changed considerably in the second half of the sixteenth century. While Henry VIII had been a builder of palaces, Elizabeth I, well equipped with those her father had bequeathed her, let her suitors do the building for her. Across the country, they built mansions in the hope of impressing her; many of them were even laid out in the shape of an 'E' for 'Elizabeth'. The key aesthetic for these prodigy houses, such as Burghley House, Kirby Hall, Holdenby House and Hardwick Hall, was symmetry. From the outside, a house needed to reveal a graceful order and proportion. This meant drawing on the expertise of master masons (the word 'architect' only began to be introduced to England at this time) such as Robert Smythson, John Symonds and William Arnold, who constructed many of the best.

As well as impressing the Queen, a grand house could also demonstrate one's classical learning: this explains the rising fashion for classical columns and pilasters (flattened columns), and the replacement of the serpentine, corkscrew brick chimneys of the early Tudors (seen at Thornbury, Ludlow and

Framlingham) with chimneys instead shaped like columns, in small groups of twos and threes. Domes, cupolas, turrets and pinnacles all adorned the rooftops of these wonder houses, proclaiming wealth and magnificence from afar.

The Elizabethan courtier's house was expected to have big, decorative windows. The little rhyme, 'Hardwick Hall, more glass than wall' referred to this trend for huge expanses of expensive glass. The effect was to create houses that glittered brightly at night, lighting up the surrounding area so much that they became known as 'lantern houses'.

Inside, however, the purpose and arrangement of the rooms was much the same as the early Tudor great house. The Great Chamber became increasingly important and, as such, was usually the most richly dressed room in the house. Precious tapestries from the Low Countries were the wall covering of choice. Failing that, the early Tudor linenfold panelling (wood carved to mimic folds of cloth) was replaced by more ornate, ostentatious designs. Either way, the walls were surmounted by plasterwork or painted friezes. Ceilings dripped with plasterwork arranged into elaborate geometric patterns, and stained glass, inlaid panelling, flamboyant overmantles, coats of arms and other heraldic devices displaying the family's powerful connections were on show for all to see. As Great Chambers were frequently on the first floor, the stairs too became more ornate. The classical Tudor staircase at Burghley House is a splendid example of this.

Another Elizabethan addition was the Long Gallery. These had been around earlier in the century – Lord Sandys added one to the The Vyne in the 1520s and Henry VIII installed one at Nonsuch Palace in 1538 – but they really took off in the last decades of Elizabeth's reign. They were places to exercise indoors in poor weather, and even when it was sunny: for both men and women of high status, pale, alabaster skin was desirable. Combine a long gallery with decorative oriel windows, as at Montacute House, and you have a room with a view.

East of
England

St John's and Trinity Colleges
Cambridge, Cambridgeshire

'John Dee, a married priest,
given to magic and uncanny arts.'
Secret (and erroneous) report sent to Jesuit Francis Borgia, 1568

Many of the colleges of Oxford and Cambridge are rich in Tudor architecture and history, but there are two neighbouring colleges in Cambridge that are worth particular attention. The gorgeous red-bricked front of St John's was built in 1515 by John Fisher, Bishop of Rochester to honour Lady Margaret Beaufort, Henry VII's mother. On its Great Gate, two yales (mythical creatures that are part goat, part antelope, part elephant) proudly bear her coat of arms. In 1546, Henry VIII amalgamated two earlier colleges with a new one to create Trinity, now the largest college in Cambridge. Trinity's Great Gate of 1530 flaunts a statue of its founder with an orb and what should be a sceptre (the sceptre was stolen long ago, however, and ignominiously replaced with a chair leg). The two colleges are between them responsible for educating many famous alumni, including a trifecta of Williams

(Cecil, Wordsworth and Wilberforce); Isaac Newton; and Lord Byron; while there is one person whose story they share: the fascinating, enigmatic and mysterious Dr John Dee.

Dee – astronomer, mathematician, astrologer, cartographer, alchemist, secret agent and magician – is without doubt one of the most colourful characters of the Tudor, or any, period. Dee joined St John's in 1542 at the age of fifteen to read for his undergraduate degree. St John's would have looked very similar to how it looks today, at least in the first courtyard (First Court), which already had the stunning red-brick east wing that can be seen from the street and the ornate carved Tudor rose and portcullis above the entrance to Screens Passage. Dee would have studied in the college's first library, to the left of Great Gate as you enter, on the first floor. An additional brick courtyard, Second Court, was constructed in Dee's lifetime in 1598–99 (look out for the gutter heads spelling out the year of completion), with two fashionable oriel windows and a long gallery on the first floor of the north side, which retains its Elizabethan plaster ceiling and wood panelling.

In recognition of his success at St John's, Dee was elected a Fellow and Under-Reader in Greek at next-door Trinity in 1546. Fifty years later, in 1593, Trinity was substantially overhauled by its master, Thomas Nevile, who moved the clock tower from its original position by the sundial to create Great Court – which was the largest courtyard in Europe – and added Queen's Gate at the far side of the court, with its statue of Elizabeth I. But the Trinity of Dee's youth is not all gone. Henry VIII had created Trinity out of King's Hall and Michaelhouse, and the medieval buildings of King's Hall are still standing, including part of the cloister walkway and Vigani's Room. This room has remained essentially unchanged since the time of Richard II while, in the early eighteenth century, it was used as a laboratory by Isaac Newton himself. The spandrel at the entrance arch bears the arms of Richard III. One can imagine

Dee looking up at King's Hall or pacing on the Bowling Green, then the Fellows' Garden, as he prepared to stage his production of Aristophanes's *Pax* with its mechanical flying scarab beetle – the act that first convinced everyone he was a conjuror.

In these early years, Dee was furiously absorbing knowledge about science, astrology and mathematics, which he was later to align with alchemy, magic and the supernatural. People like Dee gave rise to the concept of the Renaissance man, in an age where it was still possible to be expert in many fields of knowledge that were not yet fully separated by the rigid divisions that characterise them today. He visited the Continent soon after his election to Trinity and met the famed cartographer Gerardus Mercator. Dee returned with two Mercator globes and various wonderful mathematical instruments that he donated to the college. After Trinity, he spent a further two years studying at the University of Louvain, and in 1550 was asked to lecture, to packed halls, in Paris.

Dee's activities soon found him in need of financial patronage to continue his scholarship. William Cecil, Lord Burghley recommended him to Edward VI in 1551 and from this, Dee received an ongoing living from two rectories. He did not initially favour so well under Mary. He was arrested in 1555 for calculating the 'nativities' of Mary, her husband Philip and the Princess Elizabeth in order to cast their horoscopes, and accused of conjuring and witchcraft. Here we have the first indication of Dee's incredible, persuasive charm: he convinced the fearsome Bishop Bonner of his orthodoxy and, rather than burning for heresy, was named Bonner's chaplain. He was even commissioned by Mary to collect and preserve the ancient and medieval manuscripts dispersed from the monasteries by the Reformation, which became the basis of an extraordinary library: by 1583, with 3,000 books and 1,000 manuscripts, Dee had the largest private library in England. Nor did his favour with Mary hamper his relations with the new monarch,

Elizabeth, whose handlers hired him to calculate the most astrologically auspicious day for Elizabeth's coronation.

Dee's work was developing a reputation. His *Propaeduemata Aphoristica*, published in 1558, explored what might be called astrological physics: the influence of the movements of the sun, moon and planets on earthly events, and the forces of attraction in the cosmos. From the perspective of the modern mind, his thinking was part scientific: he was interested in the ebb and flow of tides, as if prefiguring Newton's work on gravity; and part magical: he believed the rays emanating from these heavenly bodies could affect human souls.

In an age when the lines between what was science and what was magic were less clear than today, Dee was vulnerable to the charge that he was a 'conjuror' – something he always strongly denied. As he explained in his 'Mathematical preface' to an English translation of Euclid's *Elements of Geometrie*, he was simply interested in putting mathematical principles into practice. Science and magic also mixed in Dee's increasing preoccupation with alchemy. In 1565, he settled in Mortlake, Surrey, and built laboratories in which to search for the philosopher's stone – the fabled substance that would turn lead into gold. Ten years later, Elizabeth I paid him a visit at a most inopportune time: the day that Dee was burying his wife, Katherine. Nevertheless, he found time to show her some of his magical equipment including a distorting mirror, which might be the black obsidian mirror that can be seen today in the British Museum. (Dee soon remarried, to Jane Fromond of Cheam, who was thirty years his junior.)

Dee was also called on for his geographical and navigational skills. In 1580, he presented two rolls to the Queen and Lord Burghley 'proving' that early Britons, including King Arthur, had visited North America which, he argued, gave England rights to conquest and colonisation in the New World: a brilliant piece of *ex post facto* history serving political interests. Remarkably, he was the first to coin the term 'British Impire' (in its original spelling). He was also frequently consulted on the search for passages through the north-east and north-west, and advised Martin Frobisher, who brought back a piece of ore from the New World that was mistakenly believed to be gold. It was in this role as 'intelligencer' on new lands and voyages that he may have worked as a secret agent for Elizabeth I. He signed his secret messages to the Queen with two zeros and a reverse long-division sign, making him the original '007'.

Things began to go wrong for Dee in 1582. In his alchemical search, he became obsessed with the esoteric world of scrying (almost literally crystal ball gazing), and was assisted by a man of dubious integrity called Edward Kelley. Kelley and Dee believed they could receive knowledge direct from angels that had been lost to mankind since the prophet Enoch. Over the next seven years, the pair became inseparable, and their search for the secret of transmuting metals into gold took them as far away as Bohemia and Poland. They finally fell out after Kelley received the message that he and Dee should hold everything in common, including swapping wives for one night.

Dee returned home destitute in 1589, and things deteriorated from there: his library and laboratory had been ransacked; his brother-in-law refused to return his house; and his eight children needed feeding. Little is known of his life in his later years, when his diary falls silent, except that forced by poverty he took a post as Warden of Christ's College, Manchester, where many of his children and his wife died of the plague in March 1605.

Dee died in 1609. Despite his many works and great renown, his early promise, which first emerged at St John's and Trinity, was never fully realised. He spent his life and brilliance chasing white rabbits, but found only dead ends.

❀

Other Tudor treasures to see: Trinity has a copy, after Holbein, of the portrait of Henry VIII from the Whitehall Mural, which presides over the hall. Here, too, are portraits of Francis Bacon; Robert Devereux, Earl of Essex; and Mary I in 1554, after Antonis Mor. The Elizabethan Master's Lodge also has a Tudor drawing room that contains portraits of all six of Henry VIII's wives: this is open to the public once a year. Trinity Chapel was completed in 1567, although the woodwork is baroque and Georgian. In Vigani's Room are Elizabethan bowls, made of negrum (a tropical hard wood), and the Wren Library, designed by Sir Christopher Wren in the seventeenth century, contains great treasures including, on display, a copy of Shakespeare's first folio.

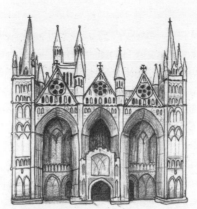

Peterborough Cathedral
Cambridgeshire

*'I beseech you for the love that has been between us,
and the love of God, let me have some justice.'*

Peterborough Cathedral is the final resting place of Katherine of Aragon: possibly the most abused and neglected Queen in England's history.

People have worshipped on the site of Peterborough Cathedral since 655. The current cathedral (it was an abbey until 1541) was started in 1118 after a fire destroyed an earlier building. With its beautiful thirteenth-century Gothic west front, this striking cathedral looks very much as it would have done when Katherine of Aragon was buried here in 1536. Even the early sixteenth-century blue and gold starred ceiling at the east end above the High Altar and the intricate vaulted ceiling of the New Building would have been in place.

Although it is also the former burial place of Mary, Queen of Scots (her son, James VI and I, removed her body to Westminster Abbey in 1612), it is Katherine's grave that has become a place of pilgrimage. When I last visited, someone had laid pomegranates, fresh flowers and palm crosses on her tomb. The cathedral still holds a remembrance service for her every year in January. There is still sympathy for this constant, faithful but abandoned first wife after 500 years, and after what she went through, who would begrudge her this honour?

Katherine, born 'Catalina' in December 1485, was the fifth child of Ferdinand of Aragon and Isabella of Castile. Her early life was spent travelling through Spain with her illustrious parents, and she lived at the Palace of the Alhambra from 1499 to 1501. She later adopted the pomegranate, the symbol of Granada, as her badge.

At the age of three, she was betrothed to the English prince, Arthur. Since the wedding was scheduled to take place after Arthur turned fourteen, Katherine lived her entire life knowing she would be Queen of England. Highly educated, with pretty auburn hair, she left her parents and her homeland in September 1501, as a teenager, landing in Plymouth on 2 October. Apart from a very brief visit by her sister, Juana, in February 1506, Katherine would never see her family again.

The would-be Queen arrived in London on 12 November 1501 in a magnificent procession. Just two days later she married her young bridegroom at St Paul's. But within six months, Katherine was a widow: Arthur died on 2 April 1502 [see LUDLOW CASTLE]. Later, when her marriage to Arthur's brother, Henry, was challenged, she would swear that her marriage to Arthur had never been consummated.

Katherine was moved to Durham House in London and, on 23 June 1503, it was agreed that she would marry the new heir, Henry, when he reached fifteen, three years later. So she waited. It must have been a terrible time for her. Consider: widowed, purposeless, her planned marriage far from certain, separated from her family in a country where she did not speak the language and kept in relative poverty by her father-in-law: it is no wonder that she was frequently ill. A recent biography by Giles Tremlett suggests that during these years Katherine displayed the symptoms of an eating disorder, such as anorexia nervosa, and regularly went several months without menstruating. In the spring of 1509, she wrote to her father, 'it is impossible for me any longer to endure what I've gone through... I'm still suffering from the unkindness of the King and the manner in which he treats me'. She begged to return to Spain to join a convent.

Luckily for her, Henry VII died on 21 April 1509, and the new King, Henry VIII, promptly married Katherine on 11 June at Greenwich Palace. Observers noted that the young couple were very much in love, a claim borne out by the fact that Katherine was frequently pregnant. Sadly, however, she miscarried in January 1510 and had a stillborn boy in 1514, while two children died in infancy, including a son and heir, Henry, at seven weeks old in 1511.

Henry evidently trusted his wife: in 1513, when he went to war in France, Katherine was appointed Queen-Regent and Governor of the Realm. In this role, she presided over the war with Scotland, including the slaughter at the Battle of Flodden Field.

In February 1516, Katherine finally gave birth to a healthy baby, Mary, but by the early 1520s she was no longer regarded as attractive, and it was becoming clear that she was now infertile. It must have been especially galling for her when Henry's bastard son Henry Fitzroy [see FRAMLINGHAM] was titled in 1525.

Katherine turned a blind eye to Henry's love affairs but, in 1527, she would have realised that his latest infatuation was of a different order, after hearing about a secret tribunal held by Cardinal Wolsey to investigate their marriage. Her suspicions were confirmed when Henry paid a visit to her in June: he told her that he believed they had been living in mortal sin for the past eighteen years, and must now live apart.

The story of Henry's 'Great Matter', his love affair with Anne Boleyn and 'divorce' from Katherine, with the justification that Leviticus 20:21 forbade a man to take his brother's wife for fear of childlessness, is very familiar. Yet, it is still remarkably poignant. Katherine's appeal, on her knees, to her husband at the trial at Blackfriars under Cardinal Lorenzo Campeggio in May 1529 is heartrending:

> I beseech you for the love that has been between us, and the love of God, let me have some justice… This twenty years or more I have been your true wife and by me you have had divers children, although it hath pleased God to call them out of this world…

After twenty-two years of marriage, she saw Henry for the last time in July 1531 when he left to go hunting with Anne; he did not even wish Katherine goodbye. Soon after, she was also separated from her daughter: Katherine was sent to The More, Hertfordshire, while Mary was sent to Richmond. They would never see each other again, despite Katherine's pleading to be allowed to do so when Mary was ill in September 1534 and February 1535.

The final indignities came in September 1532, when Henry ordered Katherine to hand over her jewels for Anne's use, and in June 1533, when Anne was crowned queen and Katherine demoted to Princess Dowager, a title she never accepted. Although Rome pronounced her marriage to Henry 'valid and canonical' in March 1534, it was too little, too late.

At Kimbolton in Huntingdonshire, in December 1535, Katherine grew very ill. When her loyal friend Maria de Salinas, Lady Willoughby joined her on 29 December, Katherine had not eaten or slept properly for days, and the pain in her stomach was so great she could barely sit up. After a brief remission, she died at 2 p.m.

on 7 January 1536. Her embalmer found all her organs to be healthy except her heart, which was 'quite black and hideous to look at'. Poison was suspected, but it was probably cancer.

After lying in state, her coffin, covered in black velvet and drawn by six horses, processed from Kimbolton to Peterborough Abbey. On 29 January, three funeral masses were said; neither Henry nor Mary attended.

Katherine's original tomb was destroyed in 1643 by Oliver Cromwell's troops. The modern black slab was given in 1895 in response to an appeal to those with the name of Katherine. It is engraved with the coats of arms of sixteenth-century England and Spain, Katherine's pomegranate badge, and the words:

Here lies the body of Katharine of Aragon Queen of England: first wife of King Henry VIII: who died at Kimbolton Castle, on the 8th day of January 1536 aged 49 years.

Hatfield Old Palace
Hertfordshire

*'The burden that is fallen upon me makes me amazed,
and yet, considering I am God's creature ordained to
obey his appointment, I will thereto yield.'*

Hatfield was Elizabeth I's childhood home, but it doesn't look exactly as she might remember it. Five years after her death, another great house was built at Hatfield, giving us not one, but two great houses – Hatfield Old Palace and Hatfield House – to visit. Of all the Elizabethan royal residences, Hatfield is the most strongly identified with her, and for good reason.

One of Henry VII's ministers, Cardinal Morton, Bishop of Ely built Hatfield Palace as a grand episcopal residence between 1485 and 1497. Rather like an Oxbridge college, it was designed as four great buildings of russet-red brick around a central quadrangle. Today only one side remains: the Great (or Banqueting) Hall.

Like Cardinal Wolsey's house at Hampton Court, Henry VIII thought nothing of appropriating the Bishop's palace as he saw fit, seizing ownership of it during the suppression of the monasteries. He had, after all, already started to use it as a residence for his children.

At the tender age of three months, in December 1533, the young Princess Elizabeth was established in an independent household at Hatfield Palace. Soon afterwards, her elder half-sister Mary's own household was dissolved and Mary was sent, to her chagrin, to join Elizabeth. This humiliation was made all the worse by the fact that the couple in charge of the new joint household were Sir John and Lady Shelton, Anne Boleyn's aunt and uncle. Anne herself visited her daughter Elizabeth in spring 1534 to check that she had settled in.

Royal childhoods were peripatetic affairs, constantly on the move from one palace to another, but even after Elizabeth was made motherless and downgraded to the title 'Lady Elizabeth', she returned repeatedly to Hatfield. It is here that we can imagine her being taught by her tutors, William Grindal, and later, the classicist Roger Ascham. Unusually for the age, she received the same education as her brother Edward, learning Latin and Greek, French and Italian. She read, Ascham wrote, 'almost the whole of Cicero, and a great part of Livy'. For relaxation, the sprawling deer park at Hatfield allowed for hunting and walking. For entertainment, Elizabeth had her own court of minstrels, fools and players. Elizabeth also learnt from Ascham a taste for animal and bird baiting.

After her father's death, Elizabeth was allowed by her brother Edward VI, with whom she had an amenable relationship, to take up official residence at Hatfield at Christmas 1548, and in September 1550, the ownership of Hatfield was formally granted to her. Her position during Mary's reign, however, was not quite so favourable, and after spending time in the Tower of London and a year under house arrest at Woodstock, she was only finally allowed to return to her estate at Hatfield in October 1555. It was here, famously, that she learnt that her half-sister had died, and that she had become queen.

Legend has it that on 17 November 1558, Elizabeth was walking in Hatfield deer park when a messenger found her under an oak tree and told her that she was now queen. Elizabeth is said to have responded with the words of Psalm 118, 'This is the Lord's doing; it is marvellous in our eyes.' Sadly, this is probably apocryphal, as only one commentator records it, seventy years after the event. Another account, by Sir John Harington, recalls Elizabeth saying, only somewhat less poetically, that she was sorrowful for her sister's death and 'amazed' at the great burden which had fallen to her, but she was 'God's creature' and it was His design.

Three days later, under the marvellous chestnut and oak framed ceiling of the Great Hall of Hatfield Palace, the new Queen Elizabeth held her first ever Council of State. Her first act was to appoint Sir William Cecil (later Lord Burghley) as Secretary of State. On 23 November 1558, Elizabeth left Hatfield in a grand procession of 1,000 courtiers to travel into London to be crowned queen. She was cheered all the way by the large crowds that lined the streets to see her.

Hatfield now became one of Elizabeth's many palaces, and somewhere she stayed while on progress. After her death, James I offered Burghley's son, Robert Cecil, Hatfield in exchange for the palatial Theobalds: Cecil agreed, and promptly demolished three-quarters of the palace in order to build a beautiful Jacobean house, reusing the old bricks. He did not forget Elizabeth entirely: the new house was built in the shape of a letter E.

In Hatfield House, there are also several other reminders of Elizabeth's presence. Look out for the exquisite Ermine and Rainbow portraits of Elizabeth by Nicholas Hilliard (1585) and Isaac Oliver (c.1600). Both are rich in symbolism, including the ermine wearing a little gold crown as a symbol of royalty, the rainbow symbolising peace and Elizabeth's cloak festooned with eyes and ears: she is one who sees and hears all. Hatfield also houses a wide-brimmed straw hat, yellow silk stockings and long-fingered gloves, all said to have belonged to Elizabeth, as well as a great stash of her letters in the archives. Most intriguingly, in the library is a twenty-two-yard illuminated parchment roll tracing the ancestry of Elizabeth back to Adam and Eve.

The remaining Great Hall of the Old Palace did not fare well. For many years, it was used as stables, and all the ground-floor windows were bricked in. Still, it is rather remarkable that the land and house remained in the hands of the descendants of the one man who featured so prominently in Elizabeth's reign as Queen: William Cecil, Elizabeth's most trusted adviser. He stood by her side at Hatfield on that momentous day of her first Council of State in November 1558, and his family have lived at Hatfield ever since.

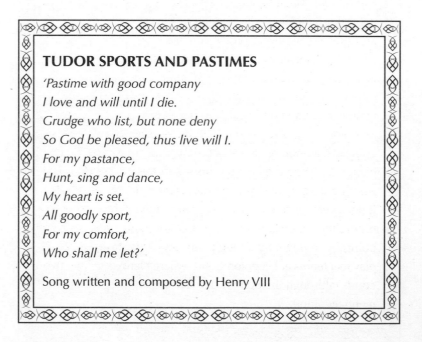

TUDOR SPORTS AND PASTIMES

'Pastime with good company
I love and will until I die.
Grudge who list, but none deny
So God be pleased, thus live will I.
For my pastance,
Hunt, sing and dance,
My heart is set.
All goodly sport,
For my comfort,
Who shall me let?'

Song written and composed by Henry VIII

The games of choice for the Tudor nobility were jousting, hunting, archery, tennis, bowls, quoits and skittles. Henry VIII excelled at them all.

Of these, jousting held a special place. It was the central event of a tournament, where two armoured riders on horseback charged at each other on either side of a wooden barrier (the tilt) holding a long lance pinned between their right arm and body, poised to hit the other knight. Striking the lance against the body or head of the other rider scored points, but the ultimate goal was to unhorse one's opponent. It demanded strength, accuracy, speed and an almost foolhardy fearlessness: when knights and kings jousted, they jousted for real. In 1559, Henri II, the King of France, died of septicaemia as a result of a jousting accident when a splintering lance entered his visor and pierced his eye. Foreign ambassadors commented on Henry VIII's expertise at the tilt, but it was his downfall, too: an accident while jousting in 1536 gave him a lifelong suppurating ulcer in his leg, an injury that directly affected his temperament and contributed to his obesity.

Henry VIII also loved to hunt – stags, not foxes. A complete glutton for the sport, he rode out early and came back late, tiring eight or ten horses in the course of a day. Another kingly sport was tennis. Henry played a complex indoor version now known as 'real tennis', which involves hitting the ball around the walls of the court, and scoring points by hitting it into netted windows. It is still possible to play real tennis at Hampton Court, where Henry VIII built two courts (although the current one dates from the early seventeenth century).

But sports were not necessarily for the masses. In perhaps one of the most mirthless (and unsportsmanlike?) laws ever passed by any ruler, an Act of Parliament in 1512 banned the lower orders from playing tennis, bowls or closh (skittles). Thirty years later, a new act reiterated that no 'artisan, husbandman, labourer, fisherman, waterman or servingman' was allowed to play tennis, dice, cards, bowls, skittles or quoits except at Christmas. It also reprimanded the 'many subtle and inventative and crafty persons' who had devised new games to replace the forbidden ones!

A game commonly, but illegally, played by the lower orders was football. Other than scoring by putting the ball between the opponent's goalposts, it was nothing like the modern game. Indeed, there were not actually any rules per se: the ball could be handled, fighting was normal, there was no limit to the number of men on each team and goalposts could easily be several miles apart. Such was its aggression that Sir Thomas Elyot in his 1531 *The Book Named the Governor* wrote that it was 'to be utterly abjected of all noblemen... wherein is nothing but beastly fury and extreme violence; whereof proceedeth hurt, and consequently rancour and malice do remain with them that be wounded'.

The Tudors loved blood sports. Elizabeth I was particularly fond of bear baiting. Bears were chained to a post and set on by mastiffs. The main bear pit in London was in Southwark, close to the site of the original Globe theatre. Archaeologists have found bones from old bears, smashed dogs' skulls and a layer of hazelnuts, the Elizabethan equivalent of popcorn, near Bear Gardens, SE1. Robert Laneham's description of the bear baiting at Kenilworth in 1575 is enough to make a modern reader shudder at what passed for pleasure for our ancestors:

> If the dog in pleading would pluck the bear by the throat, the bear with traverse would claw him again by the scalp... therefore, with fending & proving, with plucking & tugging, scratching & biting, by plain tooth & nail on one side and the other, such expense of blood and leather [skin] was there between them, as a month's licking (I think) will not recover... it was a sport very pleasant...

The Elizabethans apparently did not register any sense of animal cruelty. The Privy Council even intervened in 1591 to protect bear baiting, and prevent plays being scheduled against the usual Thursday baiting session 'because in divers places the players do use to recite their plays to the great hurt and destruction of the game of bear-baiting and like pastimes which are maintained for Her Majesty's pleasure'.

Elizabeth I also, like her father, took great pleasure in the less violent pastimes of music and dance. Henry VIII was a composer who played many musical instruments. On his death, he left a large collection of viols, virginals (a keyboard instrument of the harpsichord family), flutes, clavichords, lutes, shawms (early oboes), sackbuts (early trombones), citterns (a stringed instrument like a mandolin) and recorders. Elizabeth I herself could play the lute and the virginals, and patronised composers such as William Byrd and Thomas Tallis. But if she liked to play music, Elizabeth loved to dance, choosing either the stately, serene pavane, or the energetic galliard, which

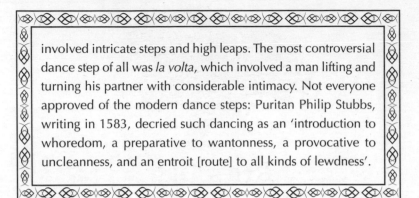

involved intricate steps and high leaps. The most controversial dance step of all was *la volta*, which involved a man lifting and turning his partner with considerable intimacy. Not everyone approved of the modern dance steps: Puritan Philip Stubbs, writing in 1583, decried such dancing as an 'introduction to whoredom, a preparative to wantonness, a provocative to uncleanness, and an entroit [route] to all kinds of lewdness'.

Kett's Oak
Wymondham, Norfolk

'Woe be to you that join house to house, and field to field!
Shall ye alone inhabit the earth?'

A t the side of the B1172, the former main road from Wymondham (pronounced 'Windham') to Norwich, stands a tree
known as Kett's Oak. Now propped up and filled with concrete to
keep it standing, it is said to be the very oak at which Robert Kett,
a wealthy tradesman from Wymondham, gathered the Norfolk rebel
armies in July 1549 before marching on Norwich (then England's
second city), in protest against religious, social and economic
changes that the common folk found oppressive and unfair. The
rebellion plunged Norfolk into great social crisis and, before it was
over, the county had experienced intense upheaval, vicious fighting
and the execution of as many men within a couple of weeks as died
in the whole of 'Bloody' Mary I's reign as martyrs. It was a pivotal
moment in the history of Tudor England, and the story starts at
the oak that still stands today.

Norfolk was not the only county to rebel in 1549. In many
parts of the country, ordinary people in Edward VI's reign were
angry about rising social inequality, religious changes imposed

from above and a rapidly deteriorating economic situation. Most peasants paid rents to their lord of the manor, and suspected their lords of being increasingly corrupt, greedy and oppressive – with good reason. Lords were raising rents and dues, turning vast swathes of land into deer parks for the leisure of hunting and, worst of all, enclosing common lands to graze their sheep. The common lands were a vital resource for poor people: a place to gather firewood, graze the odd cow and forage for wild berries and fruit. 'Stealing' common lands through enclosure was therefore seen as a great evil, which would lead to depopulation and pauperisation. Hugh Latimer, Bishop of Worcester railed against it in one sermon, 'Woe be to you that join house to house, and field to field! Shall ye alone inhabit the earth?'

This was coupled with unpopular religious changes under Edward VI's fervent Protestant government. The state was considered to be meddling in the affairs of the Church and handing the shared belongings of the Church to avaricious gentry in the aftermath of the dissolution of the monasteries. Both issues concerned social conflict, and the rights of the nobility and the Crown to interfere in the traditional, reciprocal relations between rich and poor. Matters came to a head in 1549 as food prices had soared, impoverishing new swathes of society.

On 6 July, crowds gathered in Wymondham to watch the *Wymondham Game*, a traditional play about the life of Sir Thomas à Becket. In festive spirit, and having heard news of uprisings in Kent and Cambridge, a commotion arose, targeting John Flowerdew, a minor gentleman who had acted as the King's agent in stripping Wymondham Abbey of its assets following the dissolution. Next, the crowd turned on his enemy, Robert Kett, who had initially led the opposition to Flowerdew.

Kett was a wealthy yeoman, who owned land and a profitable tanning business, and was thus an unlikely rebel. But he quickly persuaded the crowd not to target him, but instead to adopt him and his brother William as their leaders. Kett led the crowd to congregate at the oak, and on 9 July, they set off for Norwich, liberating enclosures, capturing gentlemen and amassing support along the way. By the time they reached the city, the mob numbered at least 8,000 men strong (some said as many as 20,000). The rebels set up camp on Mousehold Heath (an expanse of common land to the east of the city that still exists), with Kett himself occupying the former palace of the Earl of Surrey.

Establishing a council under another tree, dubbed the Oak of Reformation, Kett's rebels drew up a list of their grievances that they sent to Protector Somerset, Edward VI's regent. A royal herald was sent back granting a pardon for those who would disband. Refusing to believe he had done anything requiring pardon, Kett turned it down. Consequently, he and his followers were officially branded traitors. That being the case, they decided to launch a dramatic armed attack on the city of Norwich.

They were, at first, remarkably successful. The rebel fire trounced the city's retaliations, and they managed to seize the municipal artillery. When the Crown sent a small force of 1,500 men under Sir William Parr, Marquess of Northampton (brother to the late Kateryn Parr) in late July, the rebels were able to overwhelm them in the resultant clashes. Northampton's right-hand man, Lord Sheffield, was killed in battle by a butcher called Fulke, and the royal forces fled in dismay. The rebels captured more artillery, took control of the city and terrorised the gentry.

By mid-August, the King's Council redoubled their efforts and assembled an impressive force of at least 6,000 footmen and 1,500 cavalry, led by John Dudley, Earl of Warwick. On arrival at Norwich in late August, and after failed peace negotiations with Kett, Warwick forced his way into the city. For the next three days and nights, battle raged through the narrow lanes of Norwich. In the city, where cavalry and artillery could not easily be deployed, the rebels, with their local knowledge of the crooked, warren-like streets, held the advantage.

But on 26 August, Warwick received back-up. One thousand foreign mercenaries cut off the rebels' supply lines into the country-side, and Kett and his army were forced to move from Mousehold Heath down towards the valley of Dussindale. The next day, the two sides engaged in a vicious pitched battle. Each bombarded the other with arrow fire and gunshot. While the rebels had the benefit of numbers, the royal forces had cavalry and, by sunset, the rebel ranks had been broken. Kett fled, but was captured the next day. It is not known how many died (accounts vary from 1,000 to 10,000 dead), but all agreed that the losses were horrifying.

For the next ten days, Warwick remained in Norwich, exacting his retribution. Under martial law, he authorised the executions of at least 300 rebels: in one area, at the Magdalen gates (which were where Magdalen Street meets Magpie Road today) thirty rebels were hanged, drawn and quartered on just one day.

Kett and his brother were interrogated in Norwich Castle, transported to London to stand trial in November and convicted of high treason, before being taken back to Norfolk to receive punishment of the most awful kind. On 7 December, William Kett was hanged from Wymondham Abbey's West Tower, while Robert was hanged in chains – in the gibbet irons over several days – from Norwich Castle.

The town sign of Wymondham depicts Kett, while everything in the town, from schools to garden centres, bears his name. Kett is, appropriately, commemorated by a plaque on the former Becket Chapel (once owned by the abbey and now Wymondham Arts Centre), next door to the fifteenth-century Green Dragon Inn, which Kett and his rebels would have known.

The Shrine at Walsingham
Norfolk

*'For the King's Candle before Our Lady of Walsingham,
and to the Prior there for his salary, NIL.'*

Walsingham is a small, peaceful, rural village in north Norfolk
that was once home to the most important shrine to the
Virgin Mary in Britain, and that still attracts hundreds of thousands
of visitors each year to walk in the footsteps of medieval and Tudor
monarchs on pilgrimage.

Legend has it that in the mid-eleventh century Richeldis de
Faverches had a vision of the Virgin Mary, who asked her to build
a replica of the Holy House at Nazareth in Norfolk, which she did.
In 1153, her son, Geoffrey, founded an Augustinian priory next
door. The Shrine of Our Lady at Walsingham was associated with
many miracles of healing; the relic that was held in highest regard
was the 'Milk of Our Lady', preserved in a vial on the High Altar.

Nothing today remains of the original shrine, but its place can
be seen in the grounds of the abbey (accessed through Shirehall
Museum), along with the Priory Gatehouse, magnificent fourteenth-century Great East Window, refectory, undercroft and twin

wells. These peaceful grounds, with their carpet of snowdrops at the beginning of spring, still have a tangible sense of awe and holiness. Walsingham also has the ruins of a Franciscan friary, a sixteenth-century octagonal pump house (which would have been the main water supply for the village) in the main square, many medieval and sixteenth-century timber-framed buildings and two modern shrines: a neo-Italianate Anglican shrine in town and a Roman Catholic shrine at the Slipper Chapel. The Slipper Chapel was built in 1325, and was a place where pilgrims would stop, say Mass and remove their shoes to walk barefoot for the last mile of their pilgrimage.

The height of Walsingham's fame came in Tudor times when it was common currency in moments of distress for people to call on 'Our Lady of Walsingham' for help and comfort, vowing to go on pilgrimage to see her if the danger passed.

Nor was Walsingham just for common people. Henry VII went on pilgrimage to Walsingham three times between 1486 and 1505. On his last visit, he took his son and heir, Henry, with him, marking the first visit of the man who would bring Walsingham to its tragic end. Henry VII even remembered Walsingham in his will, commissioning an image of himself kneeling, cast in silver gilt, to be given to the Lady Chapel at Walsingham. Henry VIII also made many generous payments and donations to Walsingham. In 1511, he donated a rich collar of rubies and £1 3s 4d to Walsingham, and contributed £20 for glazing the windows in the Lady Chapel. He also later made annual payments for a singing priest and the King's Candle.

Walsingham was an obvious place to go to mark victory and success. Henry VIII's first pilgrimage to Walsingham as king was made on 19 January 1511 to celebrate and give thanks for the birth of his son Henry (sadly the baby died at just seven weeks of age). Katherine of Aragon visited Walsingham to rejoice after the victorious battle of Flodden Field in 1513, and the shrine evidently remained in her affections as, in her will, she left a bequest to enable someone else to go to Walsingham on pilgrimage. Cardinal Wolsey, too, went on pilgrimage to Walsingham in 1517 having survived the sweating sickness, in order to thank the Virgin Mary and in the hope that she would 'correct the weakness of his stomach'.

Like all other abbeys and shrines, Walsingham suffered at Henry VIII's hands during the dissolution (see FOUNTAINS ABBEY and HAILES ABBEY), when the famous image of the Virgin Mary was taken to London to be burned. It was a great blow to English spirituality: who should one call on for help in times of trouble? Who praise in moments of victory?

Henry VIII's expenditure accounts sum it up most poignantly: 'September 29, 1538, For the King's Candle before Our Lady of Walsingham, and to the Prior there for his salary, NIL.'

The Church of St Mary's
Bury St Edmunds, Suffolk

*'Nature never formed anything more beautiful
and she exceeds no less in goodness and wisdom.'*
Erasmus's description of Mary Tudor, sister of Henry VIII

In the lovely town of Bury St Edmunds, at the corner of the precinct of the ruined medieval abbey, is the impressively large parish church that is the final resting place of Princess Mary Tudor, Queen of France, Duchess of Suffolk and Henry VIII's younger sister.

It is certainly a beautiful and peaceful place. Of particular note are the ceilings, which Mary would have known and which are a striking example of late medieval art. The hammer-beam ceiling with its carved angels, dating from around 1445, is impressive, but the red, gold and blue chancel ceiling, and the lozenged ceiling of John Baret's Chapel with its gold and mirrored stars that twinkle in the light, invite wonderment.

Mary's tomb lies in a quiet spot at the far eastern end of the church next to the altar. It seems an unassuming, even ignoble, grave for a woman who was daughter of a king, sister of a king, wife of a king and grandmother to a queen.

Mary was born to Henry VII and Elizabeth of York on 18 March 1496, their third daughter and fifth child of eight. Only four out of the couple's eight children lived beyond infancy, and when Mary was just six, one of her remaining brothers, Arthur, and her mother died within a few months of each other. Soon after, her sister, Margaret, left for Scotland to marry James IV. Mary must surely have been traumatised by the loss, and we know that she became close to her only surviving brother, Henry.

A princess of marriageable age was a precious commodity. In Mary's case, this was exaggerated by her great charm, graceful poise and exceptional good looks (an Italian observer described her as 'a nymph from heaven'). When she was eleven years old, terms were agreed for a marriage between the young princess and the son of Philip the Handsome, Prince Charles of Castile. The betrothal took place in December 1508 by proxy, with the Sieur de Berghes standing in for Mary's eight-year-old groom-to-be. Although Charles and Mary never met during their engagement, there was childish romance: he sent her a pendant of diamonds and pearls inscribed, 'Mary has chosen the best part, no one shall take it from her.'

After Philip the Handsome's death, Henry VIII renewed the treaty for Mary's engagement with Charles's grandfather, the Holy Roman Emperor, Maximilian. It stipulated that the wedding should take place before 15 May 1514. As the date approached, Mary's trousseau was prepared, including four coffers full of gold and silver plate. But Maximilian was considering other brides for his heir and the date passed. So, under instruction, on 30 July, Mary formally repudiated the marriage contract. A week later, ever obedient to the political concerns of her brother (and perhaps mindful of her motto, 'The will of God suffices me'), the beautiful eighteen-year-old princess promised to marry the feeble and pock-marked fifty-two-year-old King of France, Louis XII.

They were married by proxy on 18 August, with the Duc de Longueville representing Louis. The ceremony even went so far as to symbolise the consummation by the Duc pressing his bare leg against Mary as the couple laid side by side in bed, fully dressed. A second wedding took place in October once Mary had travelled to France, with both Louis and Mary dressed in gold brocade trimmed with ermine. Mary was then crowned Queen of France in the Abbey of St Denis on 5 November, before entering Paris the next day in a long and extravagant procession. The celebrations were followed by days of festivities, including jousting, at which a visiting Englishman, Charles Brandon, Duke of Suffolk, excelled: a fact which did not go unnoticed by the young bride.

Louis was very proud of his young wife, and even gave her the famous 'Mirror of Naples': a pendant with a diamond 'as big as a person's finger' and a pearl beneath that was 'the size of a pigeon's egg'. He wrote to Henry VIII on 20 December to say how delighted he was with his marriage. However, as contemporary commentators had feared, the union did not agree with his health. After less than three months of marriage to his energetic young bride, Louis died on 1 January 1515.

In accordance with French tradition, the widowed Mary, dressed in white robes, remained in a swathed room for forty days (earning her the title 'the White Queen'). The next in line to the throne, Louis XII's cousin and son-in-law Francis I, could not be crowned as king until it had become clear that she had not conceived a son (in sixteenth-century France, women were not allowed to inherit the throne).

Faced with the prospect of returning to England and yet another political match, Mary remembered the promise she had extracted from her brother that if she outlived Louis, she could marry after her own heart. Fortunately, her heart chose the very man who had been sent from England to fetch her: the man who had impressed her with his skill in the tiltyard, her brother's best friend, Charles Brandon, Duke of Suffolk. She persuaded him to marry her in an immediate, clandestine ceremony in mid-February.

Henry was furious when he heard the news – after all, it was a capital offence to marry a blood relation of the King without his permission, and both Mary and Suffolk had sworn not to marry (suggesting that Henry and Wolsey had noticed some earlier attraction between the two). Oaths had been broken. Yet, Henry evidently thawed, for he allowed them a second, public wedding in Paris in March, and on their return to England in May, he attended their – third – wedding at Greenwich. He could no longer remain angry at two people whom he held so dear. He did, however, make them promise to pay the vast annual fine of £2,000 (the equivalent today of roughly £759,000) for twelve years.

After a year of five weddings and a funeral, the Duchess of Suffolk retired from court to a quieter life at her house of Westhorpe in East Anglia, and bore Suffolk four children, three of whom survived: Henry, Frances and Eleanor Brandon. Frances would go on to become the mother of Lady Jane Grey.

The notable exception to Mary's country life was her radiant appearance at the Field of Cloth of Gold in 1520. Legend has it that her former fiancé, Charles, now the Holy Roman Emperor, wept at the sight of her great beauty, and even Francis I continued to hold a candle for his former step mother-in-law.

Mary differed with her brother on just one count: she did not approve of Anne Boleyn. Some even thought that it was the shock of her brother's marriage to Anne that killed her on 25 June 1533, twenty-five days after Anne's ostentatious coronation.

It was not intended that Mary should have so modest a grave. Her body lay in state for three weeks, and was borne in a grand funeral procession to be interred in Bury Abbey. Henry VIII also ordered a Requiem Mass to be said for her at Westminster Abbey.

Six years later, after the dissolution of Bury Abbey, her body was moved next door to St Mary's for protection, where just the top of her original tomb remains today: a simple, unadorned ledger slab. It was in 1784 – in the age of morbid curiosity – that her tomb was dismantled and reduced, her coffin opened and her embalmed body plundered for locks of her famously long fair hair (Kateryn Parr received the same treatment, see SUDELEY CASTLE).

It is perhaps with this dishonour in mind that in 1881 Queen Victoria commissioned a stained-glass window, in the south chapel of St Mary's, to chart the momentous story of Mary's life and its year of five weddings and glittering fame.

❁

Other Tudor sights to see: look out for the grave of John Reeve, who conducted Mary's funeral, was the last abbot of Bury Abbey and died just four months after the dissolution. Next door, the former neighbouring parish church of St James is now St Edmundsbury Cathedral: the nave was built by the Tudor architect John Wastell, who also designed King's College Chapel in Cambridge. Also worth visiting are the beautiful gardens in the ruins of the Abbey grounds, which are vast: Bury was once the fourth largest Benedictine monastery in Europe.

The Church of St Michael
Framlingham, Suffolk

'The late Duke of Richmond, our only bastard son.'

The quiet Suffolk market town of Framlingham seems an unlikely resting place for some of the most important figures of the Tudor age but, in fact, this is just one of its two claims to Tudor fame.

The large parish church of St Michael in Framlingham dates from the twelfth century. The fourteenth-century font and wall painting in the nave and beautiful fifteenth-century fan-vaulted oak and chestnut roof testify to its medieval heritage. But you're here for the chancel, which was built in the mid-sixteenth century as a mausoleum for tombs that had to be moved from their original place in Thetford Priory in Norfolk after the priory's dissolution in 1540. Buried here are members of a family at the centre of power in Tudor England: the Howards, dukes of Norfolk.

The Howard family started the Tudor period on the back foot: John Howard, the first Duke of Norfolk fought and died for Richard III – the losing side – at the Battle of Bosworth in 1485, but Thomas Howard, second Duke of Norfolk compensated by fighting for Henry VIII against the Scots at the Battle of Flodden

Field in 1513. The helmet he wore at Flodden can be seen high on the south wall of the chancel.

His son, grandson and great-grandson are among those buried here too. His son, also named Thomas Howard, the third Duke of Norfolk, was a powerful machinator during Henry VIII's reign, and succeeded in putting two of his nieces into the royal bed [see ARUNDEL CASTLE for more on the Howards]. He lies here in effigy, with a fantastically pointed beard, beside his first wife Anne Plantagenet (who, as a royal princess, and thus his superior in rank, lies, unusually, on the right). Their tomb is one of the finest examples of Renaissance sculpture in northern Europe, decorated as it is with figures of the saints carved into Italianate shell niches.

Nearby is the colourful alabaster tomb of his son: the poet, Henry Howard, Earl of Surrey and his wife, Lady Frances de Vere, surmounted by their effigies. Surrey was executed by Henry VIII in 1547 on a charge of high treason, and this monument was built by his second son, Henry Howard, Earl of Northampton, in 1614. His first son, Thomas, who became the fourth Duke of Norfolk, was also executed for treason in 1572 [see ARUNDEL CASTLE], and this Thomas's first two wives (who both died in childbirth) and daughter are buried here too.

The most important tomb in the church is, however, deceptively plain, though it is carved with a simple decorative frieze of Old Testament scenes, including Noah's Ark. This is the resting place of Henry Fitzroy, Duke of Richmond and Somerset, Lord High Admiral of England, head of the King's Council in the North and Lord Lieutenant of Ireland. He was also Henry VIII's illegitimate son and, for years, his only male heir.

Henry Fitzroy was born to Henry VIII's mistress, Elizabeth 'Bessie' Blount, in 1519. As his surname indicates (meaning 'son of the king'), the King openly acknowledged him and, during his entire lifetime, Fitzroy was the King's only son. He was also

Henry's only recognised illegtimate child: in a letter in April 1538, Henry VIII referred to Fitzroy as 'the late Duke of Richmond, our only bastard son'.

Fitzroy evidently looked like Henry VIII, with the same red hair and good looks, and he was probably brought up in the royal nursery. At the age of six, in 1525, he was awarded the double dukedom of Richmond and Somerset, making him the highest-ranking nobleman in the land. The title 'Somerset' was particularly notable, as it had been given in 1397 to John Beaufort, a royal bastard who was later legitimised.

Throughout his early teens, Richmond (as he was now known) regularly spent time at court with his father, who was observed by the French ambassador to be very fond of him. Henry spent money on his son's hobbies, buying him new arrows for archery and a lute for music-making: pursuits that must have reminded Henry of himself as a youth. Henry VIII also chose his son to represent him at important occasions, including a feast in honour of a visiting French admiral in 1534, and the execution of the three Carthusian monks in May 1535 [see CHARTERHOUSE].

Richmond had a close relationship with the Howards. When he was eleven years old, he was entrusted to the care of Henry Howard, Earl of Surrey who was a couple of years older than him, and the two became bosom friends. They even spent a year together at the court of King Francis I of France. Surrey would later recall his years spent 'with a king's son' and their true 'friendship sworn, each promise kept so just'. In 1533, Richmond married Surrey's sister, Lady Mary Howard, the daughter of the second highest peer in the realm (after himself).

It is probable, as the Imperial ambassador Eustace Chapuys firmly believed, that in the spring of 1536, Henry VIII was seeking to make Richmond his heir. His two other children, Mary and Elizabeth, had both been declared illegitimate, and the 1536

Succession Act did not confine succession to the legitimate line, but granted Henry VIII the right to choose his successor.

Even without these considerations, it must have been devastating for the King when Richmond took ill and died suddenly and prematurely, on 23 July 1536, of a pulmonary infection. He was seventeen years old. The Duke of Norfolk was entrusted with the plans for his funeral, which was carried out privately, with minimal pomp (Henry VIII would later berate Norfolk for this). The King's son was buried with the Howards at Thetford and later moved with them here to Framlingham.

fframlingham Castle

Some 600 feet away from the Church of St Michael is Framlingham Castle. In 1547, after the arrest of the third Duke of Norfolk, Framlingham Castle passed from the hands of the Howards to Mary Tudor, Henry VIII's daughter.

In 1553, when her brother Edward VI died, and the Duke of Northumberland moved to put Lady Jane Grey on the English throne [see GUILDHALL], Mary fled to Cambridgeshire and Norfolk, before securing herself at Framlingham. It was here, at this castle, in the week of 12–19 July 1553, that Mary amassed armies that would be willing to fight for her right to rule. Thousands of troops gathered under her standard in this, her moment of greatest crisis.

Yet, the battle never came. On 19 July 1553, news reached Framlingham Castle that Northumberland had surrendered and the Privy Council in London had acknowledged her as queen. So, it was here at Framlingham that England's first crowned Queen regnant discovered that she was indeed queen. The presence of the Tudors can be powerfully felt in this apparently peaceful town.

North East, North West, Yorkshire and the Humber

Gawsworth Hall
Cheshire

'I fear they will both dwell in the Tower awhile,
for the Queen hath vowed to send them thither.'

Gawsworth Hall is, by anyone's estimation, one of the most beautiful buildings in Cheshire, if not the whole of England. A half timber-framed manor, it was built by the Fitton family between 1480 and 1600 on the site of a Norman house (the Fitton family had lived on the site of Gawsworth Hall since 1331). The original Tudor mansion was probably significantly larger, moated and enclosed a courtyard. Gawsworth Hall also has a story to tell: it was the birthplace and home of Mary Fitton, a maid-of-honour to Elizabeth I, who became infamous in 1601 for her scandalous behaviour.

Gawsworth is a rare example of a structure that is almost entirely Tudor. For the most part, the ceilings are untouched; the fireplaces are original; even the views over the park and garden wall built by Mary's father, Sir Edward Fitton, have not changed since Mary's day: it is almost just as she would remember. The major differences are that in the early eighteenth century, the Great Hall was significantly reduced in size and several rooms were demolished, but what remains is authentic. Two superbly carved decorative items deserve particular attention: the overmantle in the library, dating from 1580; and the plaster frieze of Tudor roses, birds and flowers, dating from 1540, in the Gold Room.

At some point between July 1596 and early 1598, Mary, not yet twenty years old, was sent to Elizabeth I's court to become one of her maids-of-honour. The maids were Elizabeth's companions in all things: they were professional friends whose talk brightened her days. She looked for intelligent and accomplished women, and ones with talents such as sewing, playing cards and making music, which they would use to entertain her.

Mary's father worried – rightly, as it would turn out – about her virtue, and commissioned William Knollys, comptroller of the royal household, to look out for her. Knollys promised Sir Edward that he would play 'the Good Shepherd & will to my power defend the innocent lamb from the wolvish cruelty and fox-like subtlety of the tame beasts of this place'. But William Knollys abrogated his responsibility as a chaperone. He became the wolf himself, falling headlong in love with Mary, though he was already married and she was thirty years younger than he. (It has been suggested that Knollys was Shakespeare's inspiration for the foolish servant Malvolio, with his yellow cross-garter'd stockings, in *Twelfth Night*.)

The court learned of his infatuation and Mary enjoyed a degree of celebrity. In 1600, when William Kempe, the clown of the Lord Chamberlain's Men, Shakespeare's theatre company, dedicated his *Nine Dayes Wonder* to 'Mistress Anne Fitton, Maid of Honour to the most sacred Maid Royal Queen Elizabeth', it is certain that he meant Mary. Mary's lot was not entirely happy, though. She suffered from melancholy, crying, insomnia and hysterical fits – a condition known at the time as 'suffocation of the mothers' (the womb). She was also unable to marry, as Sir Henry Wallop, one of her father's debtors, retained the money for her marriage portion.

Mary perhaps thought to swing fortune for herself. In the summer of 1600, she became mistress to William Herbert, second son of the Earl of Pembroke [see SHAKESPEARE'S BIRTHPLACE]. By January 1601, her pregnancy by him could no longer be disguised.

For the ageing Queen Elizabeth, it had become increasingly difficult to pretend that it was she, the sun, her courtiers sought, instead of her younger maids, the stars, that surrounded her. An incident like this provoked impassioned fury. She had put Ralegh and Bess Throckmorton in the Tower a few years earlier for marrying without her permission [see SHERBORNE CASTLE] but Mary Fitton had gone one further: she had become pregnant without even marrying first. It was a huge scandal. Nor would William Herbert, newly Earl of Pembroke himself, consent to wed her. A letter from Sir Robert Cecil to Sir George Carew on 5 February 1601 reports the news:

> There is a misfortune befallen Mistress Fytton, for she is proved with child, and the Earl of Pembroke being examined confesseth a fact but utterly renounceth all marriage. I fear they will both dwell in the Tower awhile, for the Queen hath vowed to send them thither.

In fact, Mary got off rather lightly. Pembroke was sent to Fleet Prison for some weeks, while Mary was put under the supervision of Lady Margaret Hawkins and gave birth to a son, who died very soon afterwards.

That, and her shame in society, was punishment enough. Mary's father took her home, back to Gawsworth. Yet, Mary had not learnt her lesson. She found herself a new lover, and only later married first Captain William Polewhele, and then John Lougher, with whom she had several children. Pembroke, meanwhile, married Lady Mary Talbot, co-heiress of the Earl of Shrewsbury, fourth husband to Bess of Hardwick [see HARDWICK HALL].

The scandal had an impact on Gawsworth itself. Sir Edward had intended to build a garden there to rival the great houses of the kingdom and had, at tremendous cost, planted avenues of lime trees, built a wall in the tiltyard and enlarged his lakes, in preparation. He had hoped to win the honour of his sovereign's visit, but after 1601, this was not to be.

There is one final story that circulates about Mary Fitton. At the end of the nineteenth century, it was suggested that she was the mysterious 'dark lady' of Shakespeare's sonnets, described in Sonnet 127 by the lines:

In the old age black was not counted fair,
Or if it were, it bore not beauty's name;
But now is black beauty's successive heir
And beauty slander'd with a bastard shame...

It is an intriguing idea, and has some logic, as scholars have tentatively identified William Herbert as the beautiful young man of Shakespeare's sonnets, who was engaged in a love triangle with the poet and the dark lady [see SHAKESPEARE'S BIRTHPLACE]. Yet, Shakespeare's mistress was black-haired, sallow-skinned and dark-eyed. Were it not for the fact that Mary Fitton had very pale skin, brown hair and grey eyes, it is a suggestion that might have been worth entertaining.

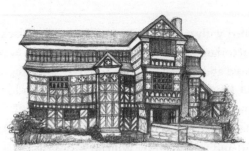

Little Moreton Hall
Cheshire

'The Speare of Destinye, whose Ruler is Knowledge.'

Little Moreton Hall is a spectacularly beautiful example of the sort of decorative timber-framed architecture that was fashionable for the homes of the sixteenth-century gentry. Of course, many of these half-timbered manor houses have not survived the fire risks of five centuries, nor would all have been as imperfectly perfect as Little Moreton. This endearingly crooked house is an outstanding masterpiece of Tudor craftsmanship and tells us much about the aesthetic tastes and, even, world-view of the Tudors.

Despite its evident beauty, this is not a grand house and was not owned by nobility. It was built by three or four generations of the Moretons, a family of prominent local landowners in Cheshire, about whom we know relatively little. Though it looks all of one piece, its construction covers the whole of the Tudor period, from extensions in the early sixteenth century; the addition of a northwest wing in 1546; and the early Elizabethan south range, through to the bake and brewhouses of the early seventeenth century. It has been little altered since.

Moated for security, the house is three storeys high with a chevron and diamond patterned exterior of ornamental oak panelling filled with white wattle-and-daub. The black and white scheme is Victorian, however: the oak beams would have originally been untreated and allowed to fade to silver, while the wattle-and-daub would have been painted ochre. The windows are also patterned and contain 37,000 leaded panes of glass.

The oldest part of the house is the east wing, dating from around 1450 and upgraded by William Moreton I in 1504–8. An essential feature of any medieval house, the Great Hall was part of this early construction, but was extended into the great gabled bay window in 1559. It still retains two pieces of the original furniture mentioned in the 1563 inventory of William Moreton II's possessions: a long refectory table and a 'cubborde of boxes', which probably held spices.

The Withdrawing Room also has a piece of original furniture – the 'greate round table' (actually octagonal) – probably made to fit the 1559 bay window. The plasterwork of the overmantle testifies to the room's Elizabethan additions: it is of Elizabeth I's arms, supported by the lion of England and the dragon of Wales.

The interior decorations of the parlour are particularly notable. In 1976, Georgian wood panelling was removed to reveal wall paintings dating from around 1580. The top frieze of biblical scenes, chiefly of the story of Susanna and the elders, was partially obscured by the subsequent lowering of the floor of the room above, but the painted *trompe d'œil*-style panelling is an unusual feature that was in fashion from around 1570 to 1610, and has by chance been preserved. If you look carefully, you can pick out the wolf's head crest of the Moretons.

The south range and gatehouse were started in 1563 to create guest lodgings, but the most striking feature here is the Long Gallery. Wonderfully wonky, and sixty-eight feet in length, this indoor exercise space – for walking, tennis or bowls – with its almost continuous windows, would have been an extraordinary and luxurious room at the time it was built.

If this gives a taste of Tudor living, so too does the irregular nature of the Upper Porch Room (the plaster coat of arms above the fireplace *is* perpendicular, despite appearances) and the Garderobe Tower. The lack of glazing in the garderobes (lavatories) means the towers are still as cold and windy as they would have been in Tudor times, while the drop for effluent into the cesspit of the moat – to be used as fertiliser – is evident. The garderobes even have their original seats.

The house is not only a testament to Tudor architecture but also to temperament and sensibilities. The plasterwork figures and inscriptions at either end of the Long Gallery attest to the Elizabethan preoccupation with learning. One end proclaims: 'The Wheele of Fortune whose Rule is Ignoraunce'; the other: 'The Speare of Destinye, whose Ruler is Knowledge'. Given that the female figure is pictured holding a globe, and that these are quotations from the 1556 book *The Castle of Knowledge* by Robert Recorde, we can conclude that the knowledge of the plasterworker was not sufficient to avoid a rather comical malapropism, and that he mistook 'sphere' for 'speare'!

There are also inscriptions in the cobbled courtyard on the front of the bay windows: 'God is Al in Al Thing: This windous whire [these windows were] made by William Moreton in the yeare of oure Lorde, M.D.LIX'; and underneath: 'Rycharde Dale Carpe[n]der Made Thies Windous By the grac of GOD'.

The Tudors knew that they lived under God, and the very design and decoration of their homes declared this.

THE TYPICAL TUDOR HOUSE

Picture a chocolate-box country cottage: it is white with black timber beams, the thick thatch curves over the top and curls down on both sides like a tortoiseshell and it has a brick chimney or two emerging from one end. It isn't more than two storeys high, looks about two rooms across and you imagine that the ceilings are low. It is quaint, picturesque, crooked and far too small for all your possessions.

What you're probably picturing is the basic Tudor dwelling, which in many ways encapsulates our very idea of a typical, traditional English home. Anne Hathaway's cottage just outside Stratford-upon-Avon is a good example, even though it has been extended since the sixteenth century. The simplest Tudor houses were built like this on a 'cruck-frame', that is, an A-frame created by growing trees so that they curved, and then splitting the trunks down the middle, so the two halves tended towards each other and met at the top. A small cottage would have at least two pairs of cruck-frames. In between the timbers, the walls were made of wattle-and-daub, which is woven hazel branches covered with a mixture of mud, dung, horse-hair and chopped straw. It was usual for wattle-and-daub to be an ochre colour, and the timbers brown or faded to silver (it was the Victorians who invented the black-and-white colour scheme). The most basic house would have two rooms: a hall with a hearth and a chamber for a bed. By the fifteenth century, central hearths were replaced with fireplaces on the inner walls, allowing rooms to be built on the floor above.

The next size of house up – one you might perhaps find in town – was still made of timber and wattle-and-daub, but was a squarer, box-framed house, with a gabled roof of hand-made tiles and leaded casement windows. It was usual for the first floor to jut out over the ground floor, so that houses appeared to lean in towards each other at the top, shutting out the light on narrow streets. Some of the gentry's manor houses in this book, such as Gawsworth Hall or Little Moreton Hall, are spectacularly beautiful examples of this style on a large scale, with elaborate timber frames in decorative patterns.

Further up the social spectrum, houses became much grander affairs. Built out of the local stone, they would all have had the minimum of a hall, a kitchen and a chapel. As the Tudor century wore on, additional chambers were added, including a great chamber and a long gallery. By the end of Elizabeth I's reign, some of these houses had reached staggering proportions, like Burghley House with its many domes and turrets, or the palace-sized Holdenby House.

The Walker Art Gallery
Liverpool, Merseyside

'Add but the voice and you have his whole self.
That you may doubt whether the painter
or the father has made him.'

Boastful inscription in Latin verse in a portrait by Hans Holbein

The Walker Art Gallery in Liverpool is the place to come face to face with Henry VIII or, at least, an arresting life-size, full-length, colour portrait of him. Dating from the 1540s or 1550s, this is the finest-quality existing copy of Hans Holbein the Younger's original painting: a wall mural at Whitehall Palace, which was destroyed by fire in 1698. This portrait type has become the definitive image of Henry VIII: one with which we're so familiar that we may easily miss the significance, symbolism and iconography of this powerful picture.

Holbein painted the original Whitehall Mural in 1537: you can see his initial cartoon, or sketch, of Henry VIII at the National Portrait Gallery, and a miniature version of the whole mural, captured in the late seventeenth century by painter Remigius van Leemput (an assistant to Van Dyck), at Hampton Court Palace.

The mural featured Henry VIII – in the first life-size, full-length portrait of an English monarch – with his parents, Henry VII and Elizabeth of York, and his wife, Jane Seymour, all standing around a stone plinth. The mural was a vast nine feet by twelve feet: in other words, a huge, arresting image of the King and his family, big enough to cover one wall in Henry's Privy Chamber at Whitehall Palace. A quick look suffices to know what a read of the Latin inscription on the plinth confirms: this picture was not to glorify the three figures of Henry's family, who are depicted with their gaze averted and with closed, even submissive body language; it was, above all, to lionise the dominant figure of Henry VIII himself.

The full-size colour copy at the Walker was produced within a decade or two of the mural: it must have been intended either for another monarch or, more probably, for a courtier. Its provenance suggests links to the Seymour family, meaning it might have been commissioned by Edward Seymour, Duke of Somerset, before his execution in 1552. This, and the fact that similar copies exist at Petworth; Chatsworth; Trinity College, Cambridge; Belvoir Castle; St Bartholomew's Hospital; Hampton Court Palace; and Parham House, suggest that this particular image of Henry had acquired an authoritative status. By ordering their own copy, courtiers felt they could demonstrate that they knew the party line; they knew what this portrait said about the King and they embraced that message.

So, what was the message? The clues are in the picture itself...

For a start, Henry is huge. He is barrel-chested, with improbably broad shoulders that are only further exaggerated by the puffed sleeves of his gown. His stance – which was considered improper, even lewd, when painted – mimics the heroic martial pose of a man in full armour. In a masterful, last-minute alteration from the original cartoon for the mural, Holbein turned Henry's face to stare confrontationally, with a sort of bovine intensity, at the viewer. This is evidently a man to be reckoned with.

Henry does not, however, bear any of the traditional accoutrements of royalty: there is no crown, orb or sceptre. The only signifiers of status are the blue ribbon of the Order of the Garter round his left leg, the magnificence of his clothing and jewellery and the sumptuousness of the setting. His attire is splendid: he wears a red velvet gown, embroidered with gold and trimmed with dark sable fur. His doublet and jerkin are cloth of silver, the former slashed to reveal the shirt below, and adorned with large jewels. He sports a heavy chain of rubies, diamonds and pearls that looks very like the 'collar of such balas [rubies] and pearl that few men ever saw the like' described by Edward Hall in 1539. His bonnet and fingers are similarly garnished with gems. He stands on a luxurious Turkish carpet with a detail of classical architecture behind him. This is Tudor bling: Henry truly matches his description by one ambassador as 'the best dressed sovereign in the world'.

Above all, it is Henry the man, not Henry the King, that this picture emphasises. The impression that this picture was designed to give is best understood by seeing Henry's body as two triangles: one formed by his vast shoulders and tapering to his waist, and the other from his splayed feet, up his legs. These triangles meet to focus the gaze on his bulging codpiece, protruding through his jerkin. His hands – holding a glove, and the cord to his dagger – frame his groin still further. This picture is about all Henry's virility and potency.

Why? The previous year had seen Henry suffer two major betrayals: a rebellion against his assumption of the title of Supreme Head of the Church of England and the dissolution of the monasteries by a large number of his northern subjects [see PONTEFRACT CASTLE]; and the alleged adultery of his second wife, Anne Boleyn. The inscription on the plinth at the centre of the original mural praised Henry's position as Supreme Head, while the characterisation of Henry himself addressed the other issue at stake.

Not only was a wife's adultery thought, in the sixteenth century, to reflect on her husband's lack of sexual appetite but, worse still, in Anne Boleyn's trial, Anne's allegation that Henry 'was not skilful in copulating with a woman, and had neither vigour nor potency' had been read aloud before a gathered crowd of 2,000. The listeners were the very group of important courtiers who would, the following year, be confronted with this ego-appeasing, myth-creating image of the King on the wall of the Privy Chamber. This, of course, is why the portrait needed to be full-length, Henry's figure so exaggerated and his codpiece centre stage.

Quite simply, this famous picture of the King was a piece of visual spin to recast Henry as a virile alpha male to those who knew better, and his courtiers bought it to suggest they believed the lie. It was so successful that it remains the dominant image of Henry VIII to this day.

The value of conveying messages through art was not lost on Henry's daughter, Elizabeth. Close to Henry in the Walker is a magnificent portrait of Elizabeth I, painted by Nicholas Hilliard in 1574, which is replete with symbolism. Elizabeth's wealth is portrayed through her elaborate red velvet gown, the painstaking blackwork embroidery of her shift and her many jewels. The central message is, though, Elizabeth's status as an unmarried Virgin Queen. The pearls with which she is drenched are a symbol of purity, as are the cherries draped over her right ear. The emblem at Elizabeth's breast gives the name to the painting: the *Pelican* portrait. A symbol of Christ's sacrifice, mother pelicans were (wrongly) believed to pluck selflessly at their own breasts to feed their starving young. Here the pelican claims the same sacrificial role for Elizabeth as the mother of her kingdom.

The Tudors certainly knew how to sing their own praises.

Pontefract Castle
West Yorkshire

'Yours as long as life endures.'

On a high blustery ridge, overlooking the town, the sandstone remains of Pontefract Castle belie its important royal history: a history of incredible bad luck.

Known as the 'key to the North', the first motte and bailey castle was built here in the 1080s by the de Lacy family. By the early thirteenth century, it had been rebuilt as a strong stone fortress, and it was here that the deposed Richard II was held prisoner and killed by Henry IV in 1400, reputedly by slow starvation. Later, Pontefract, as one of the last royalist strongholds, would be besieged three times during the Civil War. It was demolished when local people petitioned Parliament for its destruction in 1649. Before then, it had served as the setting for Henry VIII to be betrayed, twice.

Although now in ruins, Pontefract evokes its formerly grand and impressive self. In Henry VIII's day, it was described by the French ambassador, Charles de Marillac, as 'one of the finest castles in England'. Evidence remains of its large keep, the fifteenth-century Great Kitchen with bakehouse, brewhouse and ovens, the

Norman and Elizabethan chapels, Great Hall and royal apartments. However, the modern world – and nature – has encroached: trees grow in the royal apartments, modern houses sit on top of what once was John of Gaunt's Shillington Tower and a 1960s housing estate abuts the Constable Tower, creating quite a contrast between the old and new.

At this great and strategically important castle, Henry VIII would be undone by acts of treachery and disloyalty on two occasions. The first was in late 1536. In October, up to 50,000 men rose in rebellion against him across Yorkshire and Lincolnshire: it remains the largest peacetime rebellion against a reigning monarch in English history. Here at Pontefract Castle, the rebels amassed and drew up their manifesto of twenty-four demands.

The rebels' fears were partly financial: they had heard rumours that the King planned to charge taxes on cattle, white bread, cake, goose and capons, and on weddings, christenings and funerals. They were also concerned that the King's Council was made up of 'persons of low birth and small reputation' (a powerful statement about the commitment to hierarchy in Tudor England, even among ordinary people).

Above all, though, their worries were religious. They described themselves as Pilgrims of Grace fighting 'for the preservation of Christ's church'; they even marched behind a banner bearing the five wounds of Christ. They feared that the King was planning to pull down the parish churches, and steal the Church jewels and plate. As one rebel, John Hallom, stated in 1537, 'because the people saw many abbeys pulled down indeed, they believed the rest to be true'. They feared that 'heretics', like Thomas Cromwell, were infiltrating the country and, like the monks at Charterhouse, they strongly objected to Henry's adoption of the title of the Supreme Head of the Church of England. Above all, as their leader, Robert Aske, would later state: 'The suppression of the abbeys was the greatest cause of the said insurrection': they were vehemently opposed to the dissolution of the monasteries.

Their disquiet was not without reason, but from Henry VIII's egomaniacal point of view, the uprising was nothing but a completely treasonous betrayal. He was particularly affronted by the presumptuous suggestion that his subjects knew better how to rule than he, and was keen to suppress the rebellion entirely. Moreover, he had reason to be afraid of them: if they had wanted to, the rebels could easily have defeated the 9,000-strong royal army and even have deposed him.

Nevertheless, Henry was persuaded to negotiate with the rebels, which the Duke of Norfolk did on his behalf in December 1536. In exchange for their disbanding, Norfolk promised the rebels a Parliament in the north to consider their concerns, and a pardon for their rebellion. The rebels agreed and left Pontefract for home but, in the new year, when no Parliament had been called, fresh revolts broke out. It was just the excuse for which Henry had been looking to take savage revenge.

In short, Henry had set them up. In early 1537, between 144 and 153 people were executed for their involvement in the revolts, and the leader Robert Aske was 'hanged in chains' (in the gibbet irons) in York. Convinced that monks were leading figures in the rebellion, the Pilgrimage of Grace was also pivotal to Henry's decision to suppress not only the 'lesser monastic houses', as ordered in March 1536, but all 800 religious houses in England.

The second betrayal was more personal. In July 1540, Henry VIII married his fifth wife: Katherine Howard, a young, attractive girl of sixteen to twenty-four years of age (her date of birth is unknown), who was formerly Anne of Cleves's maid-of-honour. Henry VIII was delighted with his new wife, and took her on progress to York in the summer of 1541 (the only time he ever went that far north). It was while staying at Lincoln and then at

Pontefract Castle that Katherine, with the help of Jane, Lady Rochford, received Thomas Culpeper, a young gentleman of the King's Privy Chamber into her rooms, for 'many stolen interviews'.

It was not Katherine's first dalliance: it later emerged that before her marriage she had flirted with her instructor on the virginals, Henry Manox, and gone so far as to lie in 'naked bed' with a man called Francis Dereham, whom she had promised to marry (when put together, promises to marry and consummation constituted legal marriage). Four days after her arrival at Pontefract in 1541, Katherine foolishly appointed Dereham as her secretary. Some historians have suggested that both this and Katherine's meetings with Culpeper were simply an attempt to purchase their silence about her past, but a letter from Katherine to Culpeper suggests otherwise. She writes, 'it makes my heart die to think I cannot be always in your company' and signs off, 'yours as long as life endures'. We cannot be 100 per cent sure that Katherine and Culpeper were lovers, but they certainly acted very rashly indeed.

On 2 November 1541, the very day after Henry had publicly offered prayers of thanks for his happy marriage, Archbishop Thomas Cranmer reportedly left a letter on Henry's chair in the Chapel Royal at Hampton Court detailing the allegations of Katherine's misbehaviour: he was too terrified to tell Henry face to face. Katherine was immediately confined to her chambers and never saw Henry again.

Henry was utterly devastated, and took his revenge. In December 1541 Culpeper was beheaded at Tyburn, and Dereham soon after suffered the usual traitor's death of hanging, drawing and quartering. Katherine, meanwhile, was condemned by an Act of Attainder, passed through Parliament, which meant she had no chance to defend herself as she would have done at trial. The last few paragraphs of this Act created in law the general principles that consensual adultery by a queen was treasonous (previous Acts had only made provision for 'violation' of the queen) and that any queen who failed to disclose her past 'unchaste life' would also be guilty of treason (thereby creating the law and condemning her in the same document). On 10 February 1542, Katherine was transported by barge to the Tower of London, passing under Culpeper and Dereham's rotting heads on London Bridge. She was executed three days later.

If Pontefract seems desolate now, just imagine how it felt to Henry VIII.

Fountains Abbey
North Yorkshire

*'It is a lamentable thing to see a legion of
monks and nuns who have been chased from
their monasteries wandering miserably hither
and thither seeking means to live.'*

Eustace Chapuys, Imperial ambassador to England, 1537

Designated a World Heritage Site by UNESCO in 1986, Fountains Abbey has the largest monastic ruins in the country, gorgeously set in 800-acre grounds that include a beautiful landscaped Georgian water garden complete with neoclassical follies, and a deer park.

Founded as a Benedictine abbey in 1132, the monks at Fountains Abbey adopted the Cistercian rule, which meant a rigorous and austere way of life. This didn't stop Fountains becoming, by the thirteenth century, one of England's richest monasteries. It is still possible to wander through the fine cloisters, enjoy the vaulted ceiling of the cellarium and see evidence of the monastery's great wealth in the warming room with its vast fireplace, the muniment room – for the storage of documents – and the abbey's twelfth-century corn mill.

The evident beauty of the ruined medieval abbey reveals the extent of the damage and cultural trauma caused by the dissolution of the monasteries. The first sign of the coming storm came when Henry VIII's first minister, Thomas Cromwell, ordered a survey and visitation of all monastic houses in 1535. Commissioners were sent to find out the annual income of each house, and to search diligently for hints of scandal. The resulting report, called the *Valor Ecclesiasticus*, is a colourful and gossipy list of sins and abuses, which also mocks the monasteries' treasured relics. At Fountains, the commissioners reported finding four 'sodomites' and six '*incontinentia*' (monks guilty of sexual relations with women). One of the latter was the abbot, William Thirsk, whom, they said, had greatly dilapidated his house, 'wasted the wood', committed theft and sacrilege and, worst of all, 'notoriously kept six whores'.

As a result of the survey, in March 1536, an Act of Parliament was passed to dissolve the 'lesser' monasteries – those with an annual income of £200 or less – and to donate their land, plate, jewels and investments to the Crown. This was presented as an attempt to reform weak houses where scandalous misconduct was rife, with the Act drawing attention to the 'manifest sin, vicious, carnal and abominable living' in these monasteries, in comparison to the example of the 'great and honourable monasteries of religion in this realm wherein... religion is right well kept & observed'. This suggests that Henry VIII and Cromwell had no plans to dissolve all the monasteries at this stage.

This changed after the Pilgrimage of Grace [see PONTEFRACT CASTLE]. Convinced of the perfidy of the monks and the dangers of their allegiance to a power outside England, Henry became increasingly hostile to monasticism itself. Every religious house in England was now to be dissolved by the 'voluntary' surrender of their abbots, who would be induced by a combination of threats and incentives. So began the total eradication of monasticism in

England, with very few voices raised in dissent or resistance [see GLASTONBURY TOR].

The dissolution was still couched in the language of reform: abbots, monks, nuns and friars who surrendered their houses often signed documents expressing contrition and shame for their past way of life. Some went willingly: the abbot at Fountains (a wily monk called Marmaduke Bradley who bought his way into the abbotship after Thirsk resigned) surrendered the Abbey to the King's commissioners on 26 November 1539 in exchange for an annual pension of £100 – which was very handsome indeed.

Between 1536 and 1540, over 800 religious houses were suppressed, and 7,000 monks, nuns, friars and their servants were turned out into the community. It was an act of incalculable cultural vandalism: invaluable medieval libraries were ransacked, irreplaceable jewellery was dissipated, finely crafted plate was melted down and architecturally important Gothic buildings were demolished. The only ones to survive intact were those established as secular cathedrals.

It has been estimated that the dissolution brought £1.3 million (today, about £400 million) to the Crown between 1536 and 1547, through the rents from, and the sale of, confiscated lands, and the acquisition of gold, silver plate and jewels. Buildings like Nonsuch Palace and Hampton Court, or coastal fortifications [see PENDENNIS AND ST MAWES CASTLES] were funded from the proceeds of the dissolution.

The Crown sold many of these lands to the nobility and gentry: it was the largest redistribution of wealth since the Norman Conquest. The dissolution created a land market in England that enriched the aristocracy and permanently changed the religious and architectural landscape of England.

At Fountains, the ruins testify to the scale of the loss. They also typify the fate of many abbeys. When the estate was sold to Sir

Stephen Proctor, he used the sandstone from the abbey's ruins to build a grand new Elizabethan house, Fountains Hall, in the style of master mason Robert Smythson, who designed Hardwick. This elegant house, like many of the century's architectural master-pieces, could not have been completed without raiding the fabric of the old, ruined monasteries that fell increasingly into decay.

Whitby Abbey

Another abbey worth visiting in North Yorkshire is the dramatic-ally ruined eleventh-century Whitby Abbey, on its windswept, rocky headland, jutting out into the North Sea. It, too, was suppressed in 1539 and later served as the setting for Bram Stoker's novel *Dracula*.

www.suzannahlipscomb.co.uk

Twitter: @sixteenthCgirl

Acknowledgements

In writing this book, I have depended much on the expertise and generosity of others, especially at each of the fifty places featured in this book. I particularly want to thank: Lesley Smith, Curator of Tutbury Castle; Dr Gareth Williams at the British Museum; Jane Apps, Head Steward at Hever Castle; John K. Wingfield Digby of Sherborne Castle; Jon Culverhouse, Curator, and Carolyn Crookall at Burghley House; Nigel Wright, Curator, and National Trust volunteer guide, Chiara, both at Hardwick Hall; my old colleagues and friends Mark Wallis and Stephanie Selmayr at Past Pleasures; Tudor food historian Richard Fitch; Dr Kent Rawlinson, Curator of Historic Buildings at Hampton Court Palace; and Jane Spooner, Curator of Historic Buildings at the Tower of London. Particular mention must be made of all those at Trinity College, Cambridge, who welcomed me when the college was closed to the public, namely Lord Rees of Ludlow; Pauline Smith, Porter; Professor Robin Carrell; Sue Fletcher; and Sandy Paul, Librarian. I would especially like to thank Brian Jarvis, General Manager of Thornbury Castle, for his great generosity, and the time he gave up to show me around. There are also countless members of staff and volunteers at the National Trust, English Heritage, Historic House Association and independent sites along the way, whose names I didn't get a chance to learn, but who have helped me enormously. Thank you to you all.

I have also relied on the scholarship of numerous Tudor historians, too many to name (although I have recommended a good number in the list of further reading). I would also like to acknowledge my debt to the authors of the guidebooks of each historic house (even if one or two proved occasionally erroneous!). I am used to recording such debts through footnotes, and crave indulgence from scholars for their absence: this book is intended as an introduction to non-specialists. Those familiar with the field will spot my influences. Any errors are mine alone.

On my travels, I enjoyed the hospitality of some marvellous people. My thanks go to Polly and Steve Bennett, Julie and Malcolm Dunn, Rufus and Cherry Fairweather, Stephen and Alice Lawhead, and Richard and Chrissy Sturt for comforting a weary traveller with good food, good wine and good company.

I am grateful, too, for the support of my colleagues at the University of East Anglia and, latterly, at New College of the Humanities, for their input, wisdom and forbearance. Thank you, too, to my virtual history community on Twitter for thoughts and contributions along the way.

I would also like to thank my editors at Ebury, Liz Marvin and Andrew Goodfellow, and my literary agent, Andrew Lownie, for all their work on this book. Thank you to my illustrator, Angela Beal, whose beautiful drawings enhance the text greatly. I am also immensely grateful to Tony Morris for putting me in touch with Random House in the first place.

Finally and above all, my very great thanks go to my parents and to my husband, Drake, for their continuing and wonderful support. Both Drake and my mother read and commented on every chapter, and both were also taken around a good many Tudor houses! Drake encouraged me to write this book from the very start and gave up a week's holiday, and more than a few weekends, to accompany me on an intense schedule of Tudor sightseeing. Thank you to you all.

Suzannah Lipscomb
Surrey, October 2011
SDG

Further Reading

Architecture: general guides

Mark Girouard, *Life in the English Country House* (1978)

Mark Girouard, *Elizabethan Architecture: Its Rise and Fall, 1540–1640* (2009)

Maurice Howard, *Early Tudor Country House: Architecture and Politics, 1490–1550* (1987)

Harry Mount, *A Lust for Window Sills: A Lover's Guide to British Buildings from Portcullis to Pebble-Dash* (2008)

Nikolaus Pevsner, *Pevsner Architectural Guides: Buildings of England*

Simon Thurley, *The Royal Palaces of Tudor England: Architecture and Court Life 1460–1547* (1993)

Portraiture

Xanthe Brooke and David Crombie, *Henry VIII Revealed: Holbein's Portrait and Its Legacy* (2003)

Antonia Fraser and Tarnya Cooper, *A Guide to Tudor and Jacobean Portraits* (2008)

Brett Dolman, 'Wishful Thinking: Reading the Portraits of Henry VIII's Queens', in *Henry VIII and the Court: Art, Politics and Performance* ed. Thomas Betteridge and Suzannah Lipscomb (2012)

Bendor Grosvenor (ed.), *Lost Faces: Identity and Discovery in Tudor Royal Portraiture* (2007)

Tatiana C. String, 'Projecting Masculinity: Henry VIII's Codpiece' in *Henry VIII and his Afterlives: Literature, Politics and Art* ed. Mark Rankin, Christopher Highly and John N. King (2010)

Henry VII

S. B. Chrimes, *Henry VII* (1999)

Sean Cunningham, *Henry VII* (2007)

Michael K. Jones, *Bosworth 1485: The Psychology of a Battle* (2003)

Henry VIII

Lacey Baldwin Smith, *Henry VIII: The Mask of Royalty* (1971)

Robert Hutchinson, *The Last Days of Henry VIII: Conspiracy, Treason and Heresy at the Court of the Dying Tyrant* (2006)

Suzannah Lipscomb, *1536: The Year that Changed Henry VIII* (2009)

J. J. Scarisbrick, *Henry VIII* (1997)

David Starkey, *Henry: Virtuous Prince* (2009)

Alison Weir, *Henry VIII: King and Court* (2008)

Lucy Wooding, *Henry VIII* (2008)

Henry VIII's wives

David Starkey, *Six Wives: The Queens of Henry VIII* (2004)

Giles Tremlett, *Katherine of Aragon: Henry's Spanish Queen* (2011)

Eric Ives, *The Life and Death of Anne Boleyn: The Most Happy* (2005)

Lacey Baldwin Smith, *A Tudor Tragedy: The Life and Times of Katherine Howard* (1962)

Susan E. James, *Kateryn Parr: The Making of a Queen* (1999) Also republished as *Katherine Parr: Henry VIII's Last Love* (2009)

Linda Porter, *Katherine the Queen: The Remarkable Life of Katherine Parr* (2011)

Henry VIII's courtiers

Peter Ackroyd, *The Life of Thomas More* (1999)

Jessie Childs, *Henry VIII's Last Victim: The Life and Times of Henry Howard, Earl of Surrey* (2006)

Barbara J. Harris, *Edward Stafford, third Duke of Buckingham, 1478–1521* (1986)

David M. Head, *The Ebbs and Flows of Fortune: The Life of Thomas Howard, Third Duke of Norfolk* (1995)

Robert Hutchinson, *House of Treason: The Rise and Fall of a Tudor Dynasty* (2009)

Diarmaid MacCulloch, *Thomas Cranmer: A Life* (1997)

Nicola Shulman, *Graven with Diamonds: The Many Lives of Thomas Wyatt: Courtier, Poet, Assassin, Spy* (2011)

Derek Wilson, *In the Lion's Court: Power, Ambition and Sudden Death in the Reign of Henry VIII* (2002)

Edward VI

Chris Skidmore, *Edward VI: The Lost King of England* (2008)

Lady Jane Grey

Eric Ives, *Lady Jane Grey: A Tudor Mystery* (2009)

Mary I

Susan Doran and Thomas S. Freeman (ed.), *Mary Tudor: Old and New Perspectives* (2011)

Linda Porter, *Mary Tudor: The First Queen* (2009)

Anna Whitelock, *Mary Tudor: England's First Queen* (2010)

Elizabeth I

Sarah Gristwood, *Elizabeth and Leicester* (2008)

Anne Somerset, *Elizabeth I* (2002)

David Starkey, *Elizabeth* (2001)

Alison Weir, *Elizabeth the Queen* (2009)

Elizabeth I's courtiers

Stephen Alford, *Burghley: William Cecil at the Court of Elizabeth I* (2011)

Tracy Borman, *Elizabeth's Women: The Hidden Story of the Virgin Queen* (2010)

Malcolm Deacon, *The Courtier and the Queen: Sir Christopher Hatton and Elizabeth I* (2008)

Mary S. Lovell, *Bess of Hardwick: First Lady of Chatsworth* (2006)

Alan Stewart, *Philip Sidney: A Double Life* (2000)

John Sugden, *Sir Francis Drake* (2006)

Penry Williams and Mark Nicholls, *Sir Walter Raleigh: In Life and Legend* (2011)

Raleigh Trevelyan, *Sir Walter Raleigh* (2002)

Benjamin Woolley, *The Queen's Conjuror: The Life and Magic of Dr Dee* (2002)

Mary, Queen of Scots

Antonia Fraser, *Mary, Queen of Scots* (1969)

John Guy, *My Heart is My Own: The Life of Mary Queen of Scots* (2004)

War and foreign policy

David Childs, *The Warship Mary Rose: The Life and Times of King Henry VIII's Flagship* (2007)

Peter Harrington and Brian Delf, *The Castles of Henry VIII* (2007)

Joycelyne G. Russell, *The Field of the Cloth of Gold: Men and Manners in 1520* (1969)

Reformation and religious changes

G. W. Bernard, *The King's Reformation: Henry VIII and the Remaking of the English Church* (2005)

Eamon Duffy, *The Stripping of the Altars: Traditional Religion in England, 1400–1580* (2005)

Eamon Duffy, *Fires of Faith: Catholic England under Mary Tudor* (2010)

Alan Dures, *English Catholicism 1558–1642* (1983)

Christopher Haigh, *English Reformations: Religion, Politics and Society under the Tudors* (1991)

Alice Hogge, *God's Secret Agents: Queen Elizabeth's Forbidden Priests and the Hatching of the Gunpowder Plot* (2005)

Peter Marshall, *Reformation England 1480–1642* (2003)

Peter Marshall, *Religious Identities in Henry VIII's England* (2006)

Rebellions

Michael Bush, *The Pilgrimage of Grace: A Study of the Rebel Armies of October 1536* (1996)

Anthony Fletcher and Diarmaid MacCulloch, *Tudor Rebellions, fifth* edn (2004)

R.W. Hoyle, *The Pilgrimage of Grace and the Politics of the 1530s* (2003)

Andy Wood, *The 1549 Rebellions and the Making of Modern England* (2007)

Shakespeare

James Shapiro, *1599: A Year in the Life of William Shakespeare* (2006)

Michael Wood, *In Search of Shakespeare* (2005)

Appendix

Opening Times and How to Get There

LONDON AND GREATER LONDON

The Tower of London
Historic Royal Palaces, London EC3N 4AB
Tel: 0844 482 7777
www.hrp.org.uk
Opening Times: Mar–Oct Tues–Sat, 9am–5.30pm; Sun–Mon 10am–
5.30pm; Nov–Feb Tues–Sat, 9am–4.30pm; Sun–Mon 10am–4.30pm
Nearest tube: Tower Hill
Nearest train: Fenchurch Street or London Bridge
There is no parking at the Tower of London
New Armouries Restaurant; cafés
The Tower shop; The Jewel House Shop; The White House Shop; The
Medieval Palace Shop; The Beefeater Shop
For accessibility information, please visit www.hrp.org.uk/TowerOf
London/planyourvisit/disabledaccess

National Portrait Gallery
Saint Martin's Place, London WC2H 0HE
Tel: 020 7306 0055; Recorded info: 020 7312 2463
www.npg.org.uk
Opening times: Daily 10am-6pm; Thu–Fri until 9pm
Nearest tube: Charing Cross, Leicester Square or Embankment
Nearest train: Charing Cross
There are no car parking facilities at the Gallery
Portrait Café and Portrait Restaurant

The National Portrait Gallery Shop
For accessibility information, please visit www.npg.org.uk/visit/access/
in-the-gallery.php

Westminster Abbey
The Church of England
20 Dean's Yard, London SW1P 3PA
Tel: 020 7222 5152
www.westminster-abbey.org
Usually open to visitors from Mon to Sat throughout the year, Sundays
are reserved for worship
Nearest tube: St James's Park or Westminster
Nearest train: Victoria or Waterloo
No public parking facilities are available at the Abbey
There is no café at Westminster Abbey
The Westminster Abbey Shop
For a detailed disabled access guide please visit www.disabledgo.com

The London Charterhouse
Sutton's Hospital, Charterhouse Square, London EC1M 6AN
(The London Charterhouse is a private residence)
Tel: 020 7253 9503
www.thecharterhouse.org
Tours of Charterhouse run on Wed afternoons at 2.15pm Apr–Aug. Tours
and tickets must be pre-booked by letter with at least three dates and
a cheque for £10 per person made payable to 'Charterhouse'. Please
include telephone number and SAE
Nearest tube: Barbican or Farringdon
Nearest train: Liverpool Street or Old Street
Metered parking is available in Charterhouse Square
There is no café at the London Charterhouse
There is no shop, but an illustrated Guide (£7.50) is available from Clerk
to the Brothers at the address above
Limited disabled access – check website

Lincoln's Inn
The Honourable Society of Lincoln's Inn
The Treasury Office, Lincoln's Inn, London WC2A 3TL
Tel: 020 7405 1393
www.lincolnsinn.org.uk
Lincoln's Inn Fields is a public square in London and thus open to the public
The Royal Courts of Justice are open to those over 14 years, unless a notice on the doors states 'In Camera' or 'In Private'. Groups of more than 12 are asked to split up and visit different courts to cause least disturbance
Nearest tube: Temple; Holborn; or Chancery Lane
There is parking available in Lincolns Inn Fields
There are numerous cafés and shops in the vicinity
For information about accessibility, please visit www.lincolnsinn.org.uk/index.php/location/disabled-access

Guildhall
City Remembrancer's Office
Gresham Street, London EC2
Tel: 020 7332 1313
www.guildhall.cityoflondon.gov.uk
Opening times: Mon–Sat 10am–4.30pm (all year); Sun 10am–4.30pm (first weekend in May to last weekend in Sept), subject to events taking place at Guildhall. Please check that the Great Hall is available up to six weeks prior to the visit date
Nearest tube: Moorgate, Mansion House or St Paul's
Nearest train: Liverpool Street, Fenchurch Street, Cannon Street, Blackfriars or City Thameslink
Public car parking is available on London Wall, Barbican or Aldersgate
There is no café at the Guildhall, but several nearby
There is a bookshop in the Guildhall Library
Suitable for people with disabilities

Eltham Palace
English Heritage
Court Yard, Eltham, Greenwich SE9 5QE
Tel: 0870 333 1181

www.english-heritage.org.uk/daysout/properties/eltham-palace-and-
  gardens
Open daily Apr–Oct 10am–5pm; Nov–March 10am–4pm
Nearest train: Eltham or Mottingham (both ½ mile)
Parking is available at Eltham Palace
Restaurant, tea room, picnic area
Shop available
Suitable for people with disabilities

Richmond Palace, Surrey
Only traces of Richmond Palace remain, notably the Gatehouse. The site is
between Richmond Green and the River Thames. Information about Rich-
mond Palace is available at the Museum of Richmond
The Museum of Richmond, The Old Town Hall,
Whittaker Avenue, Richmond-upon-Thames, Surrey TW9 1TP
Museum Tel: 020 8332 1141
www.museumofrichmond.com
Museum opening times: Tue–Sat 11am–5pm
Nearest tube: Richmond
Nearest train: Richmond
Car parking at Friar's Lane car park, 100 m
There is no café at the Museum, but many in Richmond itself
The Museum Shop
Suitable for people with disabilities

Hampton Court Palace, Surrey
Historic Royal Palaces
East Molesey, Surrey KT8 9AU
Tel: 0844 482 7777
www.hrp.org.uk/hamptoncourtpalace
Opening Times: Summer 10am–6pm, latest entry to maze 5.15pm; winter
  10am–4.30pm, latest entry to maze 3.45pm
Nearest train: Hampton Court
Car parking at Hampton Court Palace and on Hampton Court Green, or
  Hampton Court railway station
The Tiltyard Café
The Barrack Block Shop; The Henry Shop; The Garden Shop; The Tudor
  Kitchens Shop

Suitable for people with disabilities, for information please visit www.hrp.
org.uk/HamptonCourtPalace/planyourvisit/disabledaccess

SOUTH EAST

St George's Chapel, Windsor Castle, Berkshire
The Royal Collection
Windsor, Berkshire SL4 1NJ
Tel: 020 7766 7304
www.royalcollection.org.uk
Opening times: Mar–Oct, 9.45am–5.15pm (last admission 4pm); Nov–
Feb, 9.45am–4.15pm (last admission 3pm). Please see website for
additional closures
Nearest train: Windsor
For parking information visit: www.windsor.gov.uk
Refreshments from The Undercroft Café. A re-entry band can be obtained
from the Middle Ward or Lower Ward shops if you wish to leave the
Castle for refreshments in the town's many cafés
There are three shops, all selling merchandise exclusive to Windsor Castle
Suitable for people with disabilities, for more information please see website

The Mary Rose, Hampshire
The *Mary Rose* Trust, Portsmouth Historic Dockyard Ltd
College Road, HM Naval Base, Portsmouth, Hampshire PO1 3LX
Tel: (Office) 023 9275 0521, (Museum) 023 9281 2931
www.maryrose.org
Open daily from 10am throughout the year; Apr–Oct: Last entry 4.30pm,
gates close 6pm; Nov–Mar: last entry 4pm, gates close 5.30pm
Nearest train: Portsmouth Harbour
Car parking at Historic Dockyard Car Park, 400 yards
Costa Coffee; Quick Crepes; Boathouse No. 7; The Georgian; Action
Stations Café
Mary Rose shop; Nauticalia; National Museum RN shop; Antiques Store-
house
Limited disabled access – all disabled visitors must be accompanied by a
carer. For more information please visit www.maryrose.org/visit/
access_poster.pdf

Winchester Cathedral, Hampshire
Dean and Chapter for the Church of England
9 The Close, Winchester, Hampshire SO23 9LS
Tel: 01962 857200
winchester-cathedral.org.uk
The Cathedral is open every day of the year, except for necessary closures
Nearest train: Winchester
There is no parking within the Cathedral Close or the immediate vicinity
Refectory
Cathedral shop
Suitable for people with disabilities

The Vyne, Hampshire
The National Trust
Vyne Road, Sherborne St John, Basingstoke, Hampshire RG24 9HL
Tel: 01256 883858
www.nationaltrust.org.uk/main/w-thevyne
Please see website for seasonal opening times
Nearest train: Bramley (2½ miles) or Basingstoke (4 miles)
Free car parking, 40 yards
Tudor Brewhouse Restaurant
Coach House Shop
Good disabled access to ground floor, upper floors only accessible via stairs

Hever Castle, Kent
Estate Office, Hever Castle
Hever, Nr Edenbridge, Kent TN8 7NG
Tel: 01732 865224
www.hevercastle.co.uk
For detailed seasonal opening times see www.hevercastle.co.uk/hever-
    castle-opening-times.aspx
Nearest train: Edenbridge or Hever
Ample car parking
The Moat Restaurant, Guthrie Pavilion, plus four kiosks
The Courtyard shops; The Hever Shop
Limited disabled access, please visit www.hevercastle.co.uk/accessibility.
    aspx

Leeds Castle, Kent
Leeds Castle Enterprises Ltd
Maidstone, Kent ME17 1PL
Tel: 01622 765400
www.leeds-castle.com
Opening times: Apr–Sep 10am–6pm, (castle open 10:30am–5pm) last
    entry to grounds 4:30pm; Oct–Mar 10am–5pm (castle open 10:30am–
    3:30pm) last entry to grounds 3pm
Nearest train: Bearsted
Free car parking
Fairfax Restaurant and the Maze Market Grill (seasonal)
The Leeds Castle Shop
Suitable for disabled visitors

Penshurst Place, Kent
The Estate Office, Penshurst Place
Penshurst, Tonbridge, Kent TN11 8DG
Tel: 01892 870307
www.penshurstplace.com
House and Toy Museum open mid-Feb–Oct 12pm–4:30pm. Last entry
    4pm, grounds close 6pm
Nearest Train: Tunbridge Wells or Edenbridge
Ample free car parking
Tea Room sells light lunches
Gift shop
For information about accessibility, please visit www.penshurstplace.com/
    page/3033/Access-Facilities

Rochester Castle, Kent
Medway Council for English Heritage
Castle Hill, Rochester, Kent ME1 1SW
Tel: 01634 402276
www.english-heritage.org.uk/daysout/properties/rochester-castle
Open daily Apr–Sep 10am–6pm; Oct–Mar 10am–4pm
Nearest train: Rochester
There are car parks nearby
There is no café, but restaurants nearby

Rochester Castle Shop
Limited disabled access

Allington Castle, Kent (not open to the public)

Sir Robert and Lady Worcester since 1996, previously The Order of the
Carmelites
Castle Road, Allington, Maidstone, Kent ME16 0NB
Tel: 01622 606404
Allington Castle is not open to the public although the ground floor is
available for functions and weddings
Nearest train: Maidstone Barracks or Maidstone East
Parking is available for function guest cars only

Christ Church College, Oxfordshire

The University of Oxford
St Aldates, Oxford OX1 1DP
Tel: 01865 276150
www.chch.ox.ac.uk/visiting
Opening times: Mon–Sat 9am–5pm, Sun 2pm–5pm throughout the year.
However, Christ Church College is a working academic and religious
institution and some areas, including the Hall and the Cathedral, may
close without notice. The Hall can sometimes be closed between 12
midday and 2pm. The Cathedral closes for choir practice every day at
4:45pm.
Nearest train: Oxford
Car parking nearby
There is no café, but as Christ Church is in the centre of Oxford there are
cafés nearby
The Cathedral Shop
For accessibility information see www.chch.ox.ac.uk/visiting/accessibility

Broad Street, Oxfordshire

Oxfordshire County Council
Broad Street, Oxford, Oxfordshire
Nearest train: Oxford
Limited parking in Broad Street, but parking in nearby St Giles
There are several cafés and shops in Broad Street
Cobbled street may be difficult for wheelchairs

Loseley Park, Surrey
The More-Molyneux family
Loseley Park, Guildford, Surrey GU3 1HS
Tel: 01483 304440
www.loseleypark.co.uk
House open to the public May–Aug (except Mon). Visits to Loseley
    House are by guided tour only and last around 45 minutes
Nearest train: Guildford
Car parking is available
The Mulberry Tea Lawn and The Wisteria Courtyard Restaurant
The Loseley Park shop
Limited disabled access, please make contact direct for details

Arundel Castle, West Sussex
The Duke and Duchess of Norfolk
Arundel, West Sussex BN18 9AB
Tel: 01903 882173
www.arundelcastle.org
Open daily Apr–Oct, 10am–5pm, except Mon
Nearest train: Arundel
There is a pay and display car park directly opposite the Castle entrance
The Arundel Castle Restaurant , and the Arundel Castle Coffee Shop are
    open Tue–Sun inclusive, Bank Holidays and Mon throughout Aug,
    from 10.30am–4.30pm
The Arundel Castle Shop
Limited disabled access – please see website

SOUTH WEST

Pendennis and St Mawes Castles, Cornwall
English Heritage
Castle Close, Falmouth, Cornwall TR11 4LP
Tel: 01326 316 594
www.english-heritage.org.uk/daysout/properties/pendennis-castle
Please see website for detailed seasonal opening hours
Nearest train: Falmouth Docks

Main car park on Castle Drive
Tearoom
Castle shop
Suitable for people with disabilities, but limited access in places

Buckland Abbey, Devon
The National Trust
Yelverton, Devon PL20 6EY
Tel: 01822 853607
www.nationaltrust.org.uk/main/w-bucklandabbey
Opening times: Mar–Oct 10.30am–5.30pm; Nov–Feb 11am–4:30pm.
   Closed Jan.
Nearest train: Plymouth (11 miles)
Free car parking
14th-Century Refectory serving freshly cooked local produce
Buckland Abbey Shop
Limited disabled access, please see website

Sherborne Castle, Dorset
English Heritage for John K Wingfield Digby
New Road, Sherborne, Dorset DT9 5NR
Tel: 01935 812072
www.sherbornecastle.com
Open Apr–Oct 11am–4.30pm
Nearest train: Sherborne
Free car parking
Tea room
Gift shop
Limited disabled access, please see website

Sandford Orcas Manor House
Sir Mervyn Medlycott Bt
The Manor House, Sandford Orcas, Sherborne Dorset DT9 4SB
Tel: 01963 220206
Opening times: Easter Monday 10am–5pm; May, July–September, Sun
   and Mon 2–5pm
Nearest train: Sherborne

No tea room or gift shop
Limited disabled access

Hailes Abbey, Gloucestershire

English Heritage
Hailes, near Winchcombe, Cheltenham, Gloucestershire GL54 5PB
Tel: 01242 602398
www.english-heritage.org.uk/daysout/properties/hailes-abbey
Opening times: Apr–Oct, 10am–4pm, 5pm or 6pm (see website)
Nearest train: Cheltenham (10 miles)
Free car parking
Refreshments available
Abbey shop
Suitable for people with disabilities

Sudeley Castle, Gloucestershire

The Dent-Brocklehursts and Lord and Lady Ashcombe
Winchcombe, Gloucestershire GL54 5JD
Tel: 01242 602308 or 01242 604357(Infoline)
www.sudeleycastle.co.uk
Open daily Apr–Nov 10.30am–5pm,
Nearest train: Cheltenham Spa
Parking is available
Coffee shop
The Visitor and Plant Centre, plus Old Stable shop in the Castle
Limited disabled access – upper floors are unsuitable for those with limited
    mobility

Thornbury Castle, Gloucestershire

Von Essen Hotels
Thornbury Castle and Tudor Gardens, Castle Street, Thornbury,
South Gloucestershire BS35 1HH
Tel: 01454 281182
www.thornburycastle.co.uk
Thornbury Castle is a working hotel so to enjoy the on-site facilities it is
    necessary to say the night
Nearest train: Bristol Parkway

Parking is available for guests
Fine dining is available at Thornbury Castle
Limited disabled access

Glastonbury Tor and Abbey, Somerset
The National Trust
Near Glastonbury, Somerset
Tel: 01643 862452
www.nationaltrust.org.uk/main/w-glastonburytor
Open all year, all day
Nearest train: Castle Cary from Paddington
No parking (except for orange or blue badge holders). Use council run
    park-and-ride from centre of Glastonbury Apr–Sep, or park in free
    car park at Somerset Rural Life Museum, Abbey Farm, Glastonbury.
    Tel 01458 831197 to confirm availability. Lower entrance to the Tor
    is approximately ¼ mile from museum car park
There is no shop or refreshments at Glastonbury Tor
Limited accessibility. Steep terrain with steps

Montacute House, Somerset
The National Trust
Montacute, Somerset TA15 6XP
Tel: 01935 823289
www.nationaltrust.org.uk/main/w-vh/w-visits/w-findaplace/w-
    montacute/
Open daily Mar–Oct 10am–4pm except Tue. Open Tue in Aug
Nearest train: Yeovil Pen Mill (5½ miles); Yeovil Junction (7 miles) or
    Crewkerne (7 miles)
Free car parking
Courtyard Café
Gift shop and plant sales
Suitable for people with disabilities

WEST MIDLANDS

Ludlow Castle, Shropshire

Earl of Powis
Castle Square, Ludlow, Shropshire SY8 1AY
Tel: 01584 874465
www.ludlowcastle.com
For opening times see www.ludlowcastle.com/Pages/admission.aspx
#opening
Nearest train: Ludlow
Public car park in the centre of Ludlow near to the Castle
Café
Gift shop
Limited disabled access – see website or telephone for more information

Tutbury Castle, Staffordshire

Lesley Smith, Curator
Castle St, Tutbury, Burton upon Trent, Staffordshire DE13 9JF
Tel: 01283 812129
www.tutburycastle.com
Opening times: Apr–Sep 11am –5pm, Wed–Sun
Nearest train: Burton-on-Trent
Parking available at £1 per car
Café
Castle shop
For accessibility information see www.tutburycastle.com/visit.php?id=
special_needs

Kenilworth Castle, Warwickshire

English Heritage
Castle Green, Kenilworth, Warwickshire CV8 1NE
Tel: 01926 852 078
www.english-heritage.org.uk/daysout/properties/kenilworth-castle
Opening times: Apr–Oct, 10am–5pm; Nov–Mar 10am–4pm
Nearest train: Coventry or Leamington Spa (5 miles), or Warwick (7 miles)
Car parking available
The Stables Tea Room

No shop
For accessibility information see www.english-heritage.org.uk/daysout/
    properties/kenilworth-castle/visitor-information

Shakespeare's Birthplace, Stratford-upon-Avon, Warwickshire
The Shakespeare Birthplace Trust
Shakespeare Centre, Henley Street, Stratford-upon-Avon,
Warwickshire CV37 6QW
Tel: 01789 204 016
www.shakespeare.org.uk
Opening times: Apr–May and Sept–Oct 9am–5pm; Jun–Aug 9am–6pm;
    Nov–Mar 10am–4pm. Times may vary in the other museum houses
Nearest train: Stratford-upon-Avon
Nearest car park is Windsor Street multi-storey
There are a variety of cafés and restaurants in Stratford
Gift shops including the Shakespeare Bookshop
Visitors with restricted mobility should ring 01789 201836/806 for
    information

Harvington Hall, Kidderminster
Harvington Hall Lane, Harvington, Kidderminster,
Worcestershire DY10 4LR
Tel: 01562 777846
www.harvingtonhall.com
Opening times: Apr–Oct 11.30am–5.00 pm, Wed–Sun; Mar 11.30am–
    5.00pm, Sat–Sun
Nearest train: Kidderminster
Free car parking
Moatside Tea Room
Gift shop
Suitable for disabled visitors

EAST MIDLANDS

Bosworth Battlefield Heritage Centre, Leicestershire
Leicestershire County Council
Sutton Cheney, Nr. Market Bosworth, Nuneaton, Leicestershire CV13 0AD

Tel: 01455 290429
www.bosworthbattlefield.com
Opening times: Apr–Oct, 10am–5pm; Nov–Mar, 10am–4pm. Closed
    January
Nearest train: Nuneaton and Leicester
Paid car parking available
Tithe Barn Restaurant
Gift shop
For accessibility information, please visit www.bosworthbattlefield.com/
    visit/facilities

Hardwick Hall, Derbyshire
The National Trust
Doe Lea, Chesterfield, Derbyshire S44 5QJ
Tel: 01246 850430
www.nationaltrust.org.uk/main/w-hardwickhall
Opening times: Feb–Nov 12 noon–4.30pm, Wed–Sun
Nearest train: Chesterfield (8 miles)
Parking available at £2 per car
Restaurant and kiosk
Hardwick Hall Shop
Limited disabled access – slopes, grass paths, some cobbles. Please see
    website for more details

Burghley House, Lincolnshire
Burghley House Preservation Trust
61 St Martins, Stamford, Lincolnshire PE9 2LQ
Tel: 01780 752451
www.burghley.co.uk
Opening times: Mar–Oct 11am–4.30pm, except Fri
Nearest train: Stamford (1 mile)
Free car parking
Orangery Restaurant
Gift shop and Garden shop
Disabled access includes chair lifts and wheelchair access

Kirby Hall, Northamptonshire
English Heritage
Kirby Lane, Corby, Northamptonshire NN17 3EN
Tel: 01536 203230
www.wakefieldmuseums.org/our_sites_pontefract_cas.htm
Opening daily Apr–Oct 10am–5pm; Nov–Mar 10am–4pm, weekends only
Nearest train: Kettering, 11 miles
Car parking available
Refreshments available from shop
Gift shop
Suitable for disabled visitors

EAST OF ENGLAND

Trinity College Cambridge, Cambridgeshire
The University of Cambridge
Saint John's Street, Cambridge CB2 1TQ
Tel: 01223 338400
www.trin.cam.ac.uk
Trinity welcomes visitors to the College on most of the year. Please contact
the Porter's Lodge for specific opening times
Nearest train: Cambridge
Public parking along Queen's Road.
Cafés, restaurants and shops abound in Cambridge
Disabled visitors should seek advice from the Head Porter or the Admissions Office

Peterborough Cathedral, Cambridgeshire
The Church of England
Minster Precincts, Peterborough, Cambridgeshire PE1 1XS
Tel: 01733 343342
www.peterborough-cathedral.org.uk
Open every day of the year (except Boxing Day) 9am-5.15pm Mon–Fri,
9am–3.15pm Sat & Sun, 12 noon–3.15
Nearest train: Peterborough
There is generally only disabled public parking available in the Precincts

Cathedral Coffee Shop
Gift and souvenirs shops
Suitable for people with disabilities

Hatfield Old Palace and House, Hertfordshire

Lord and Lady Salisbury
Hatfield Park, Great North Road, Hatfield, Hertfordshire AL9 5NQ
Tel: 01707 287000
www.hatfield-house.co.uk
For opening times please see www.hatfield-house.co.uk/plan-your-visit/
    opening-times-and-prices
Nearest train: Hatfield
Free parking available
Coach House restaurant in Stable Yard
The Hatfield House Gift shop and independent shops
Suitable for people with disabilities

Kett's Oak, Norfolk

Can be found on B1172 between Wymondham and Norwich

Shrine at Walsingham, Norfolk

Entrance via Shirehall Museum, Common Place, Walsingham,
Norfolk NR22 6BP
Tel: 01328 820510
www.walsinghamabbey.com
Open daily in summer 10–4.30pm; winter (1 Nov-3 Feb) grounds only
    9am–5pm, Mon–Fri
Nearest train: King's Lynn
Public car park nearby
There is no café but there are pubs nearby
Shop available
Wheelchair users can reach some if not all of the woodland

St Mary's Church, Bury St Edmunds, Suffolk

The Church of England
Honey Hill, Bury St Edmunds, Suffolk IP33 1RT
Tel: 01284 754680

www.stmarystpeter.net/stmaryschurch
Open weekdays 10am–4pm (3pm in winter)
Nearest train: Bury St Edmunds
Limited on-street and pay-and-display parking available
Cafés and shops available in the town nearby
Suitable for people with disabilities

St Michael's Church, Framlingham, Suffolk
The Church of England
Church Street, Framlingham, Suffolk IP13 9BH
Tel: 01728 723255 (Mr Nicholas Nottidge)
www.onesuffolk.co.uk/StMichaelsChurchFram
Framlingham PCC offers conducted tours lasting approximately one hour
    for a small charge for parties of between 10 and 40. Please telephone
    number above
Nearest train: Campsea Ashe
Public parking available
There are cafés in the town
There are shops on the street opposite
Suitable for people with disabilities

NORTH EAST, NORTH WEST, YORKSHIRE AND THE HUMBER

Gawsworth Hall, Macclesfield, Cheshire
Mr and Mrs Timothy Richards
Church Lane, Gawsworth, Cheshire SK11 9RN
Tel: 01260 223456
www.gawsworthhall.com
Opening times: 24 Apr–25 Sep 2pm–5pm, Suns & special events; 27 Jun–
    2 Sep, 2pm–5pm daily
Nearest train: Macclesfield
Free car parking
The Orchard Tea Rooms
There is no shop
Limited disabled access, please contact directly for more information

Little Moreton Hall, Cheshire
The National Trust
Congleton, Cheshire CW12 4SD
Tel: 01260 272018
www.nationaltrust.org.uk/main/w-vh/w-visits/w-findaplace/w-little
    moretonhall
Closed until 4 Apr 2012. Then open weekends 11am–4pm, except Jan
    and Feb; Mar–Oct also open 11am–4pm, Wed–Fri
Nearest train: Kidsgrove (3 miles) or Congleton (4½ miles)
Car parking 100 yards
Brewhouse Restaurant
There is a shop
Limited disabled access, please see website

The Walker Art Gallery, Liverpool, Merseyside
National Museums Liverpool
William Brown Street, Liverpool, L3 8EL
Tel: 0151 478 4199
www.liverpoolmuseums.org.uk/walker
Open daily 10am–5pm
Nearest train: Liverpool Lime Street
There is limited pay and display parking just down the hill from the Walker
    on William Brown Street. The nearest car park is at Queen Square.
Walker Café
Walker Shop
Suitable for disabled visitors

Pontefract Castle, West Yorkshire
Owned by the Duchy of Lancaster, run by Wakefield Council
Castle Chain, Pontefract, West Yorkshire WF8 1QH
Tel: 01977 723440
www.wakefieldmuseums.org/our_sites_pontefract_cas.htm
Open daily, 8:30am–5:00pm Mon–Fri, 9:30am–6:15pm Sat Sun; in winter
    the castle closes at dusk
Nearest train: Pontefract
Car parking is adjacent to All Saints Church
No café
The Visitors Centre and Shop open 11:00am–3:00pm, Wed–Sun

Fountains Abbey, North Yorkshire
National Trust
Fountains Abbey & Studley Royal Water Garden, Ripon Nr Harrogate,
North Yorkshire HG4 3DY
Tel: 01765 608888
www.fountainsabbey.org.uk
Open daily Oct and Mar 10am–4pm; Apr–Sep 10am–5pm; it is closed Fri
   Nov–Jan
Nearest train: Harrogate, then bus to Ripon and on to Fountains Abbey
   (4 miles from Ripon)
Free car parking at the visitor centre, or Studley Royal lakeside
Two restaurants and refreshment stands
Two gift shops
Suitable for disabled visitors

Index